AF601458

FLOODGATE COMPANION

Robert Beatty

Floating World Comics

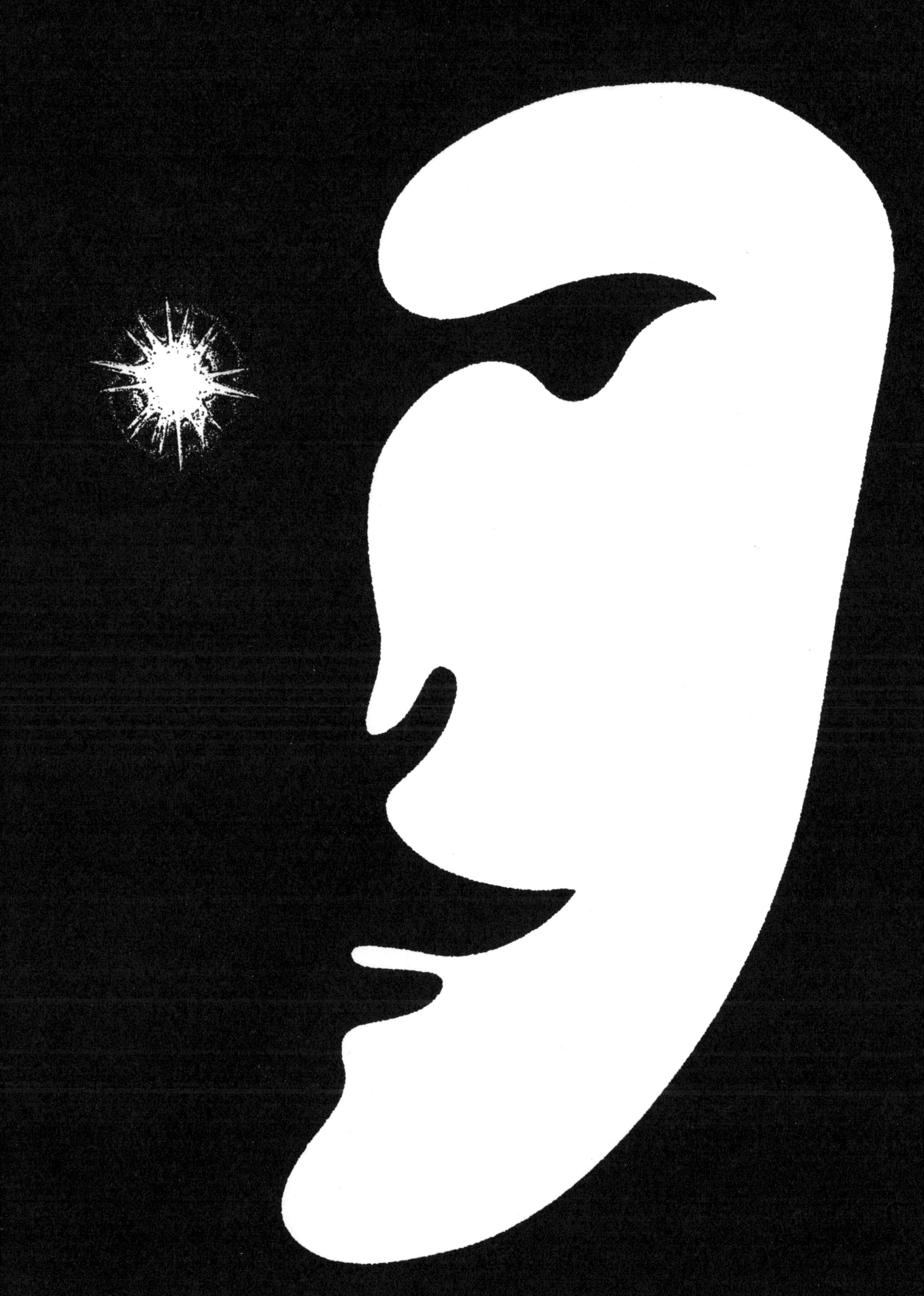

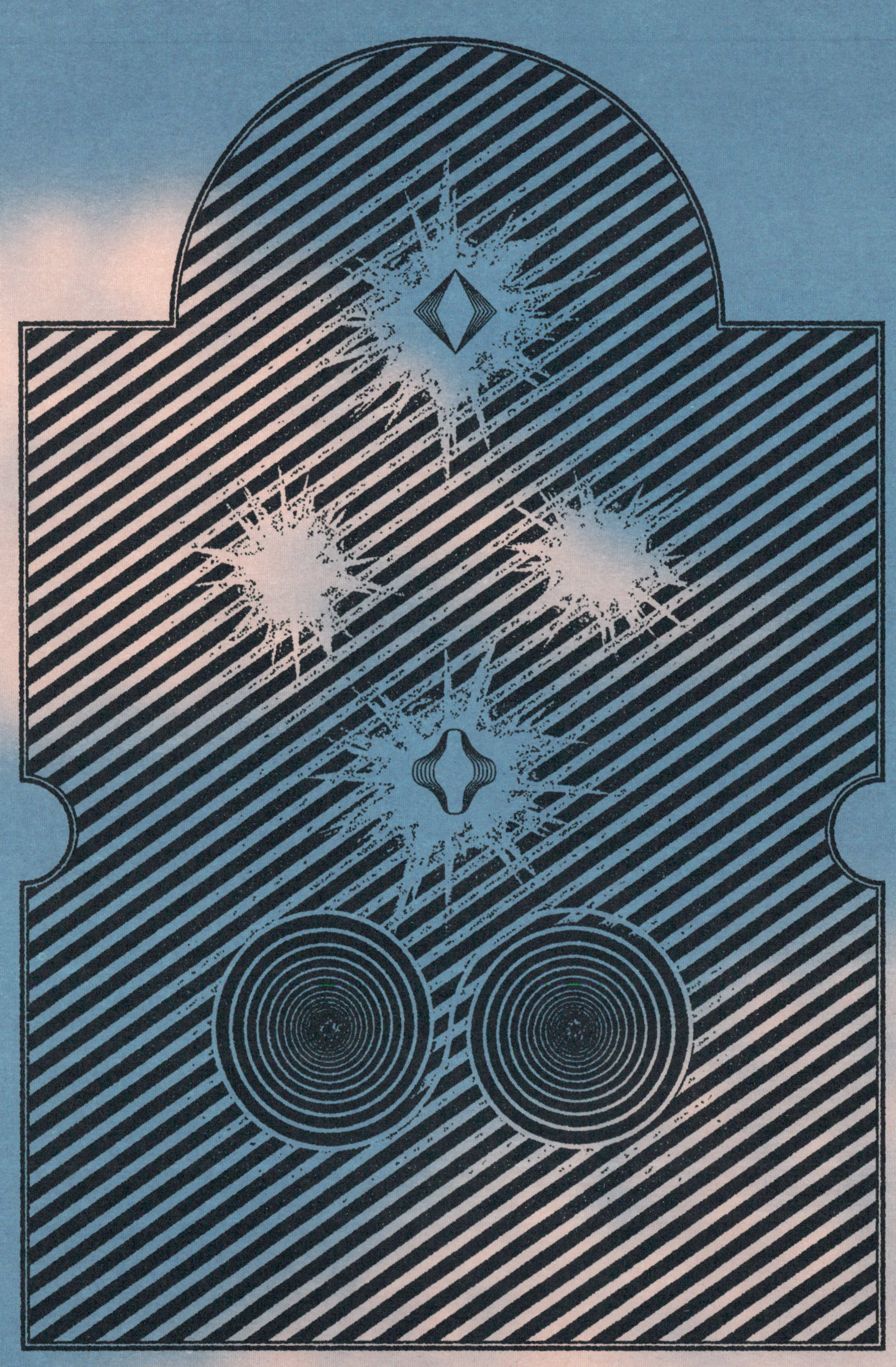

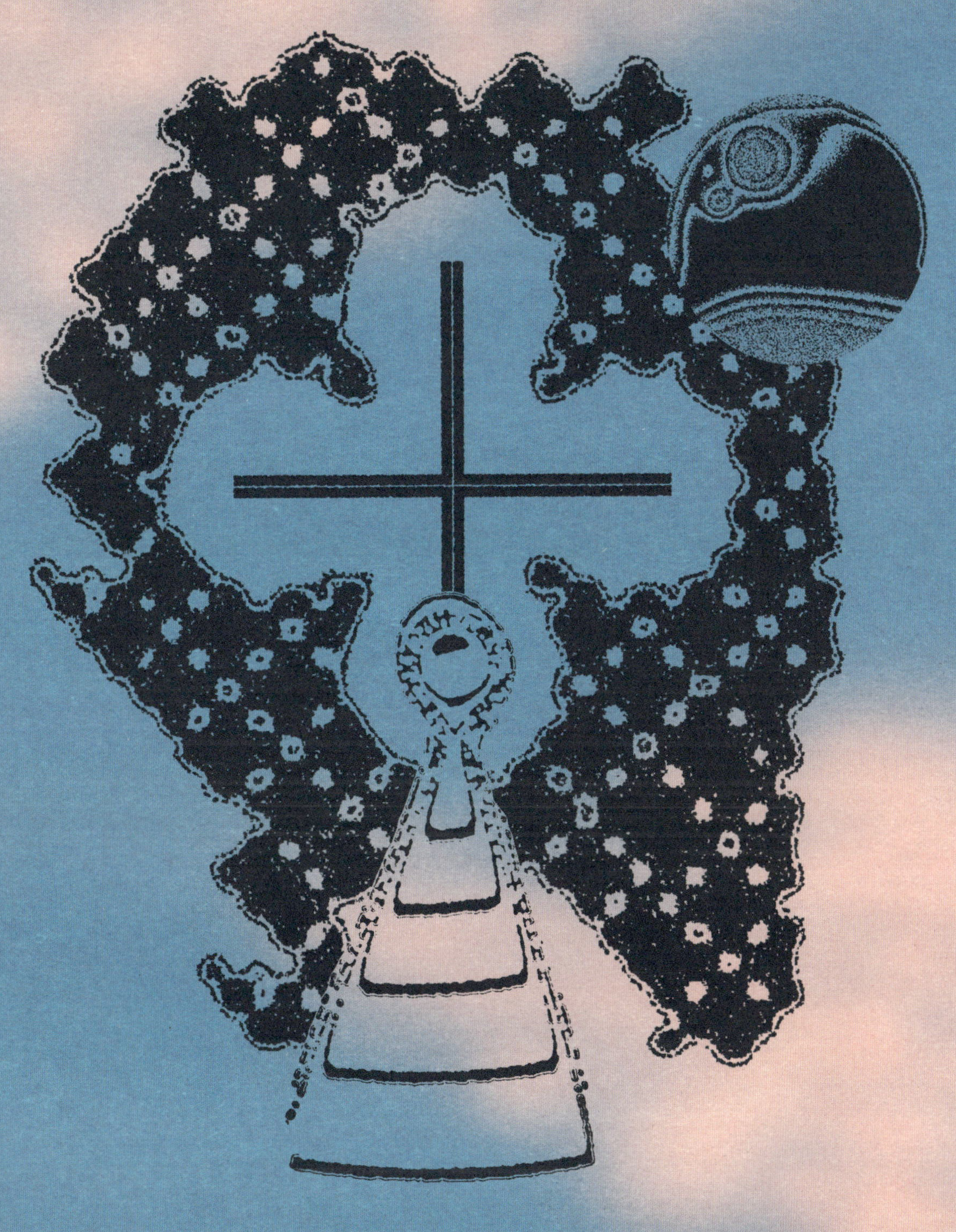

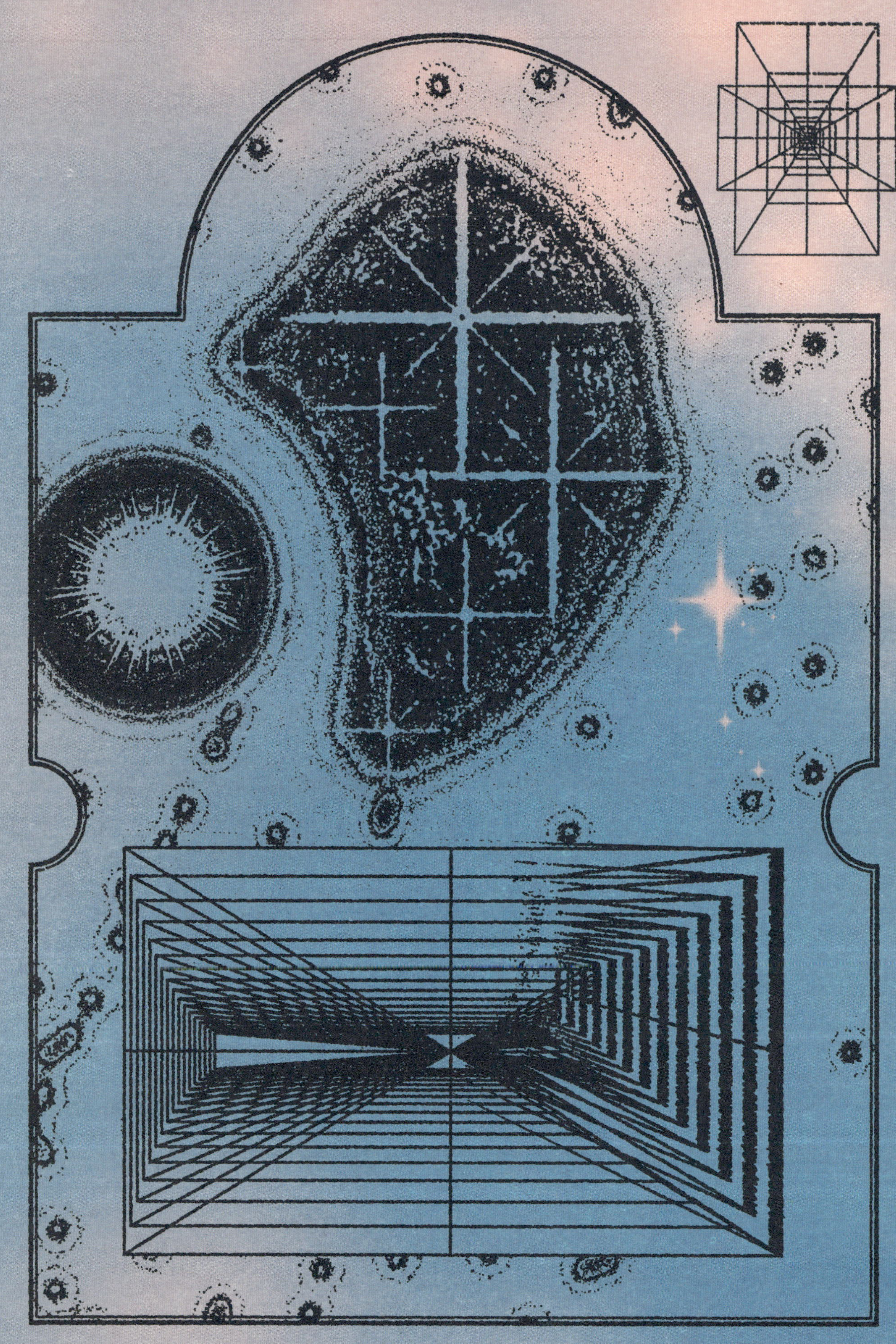

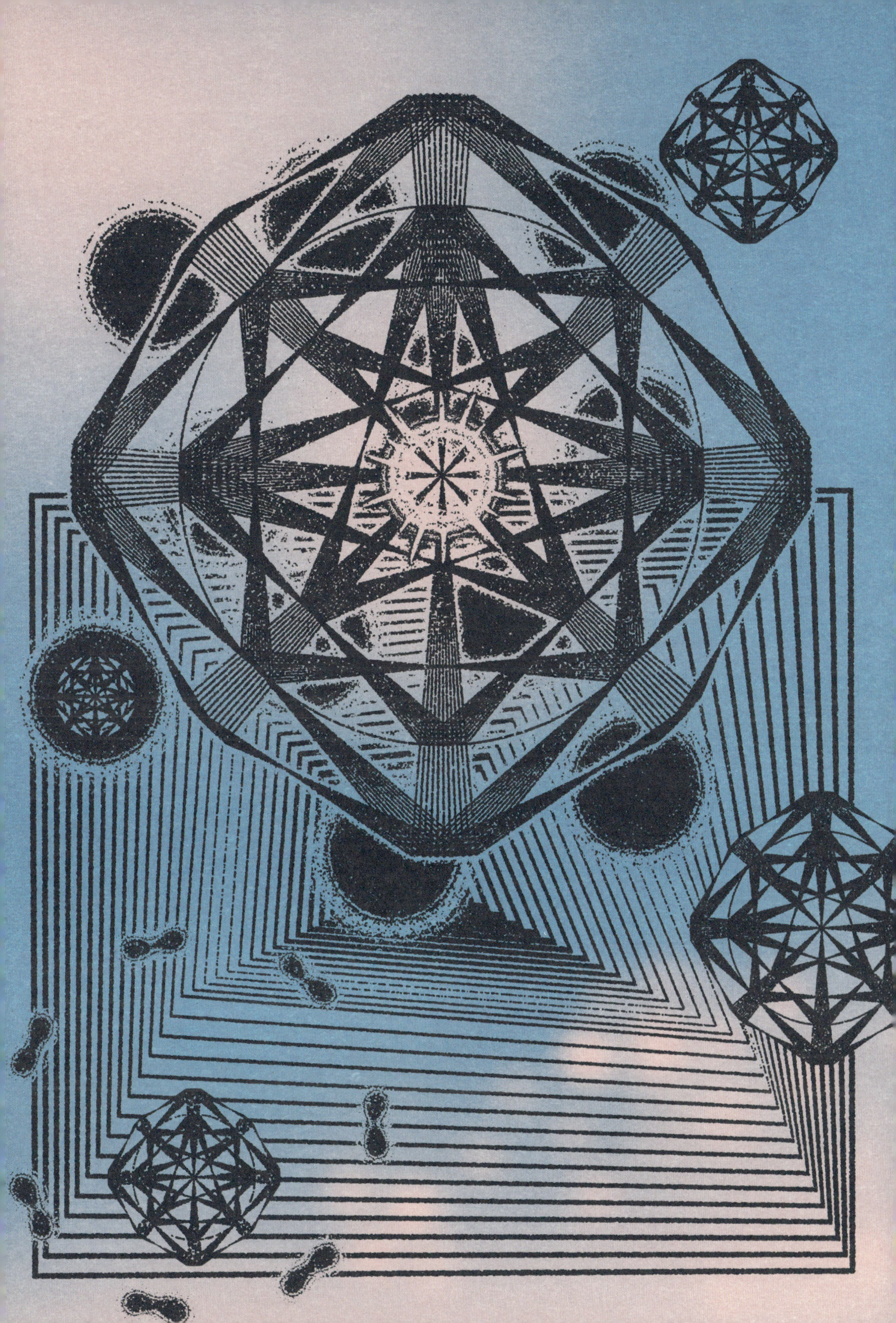

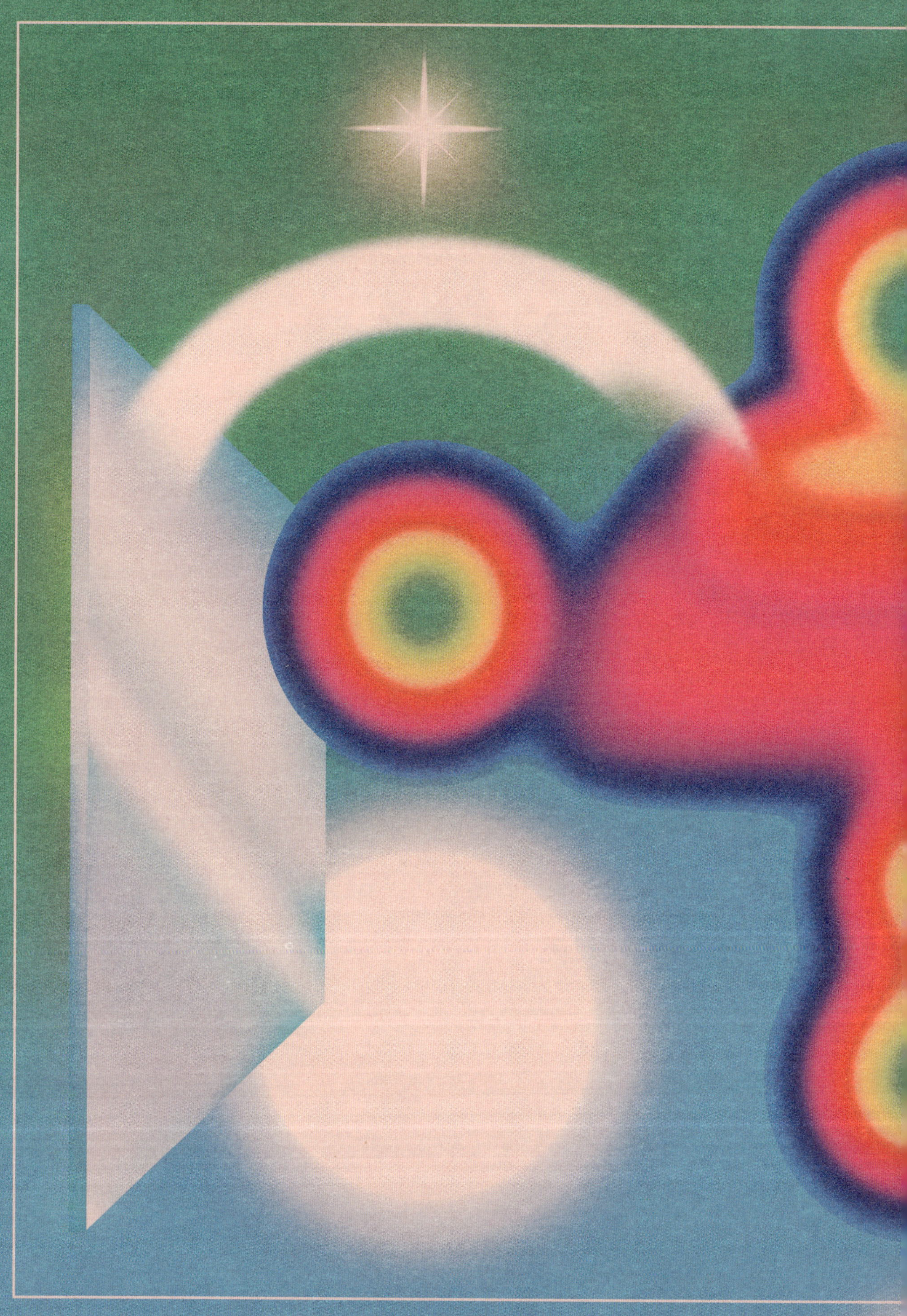

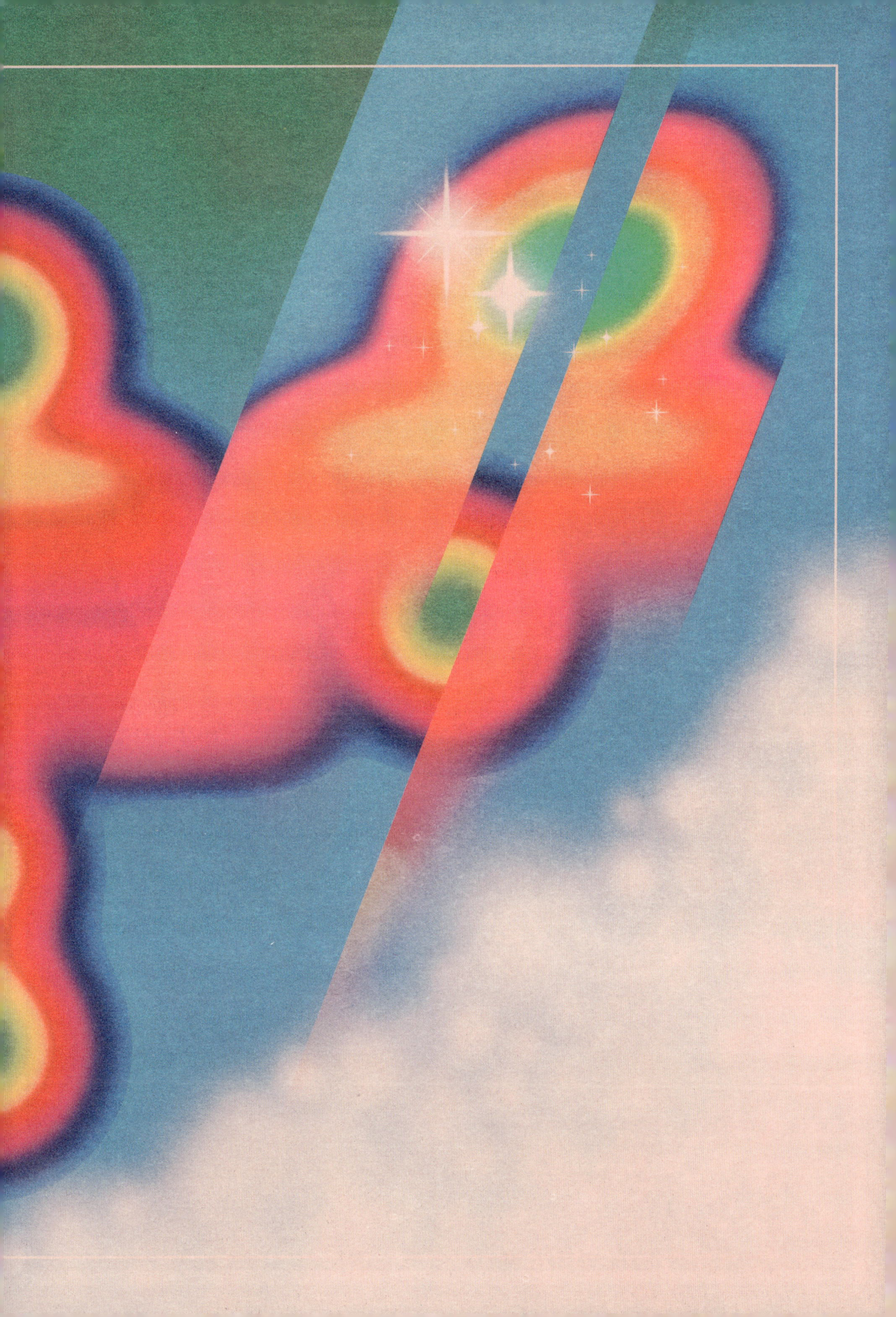

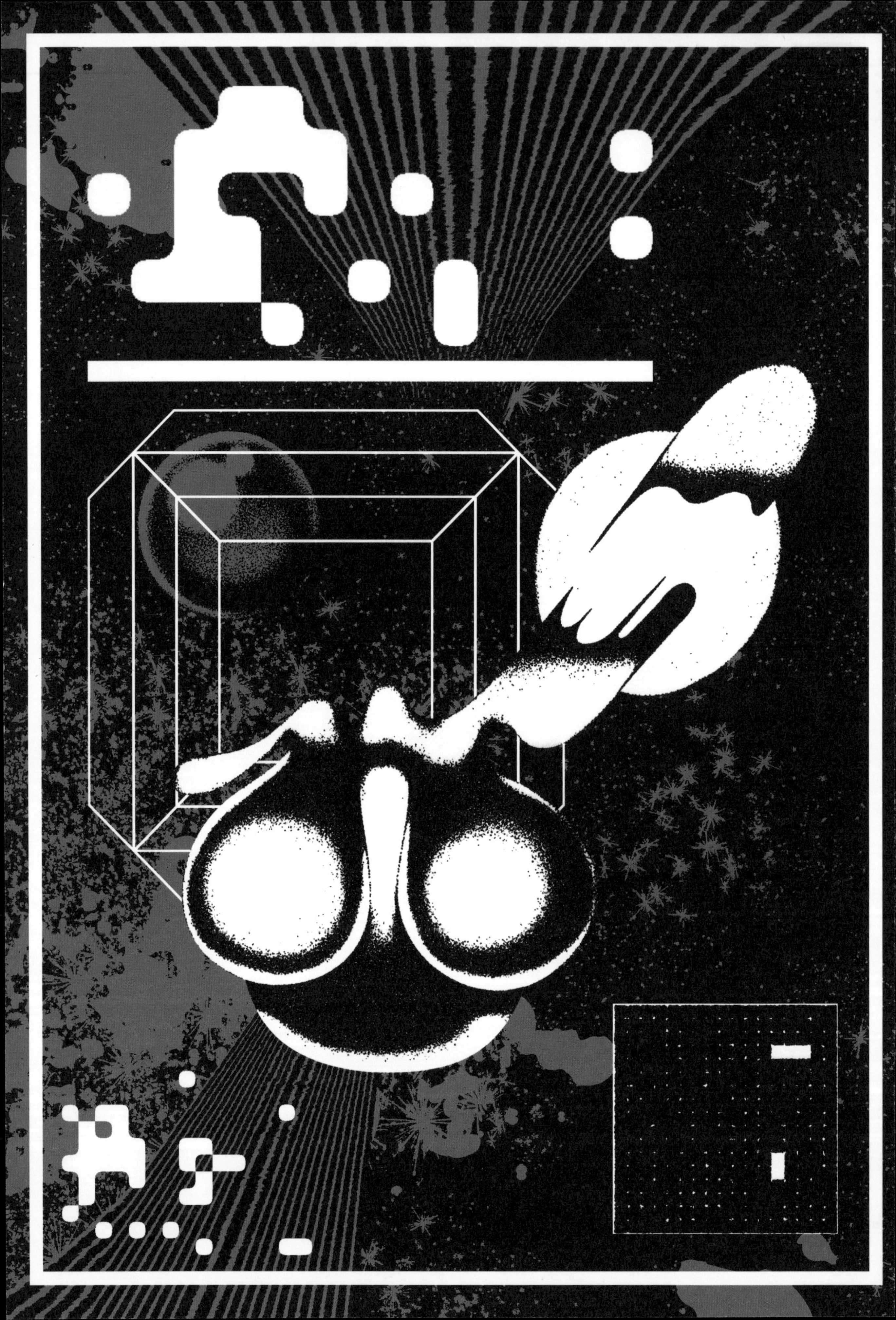

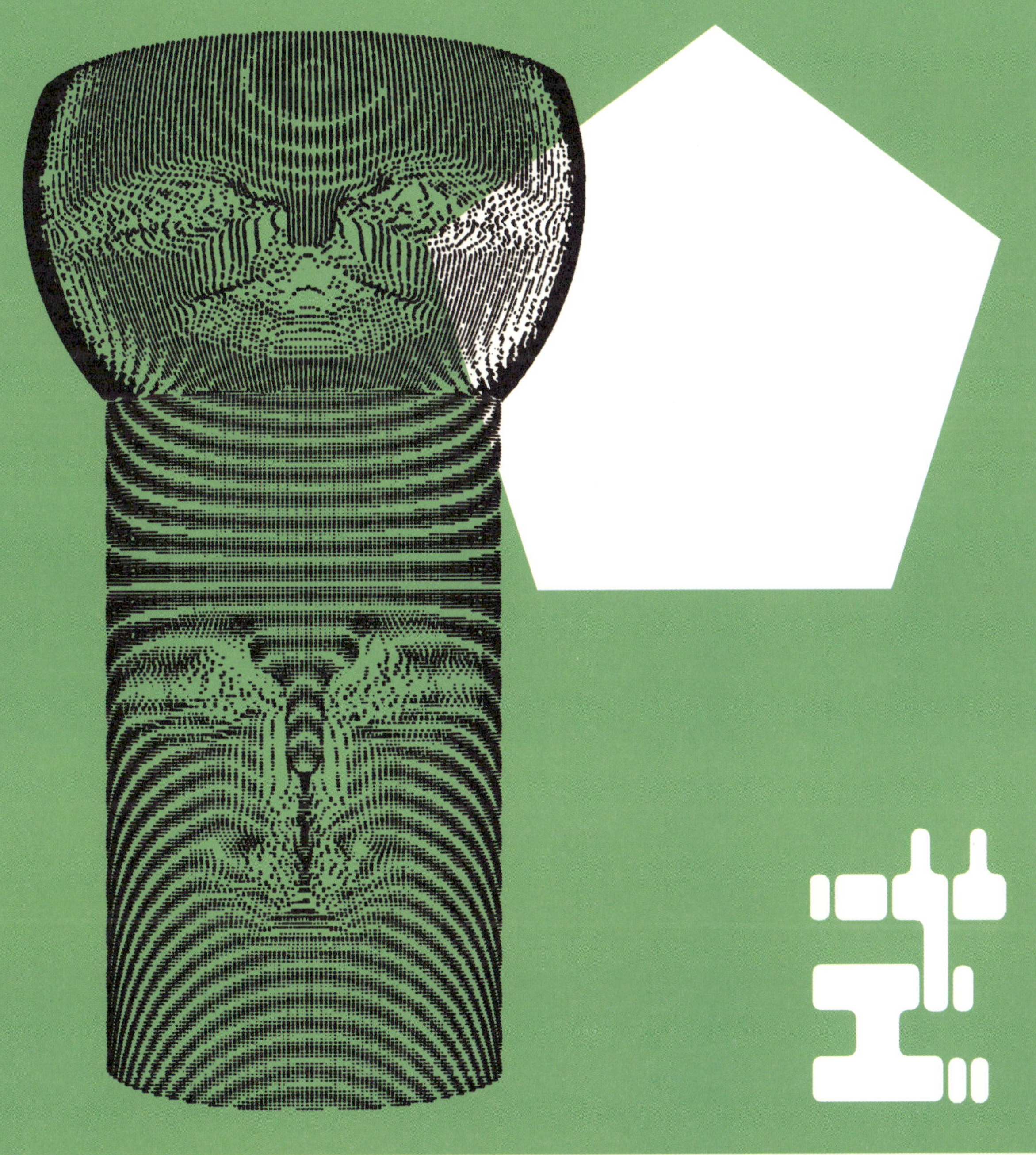

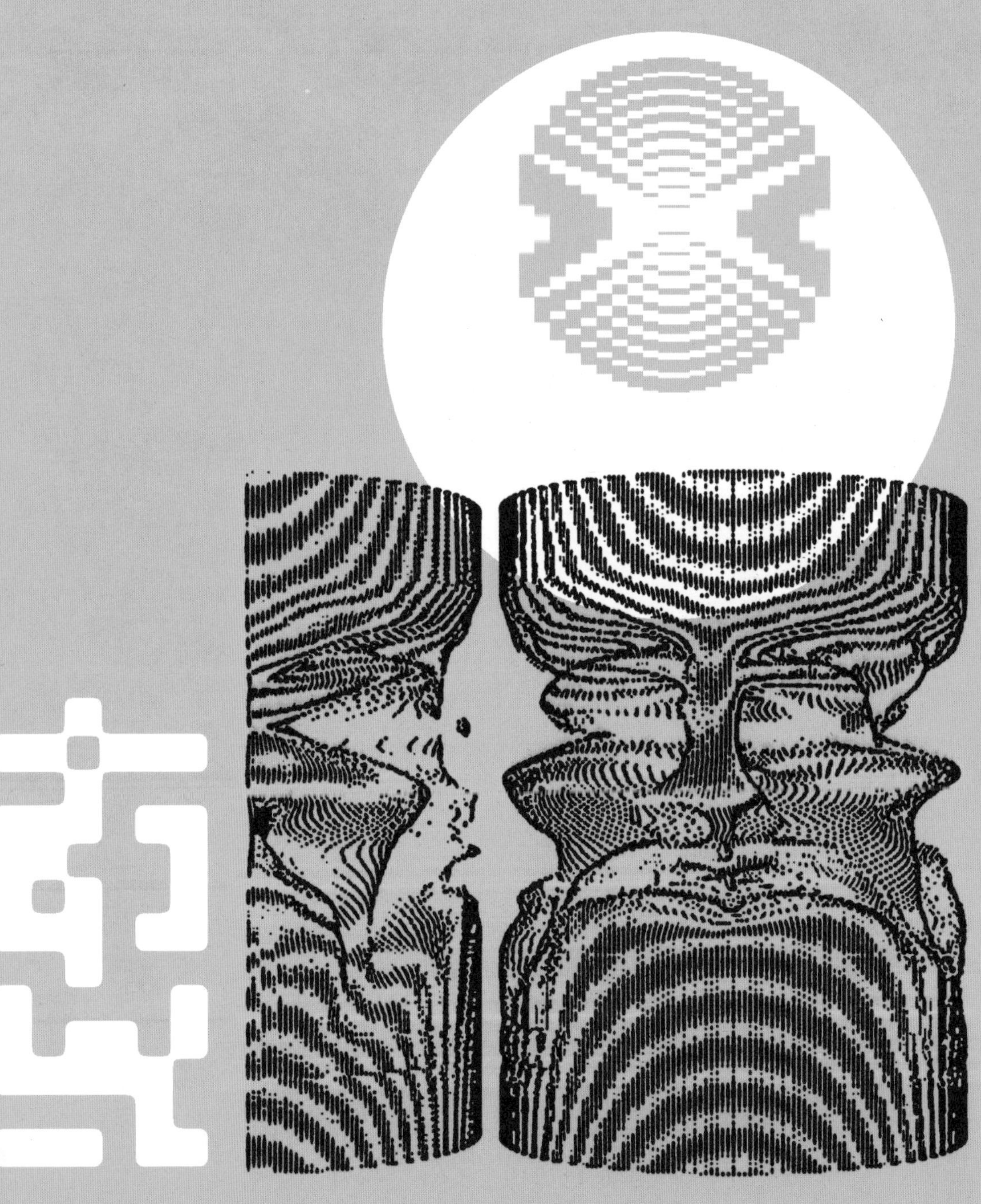

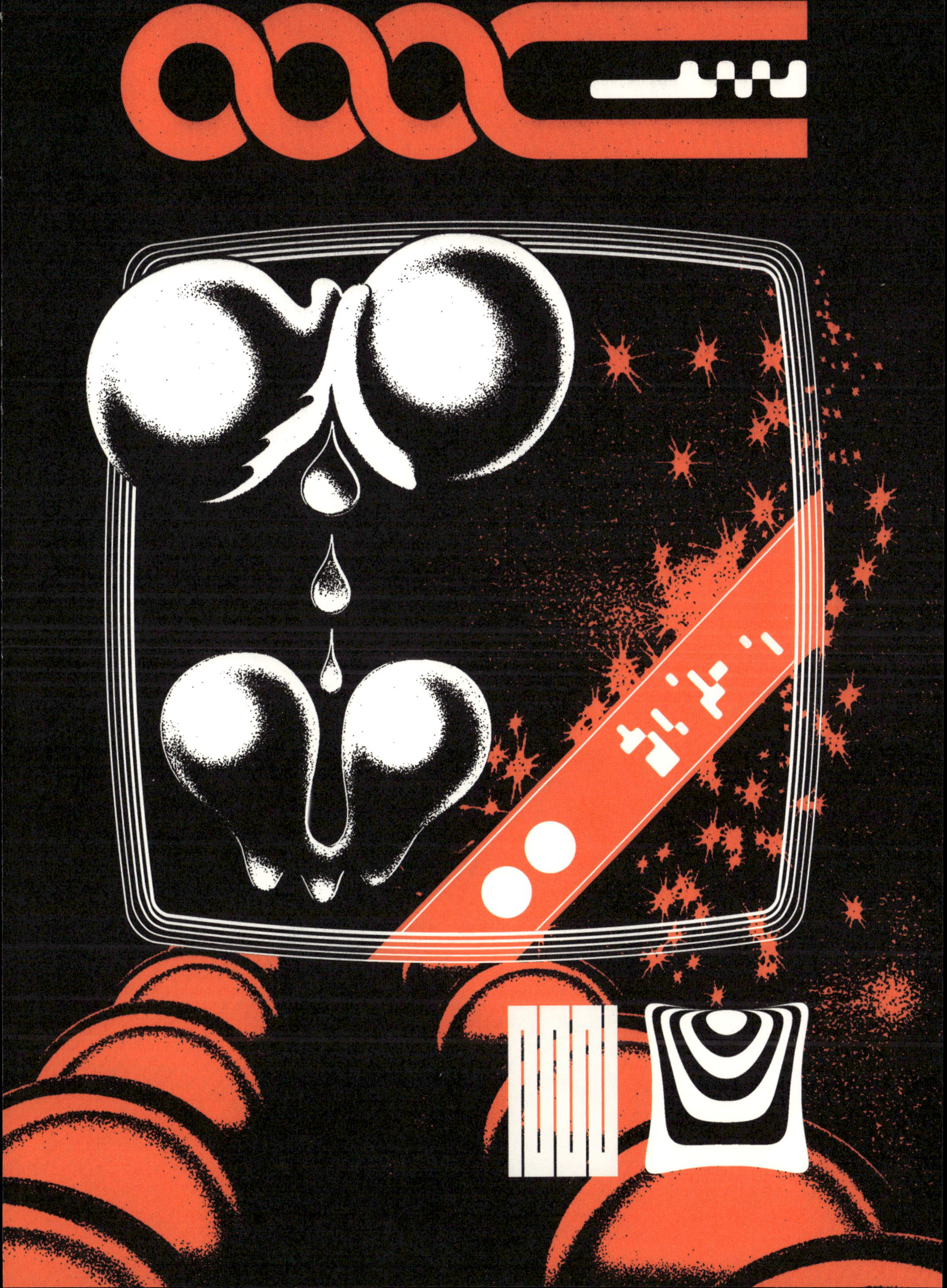

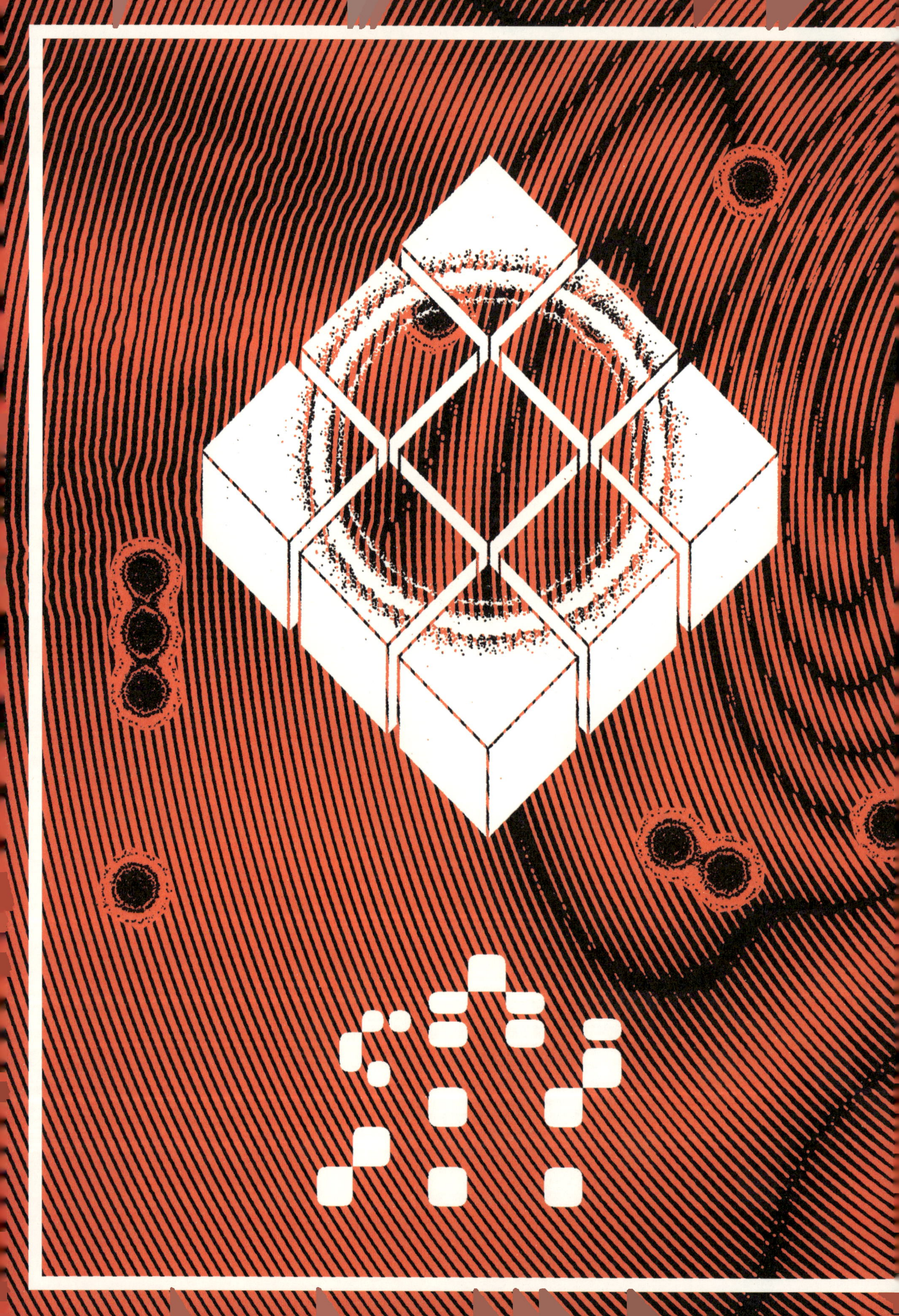

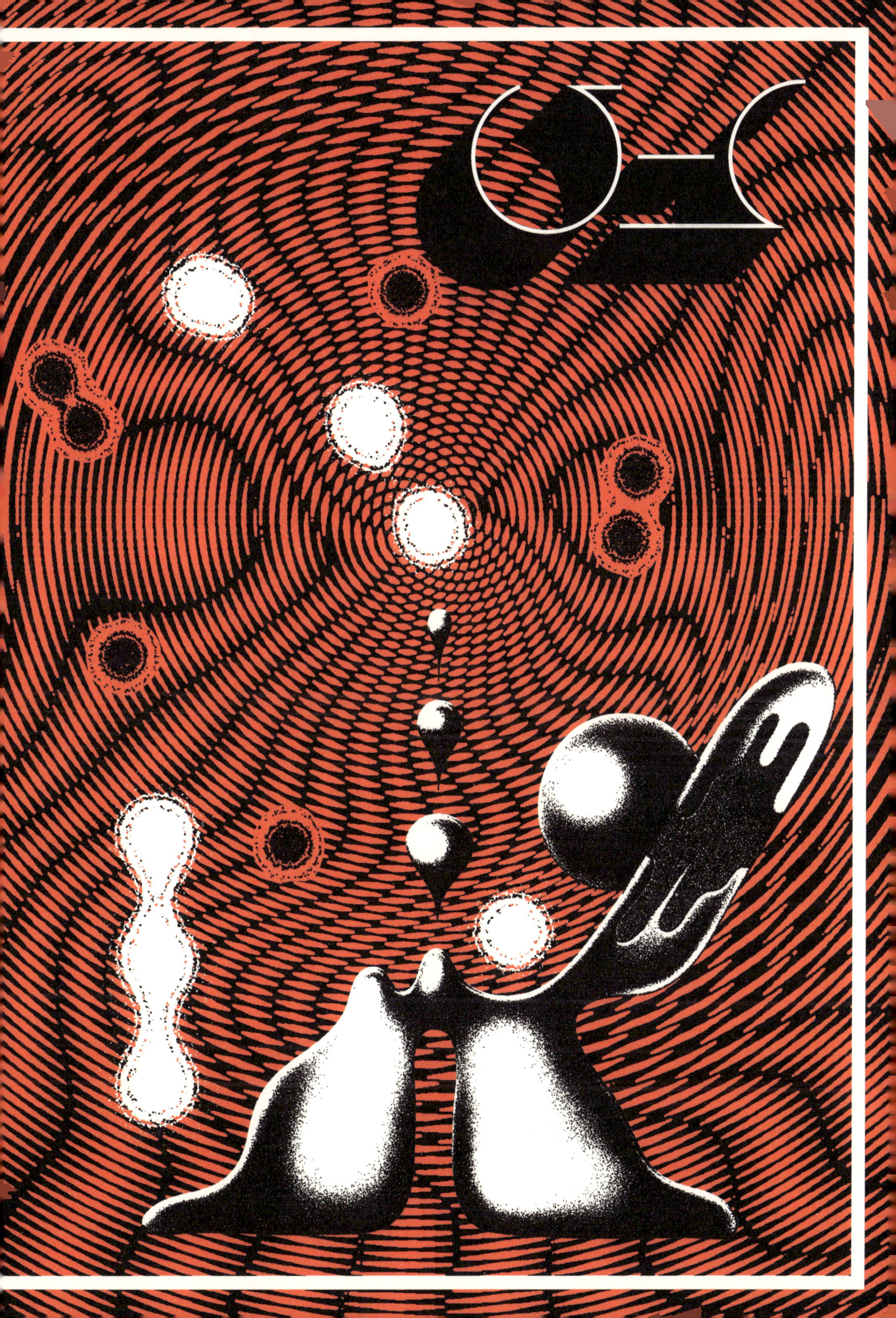

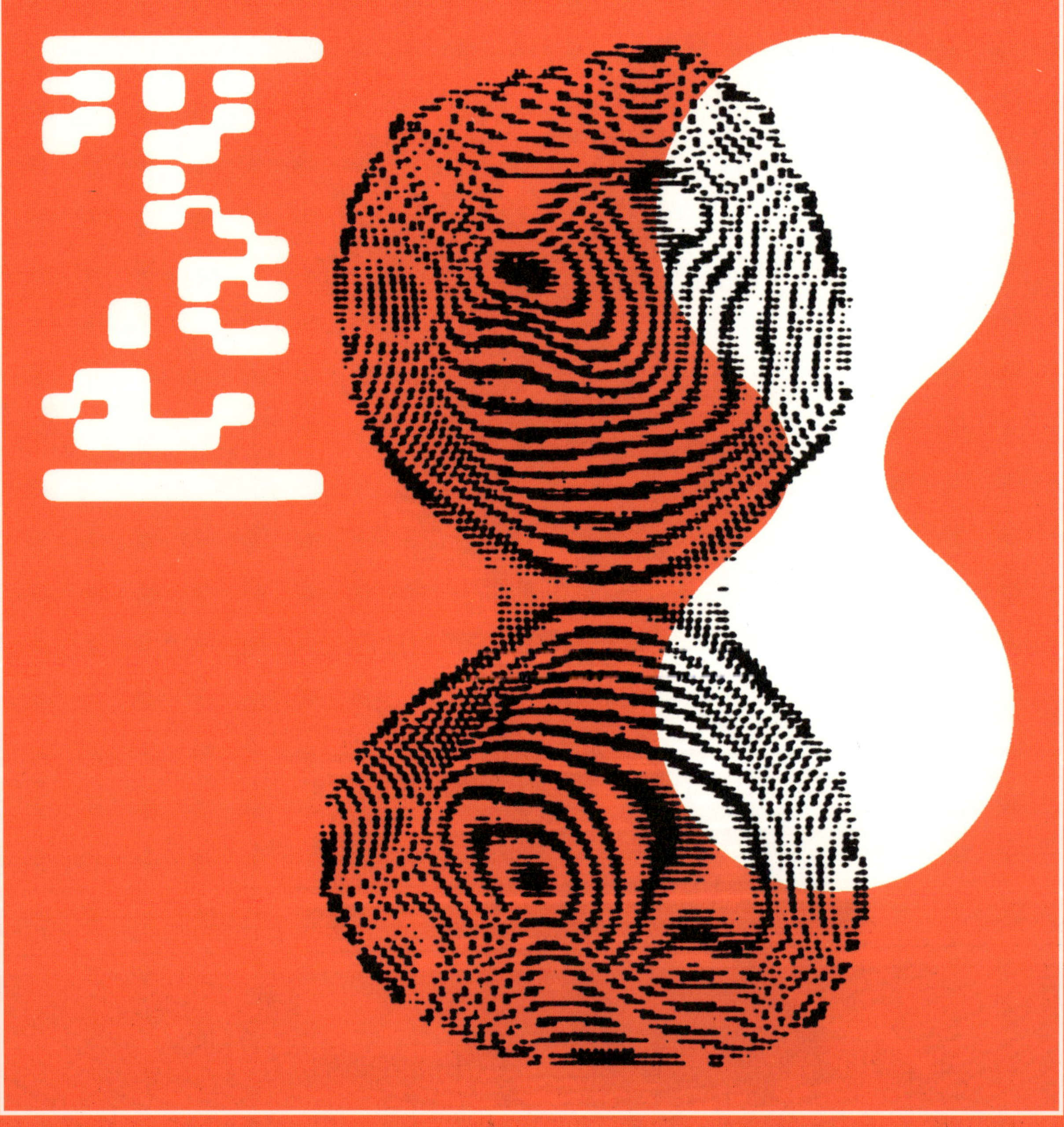

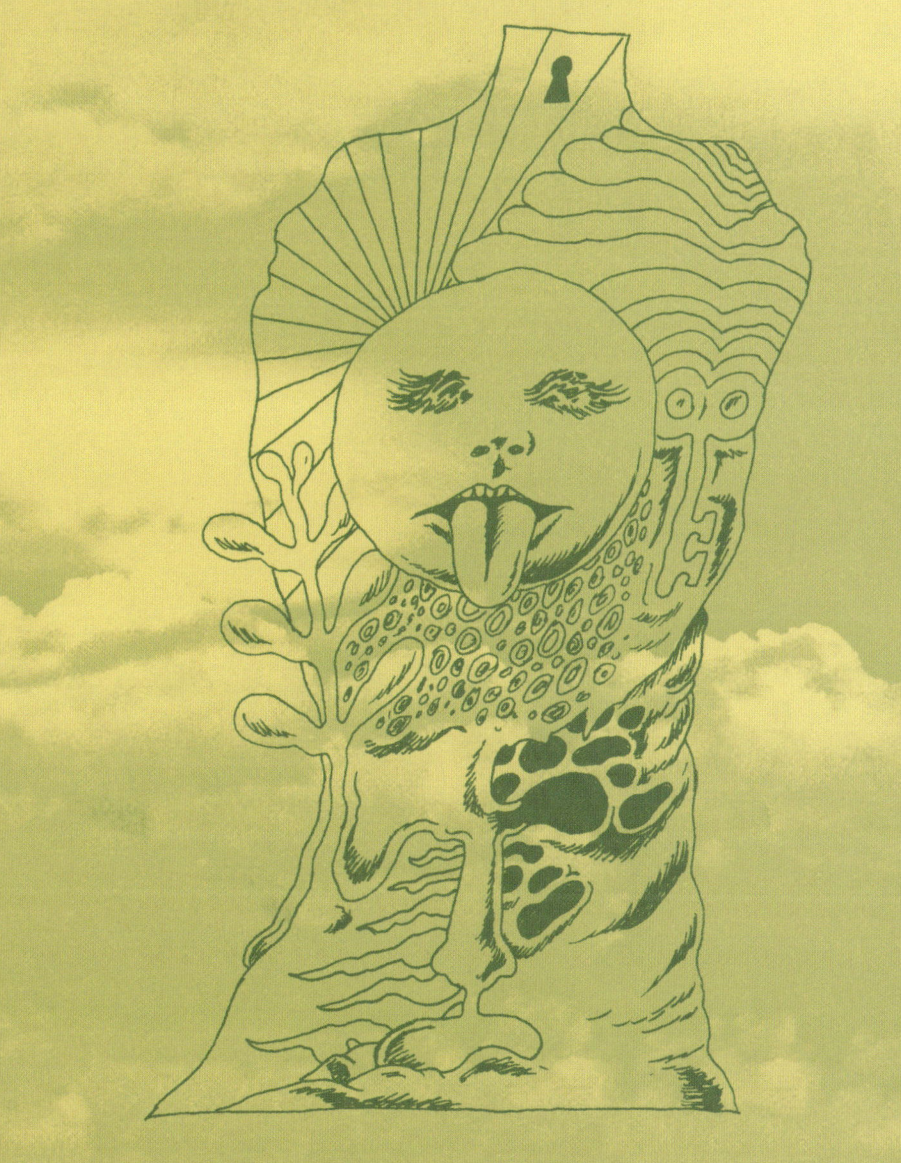

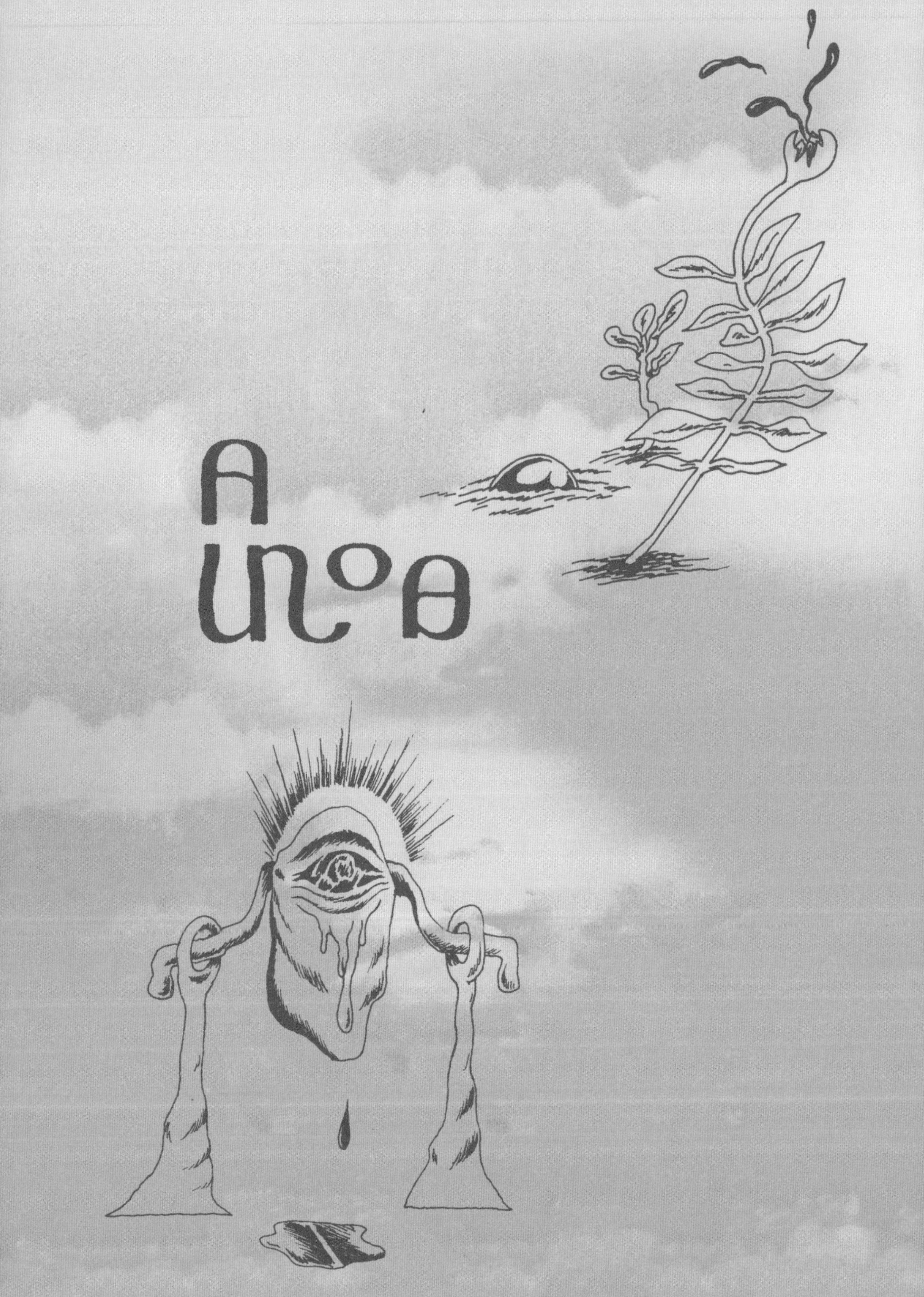

A
Ulºθ

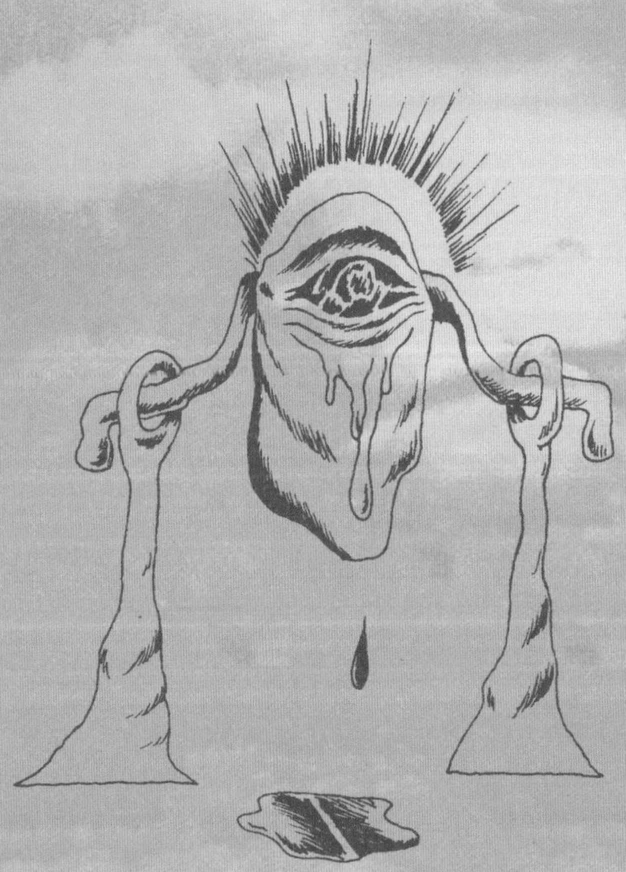

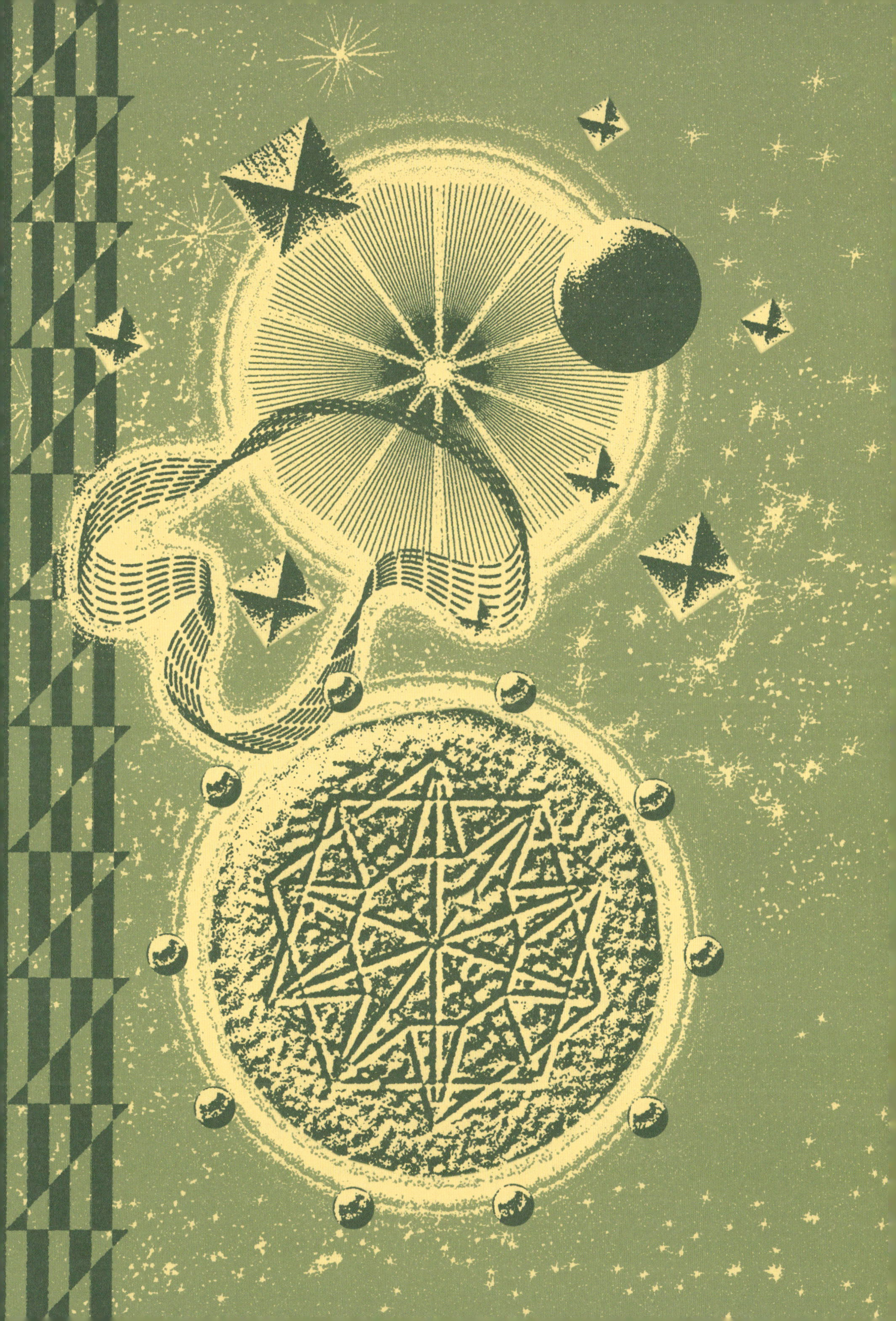

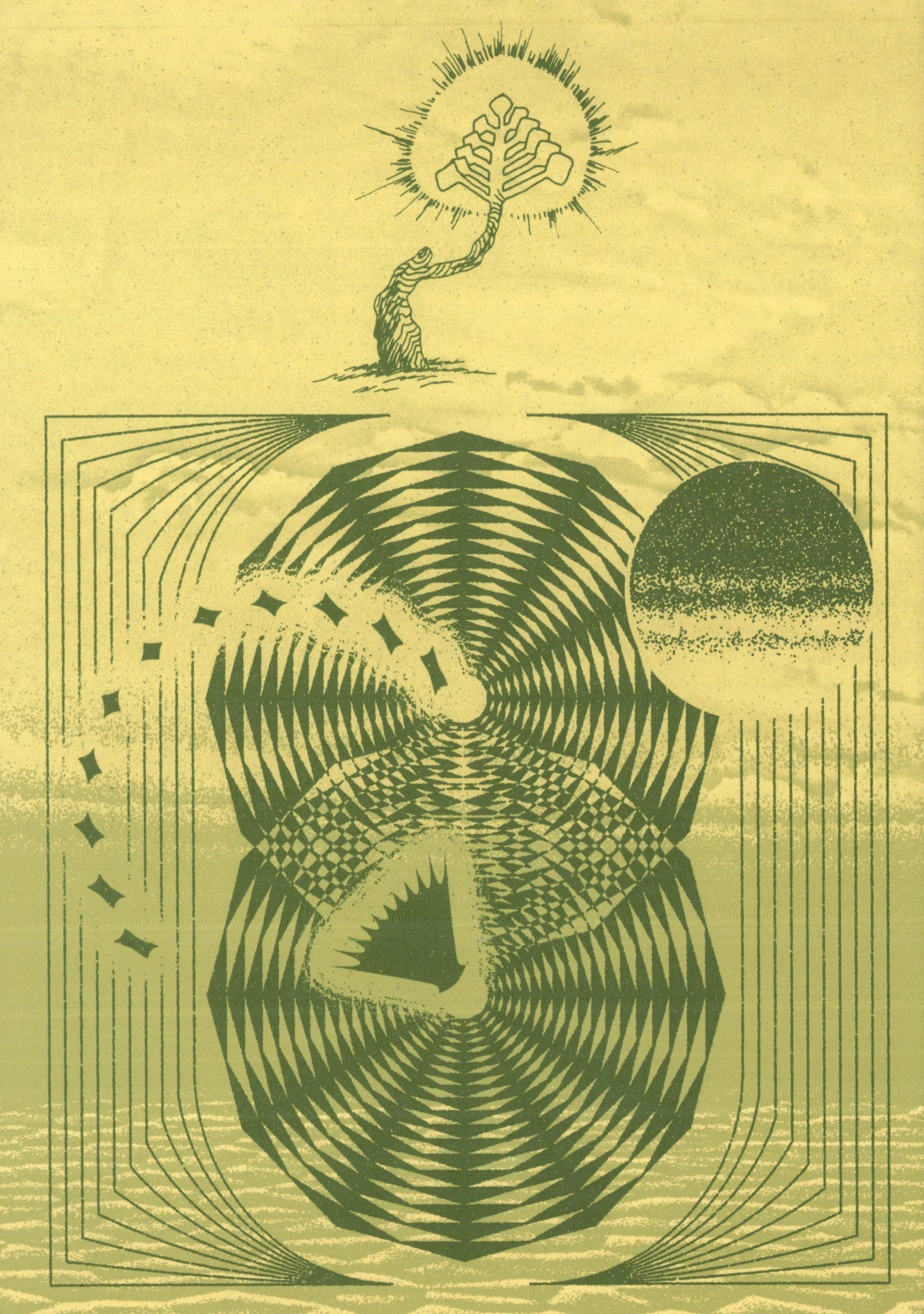

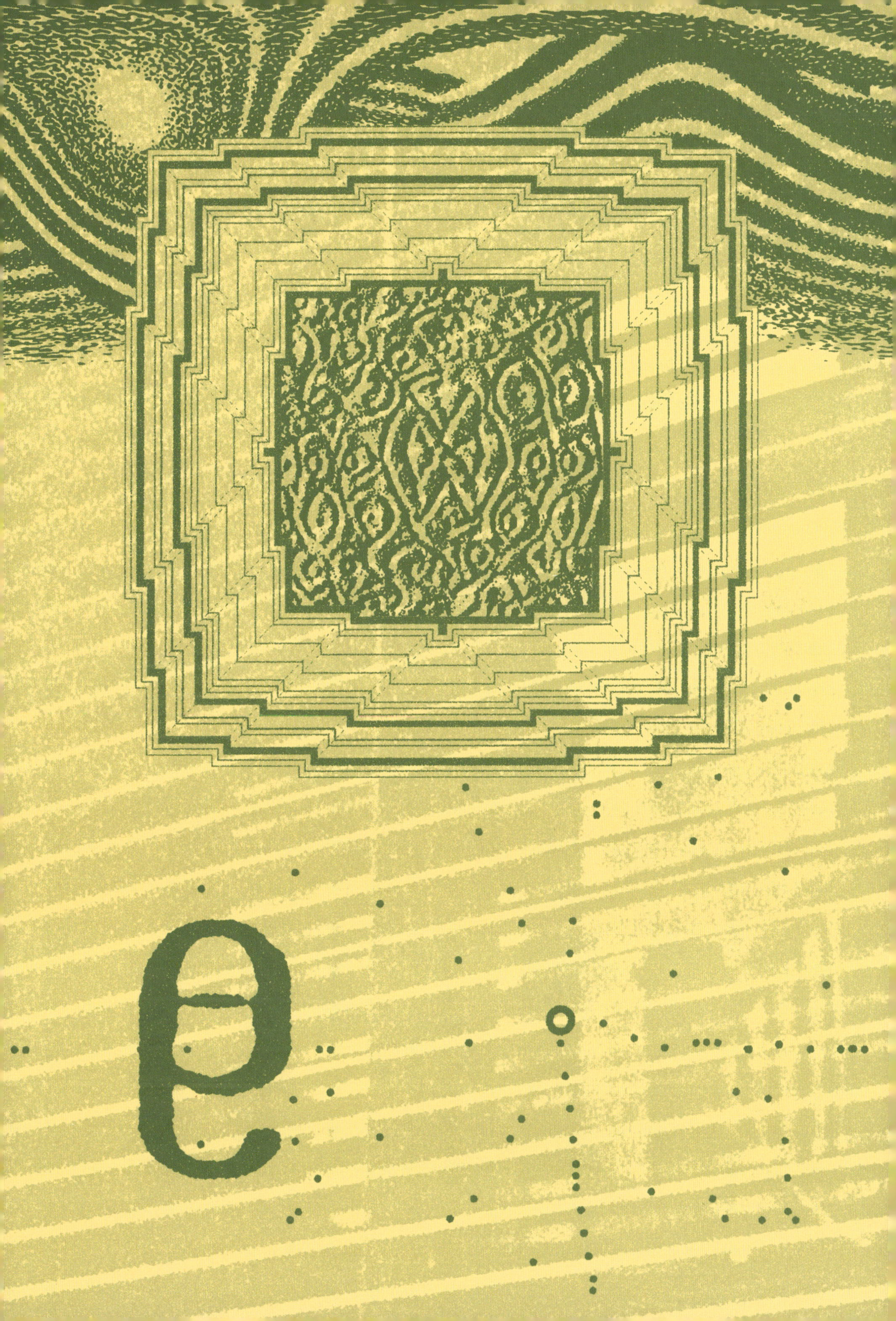

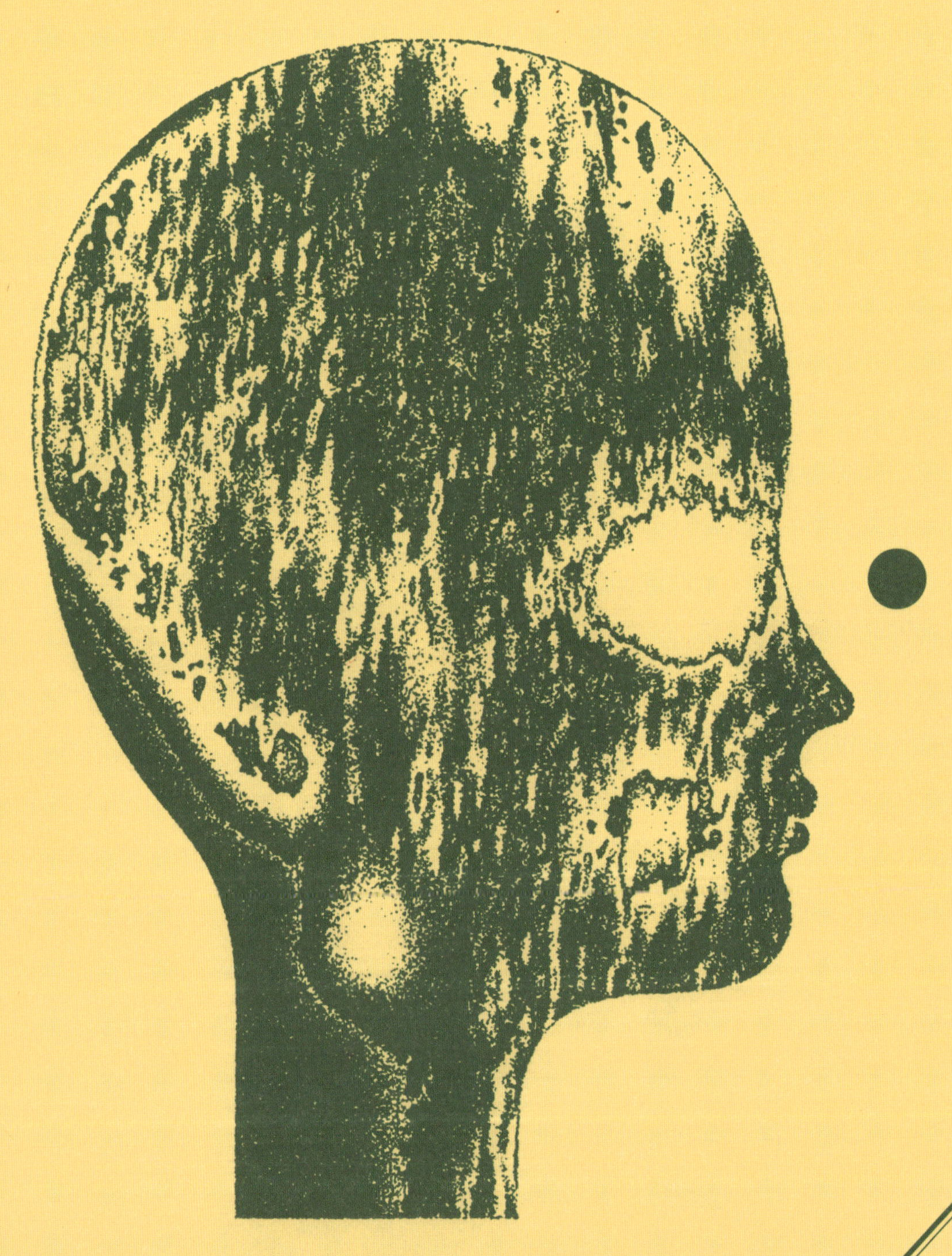

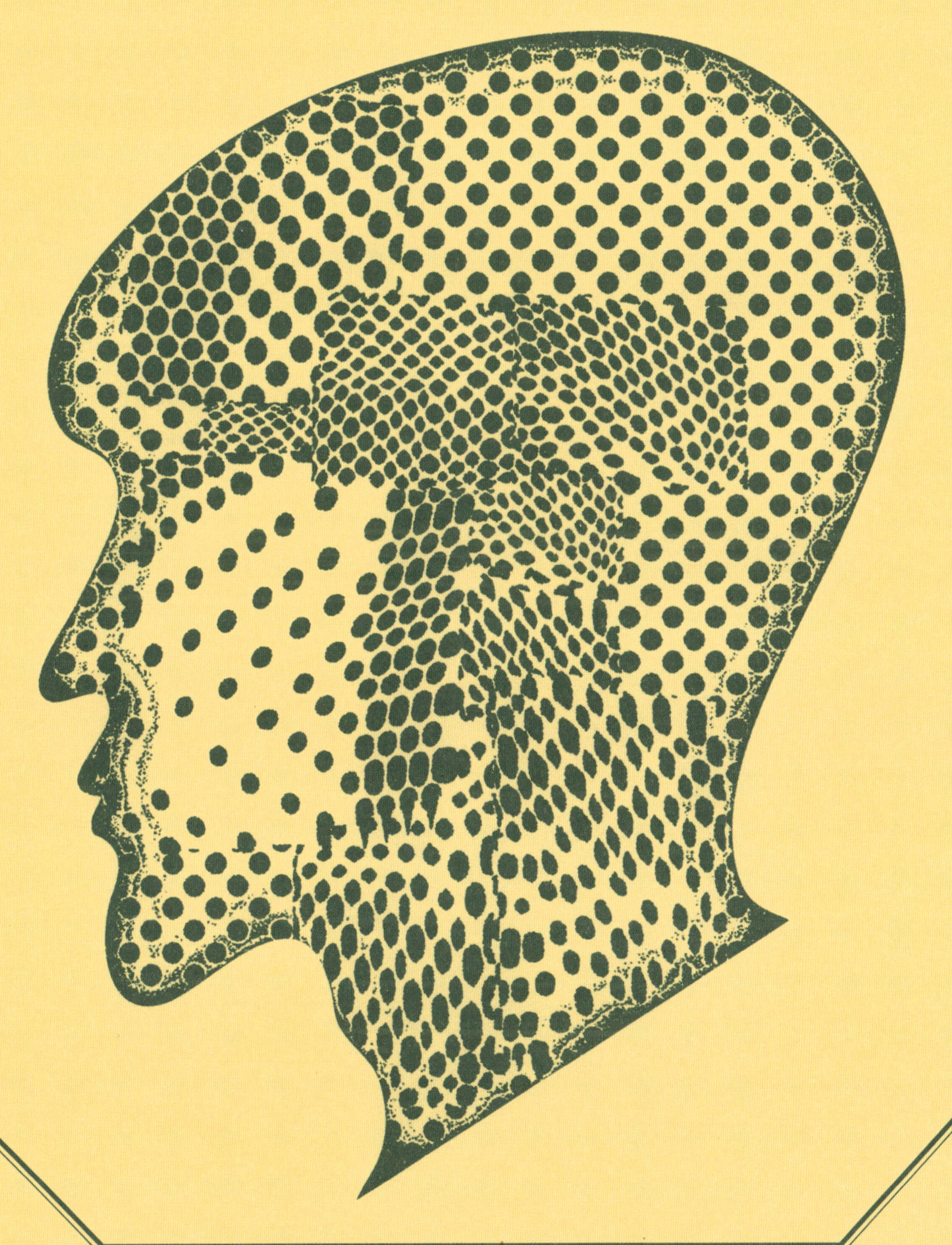

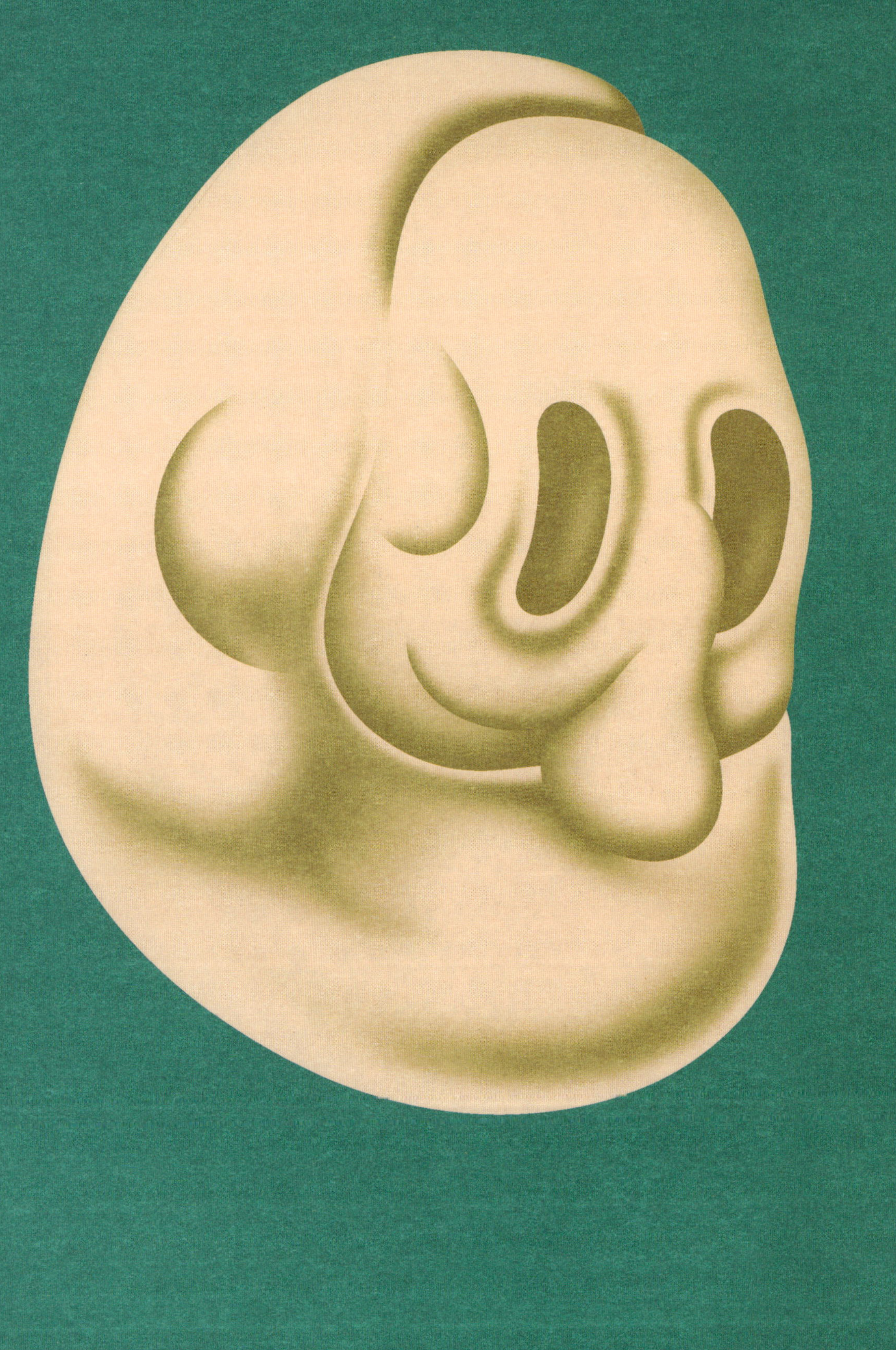

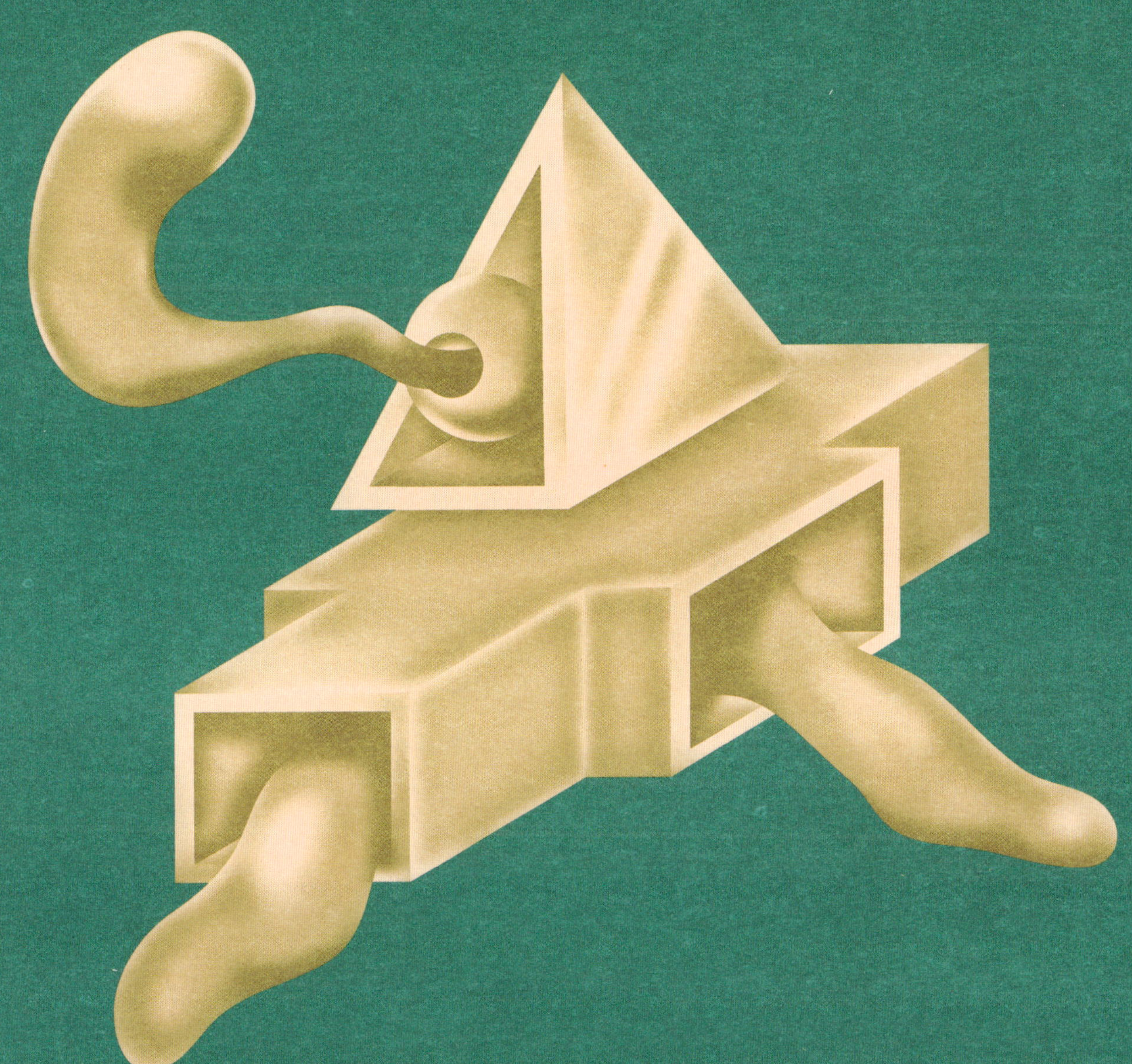

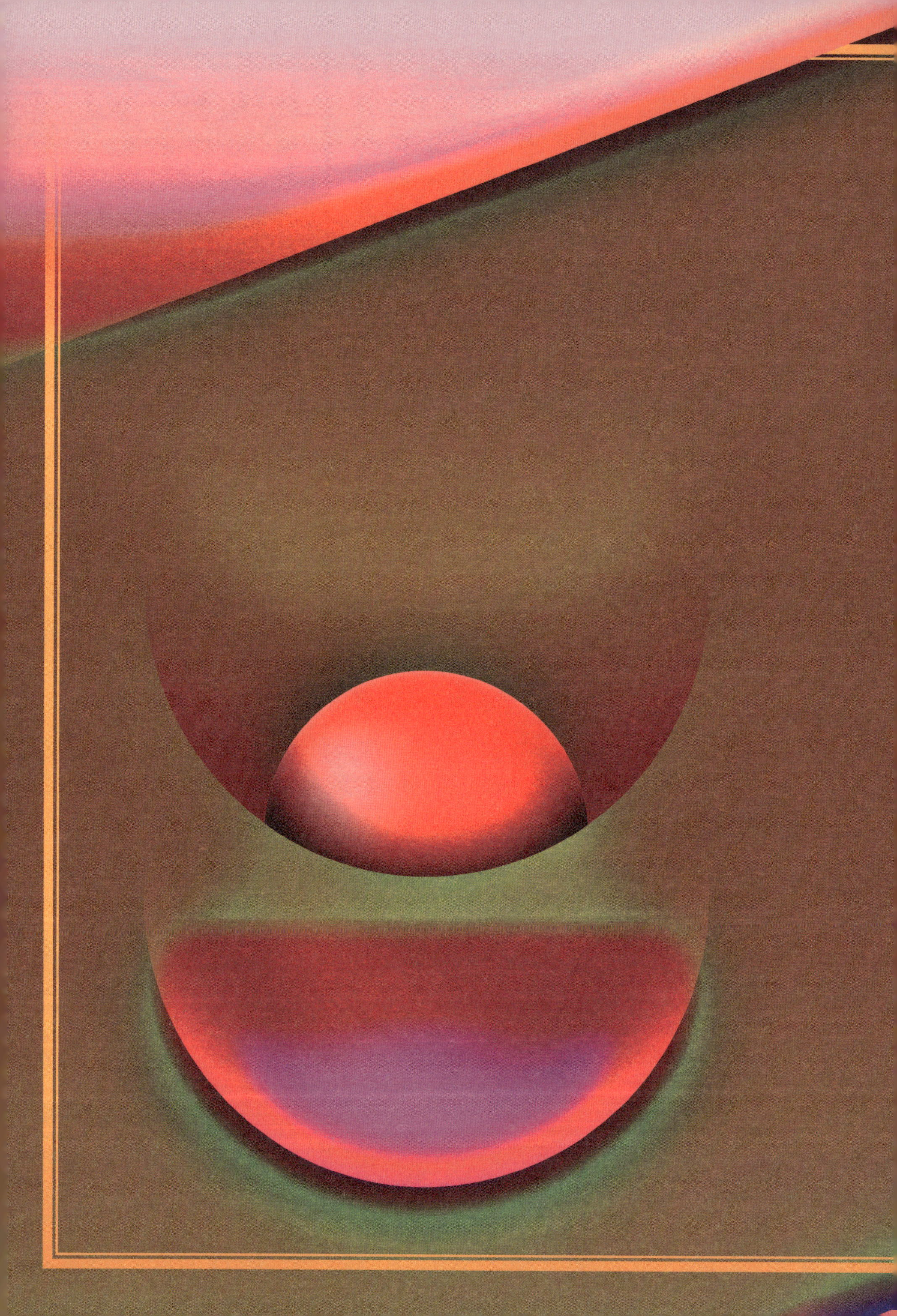

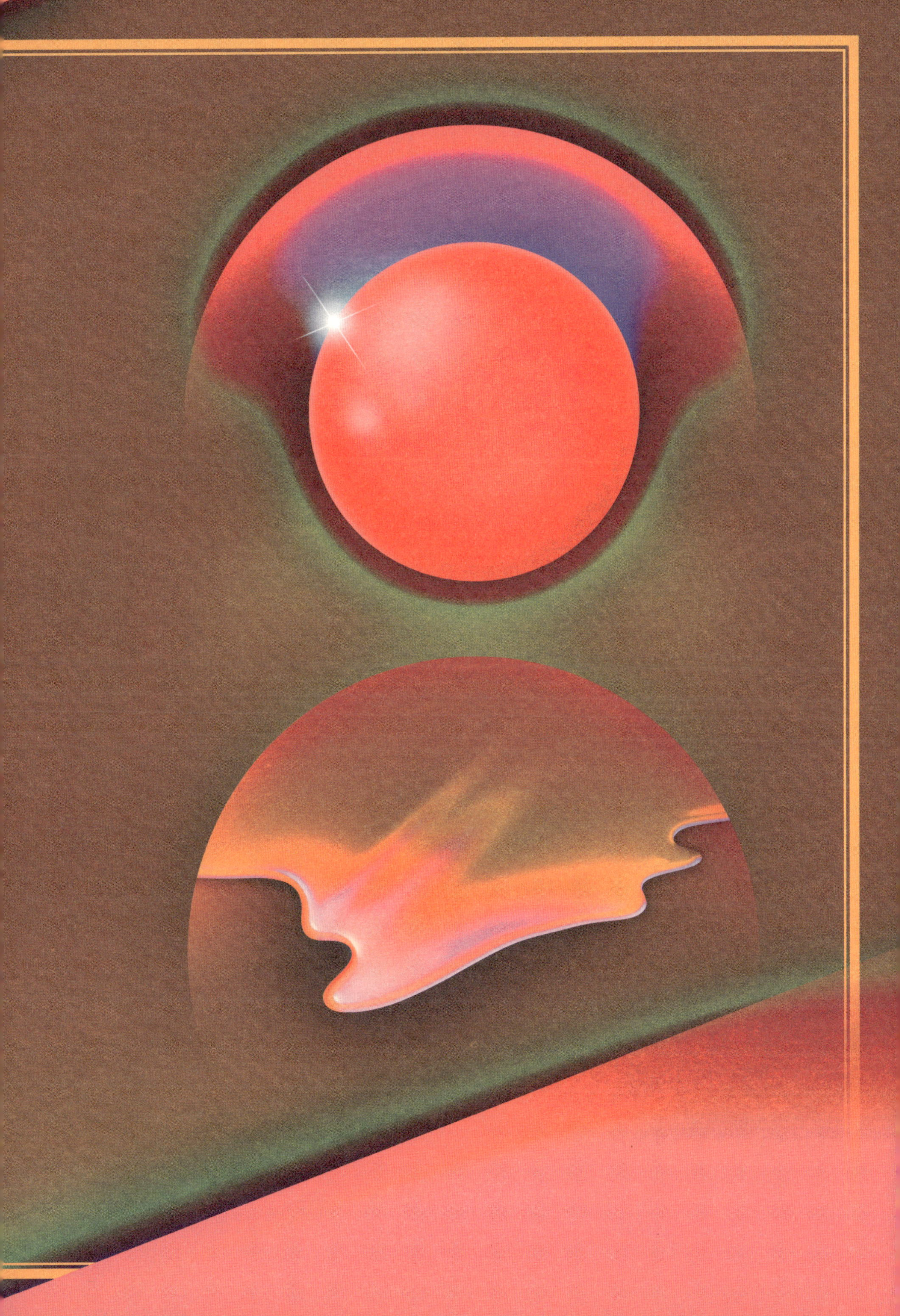

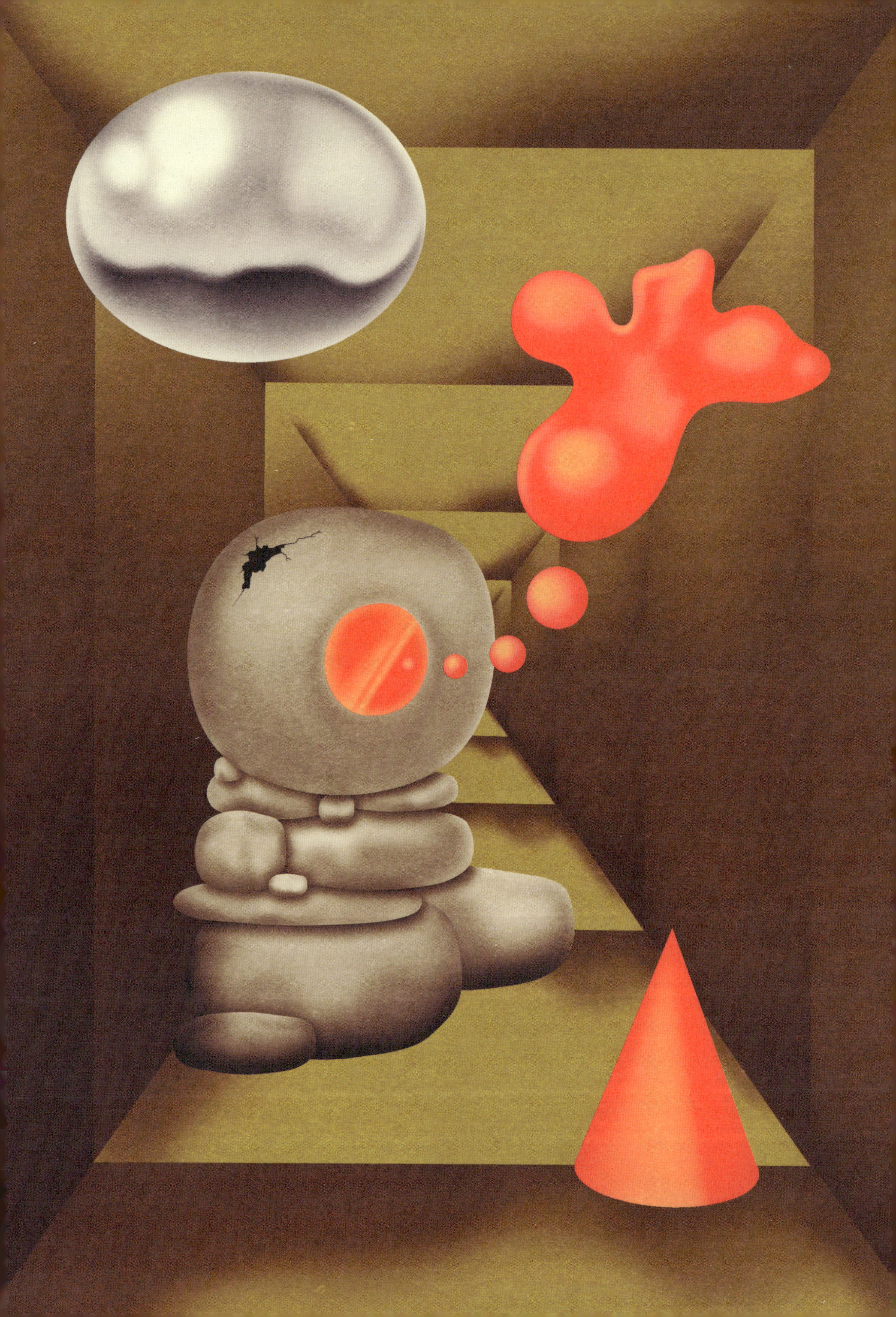

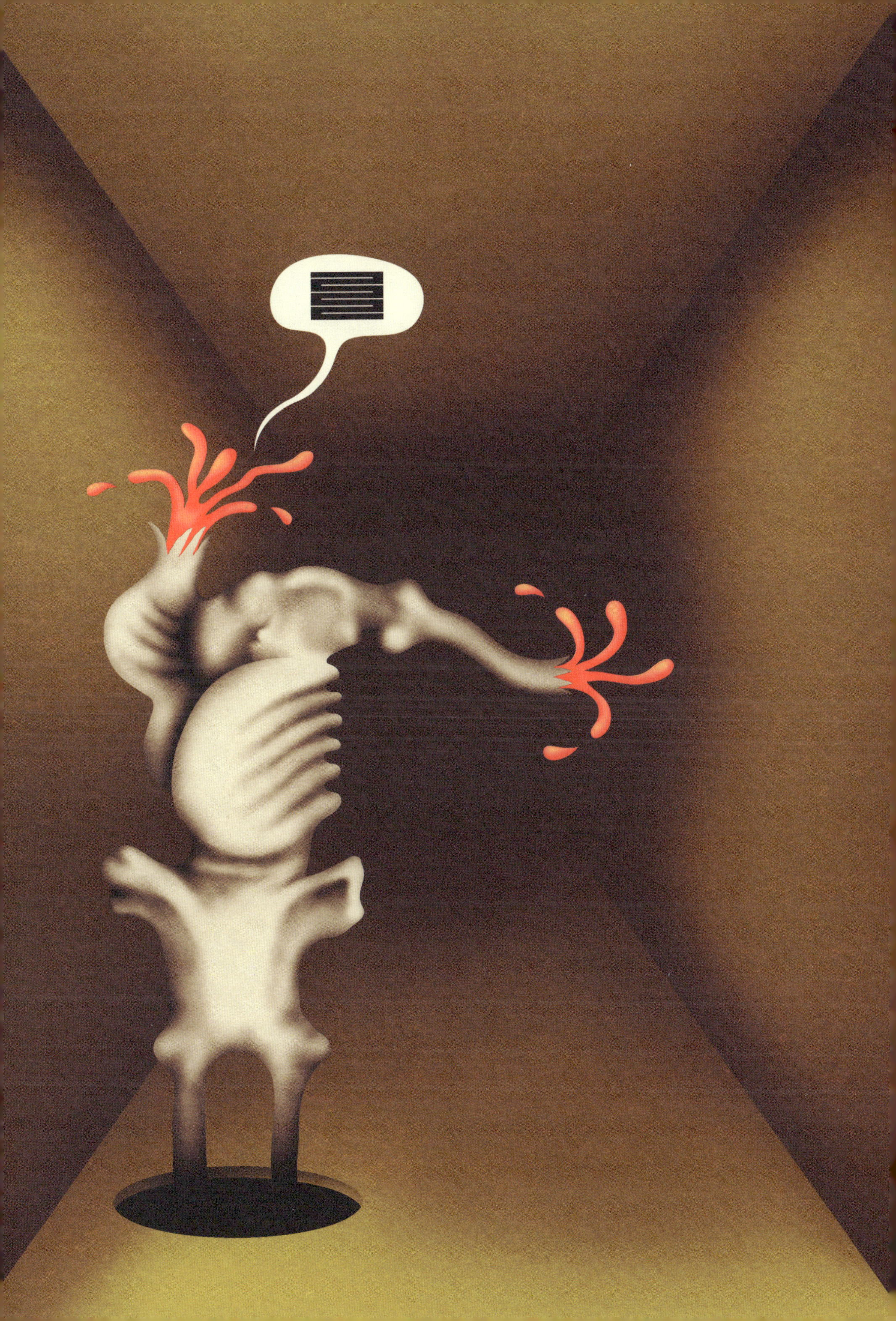

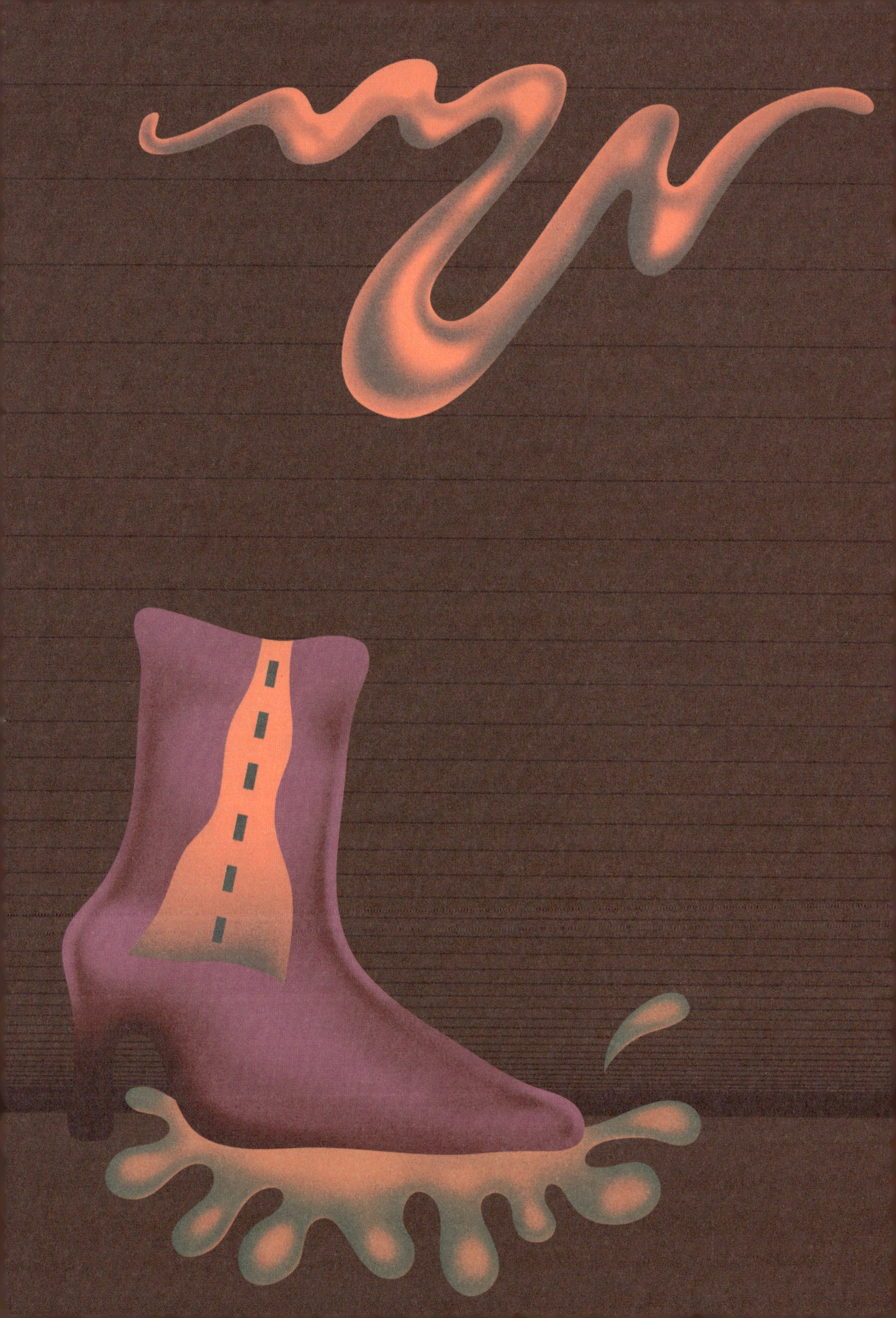

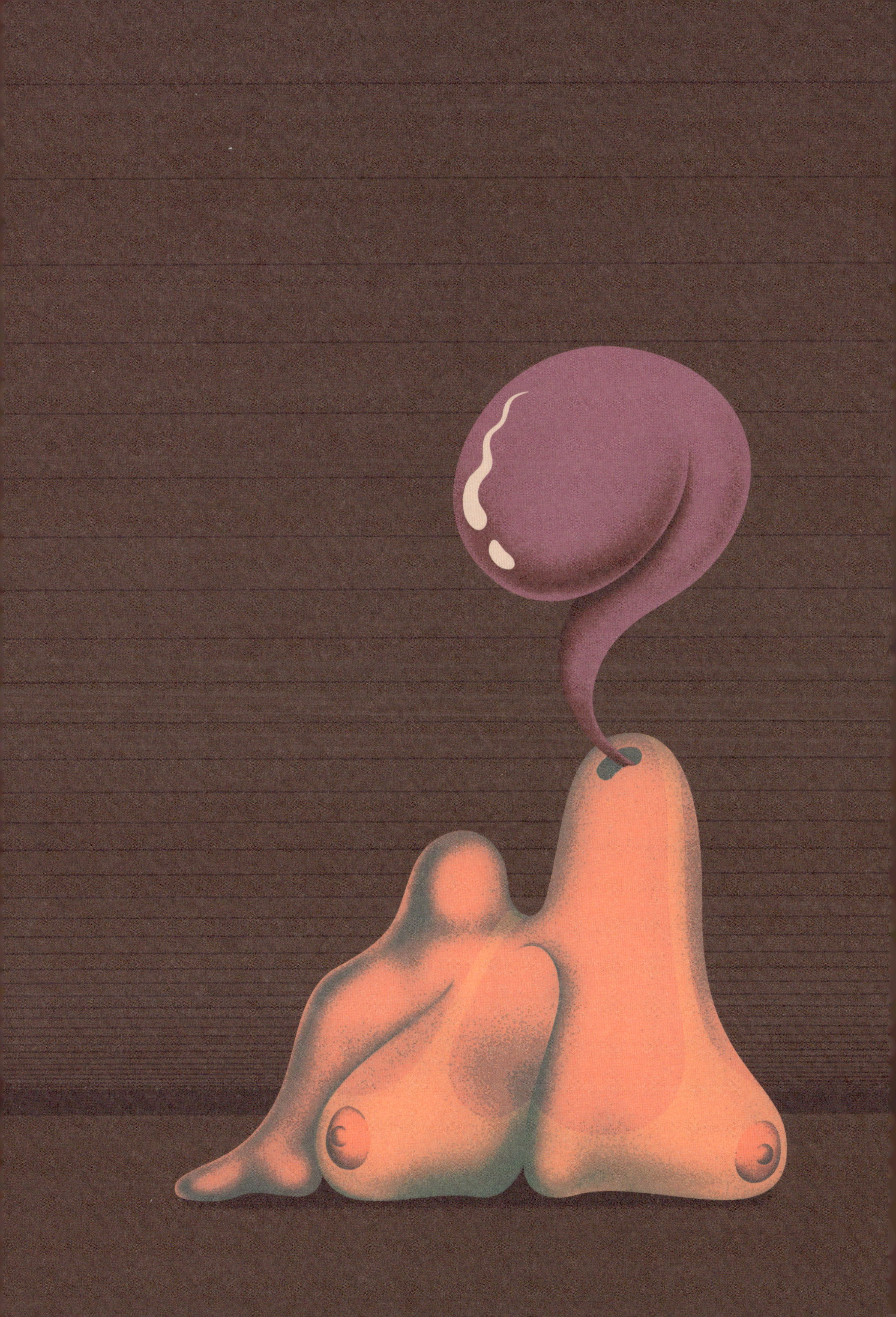

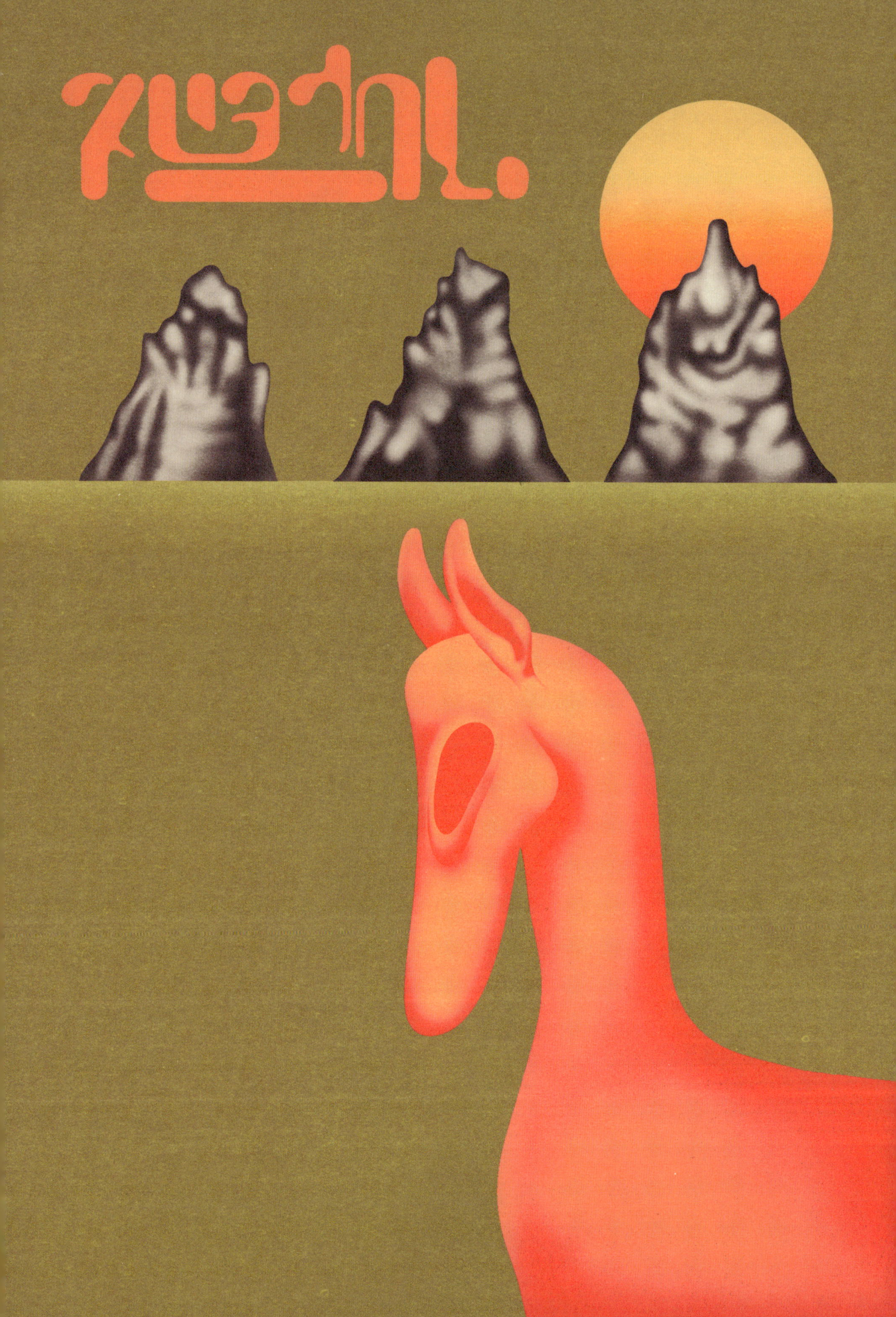

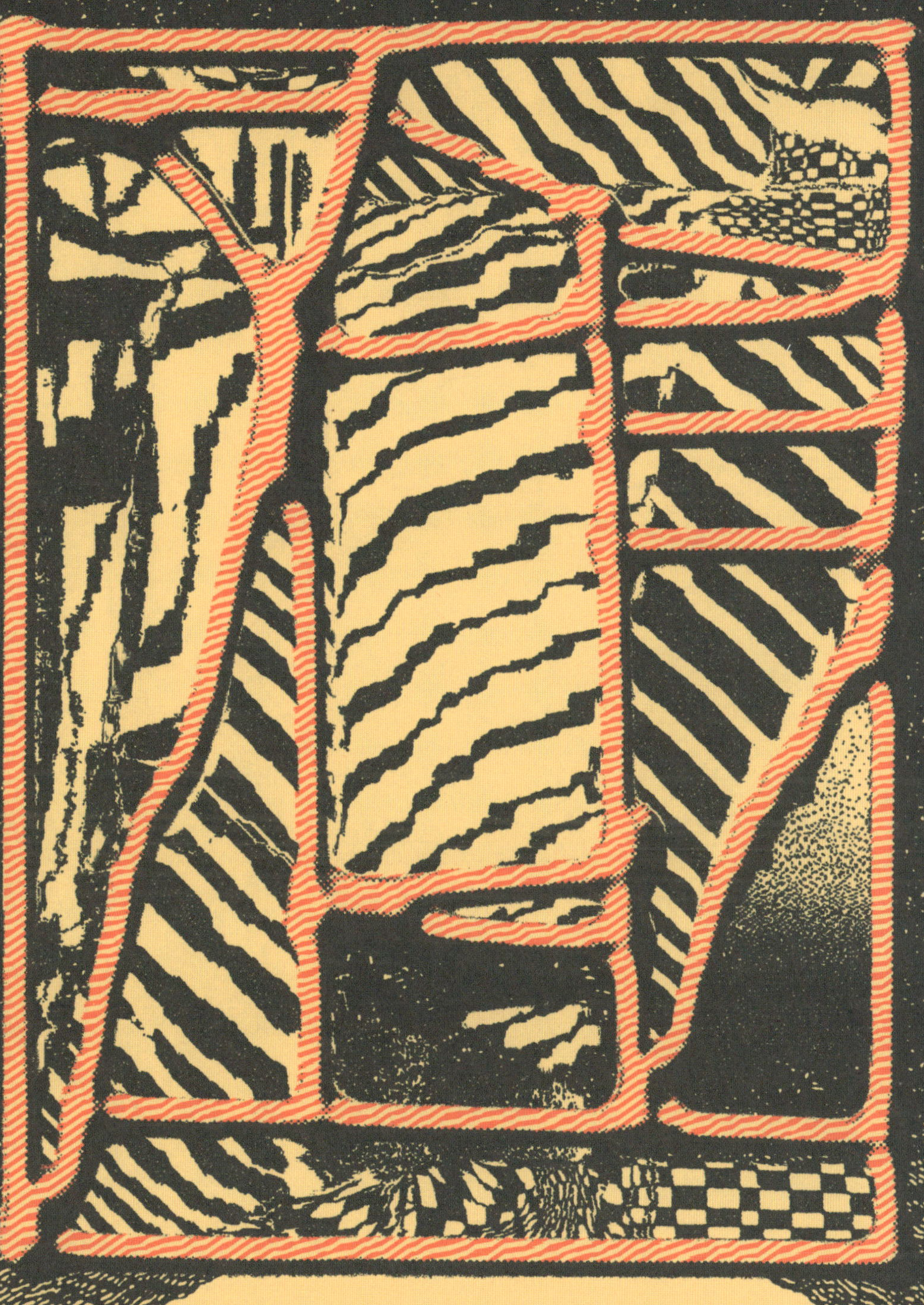

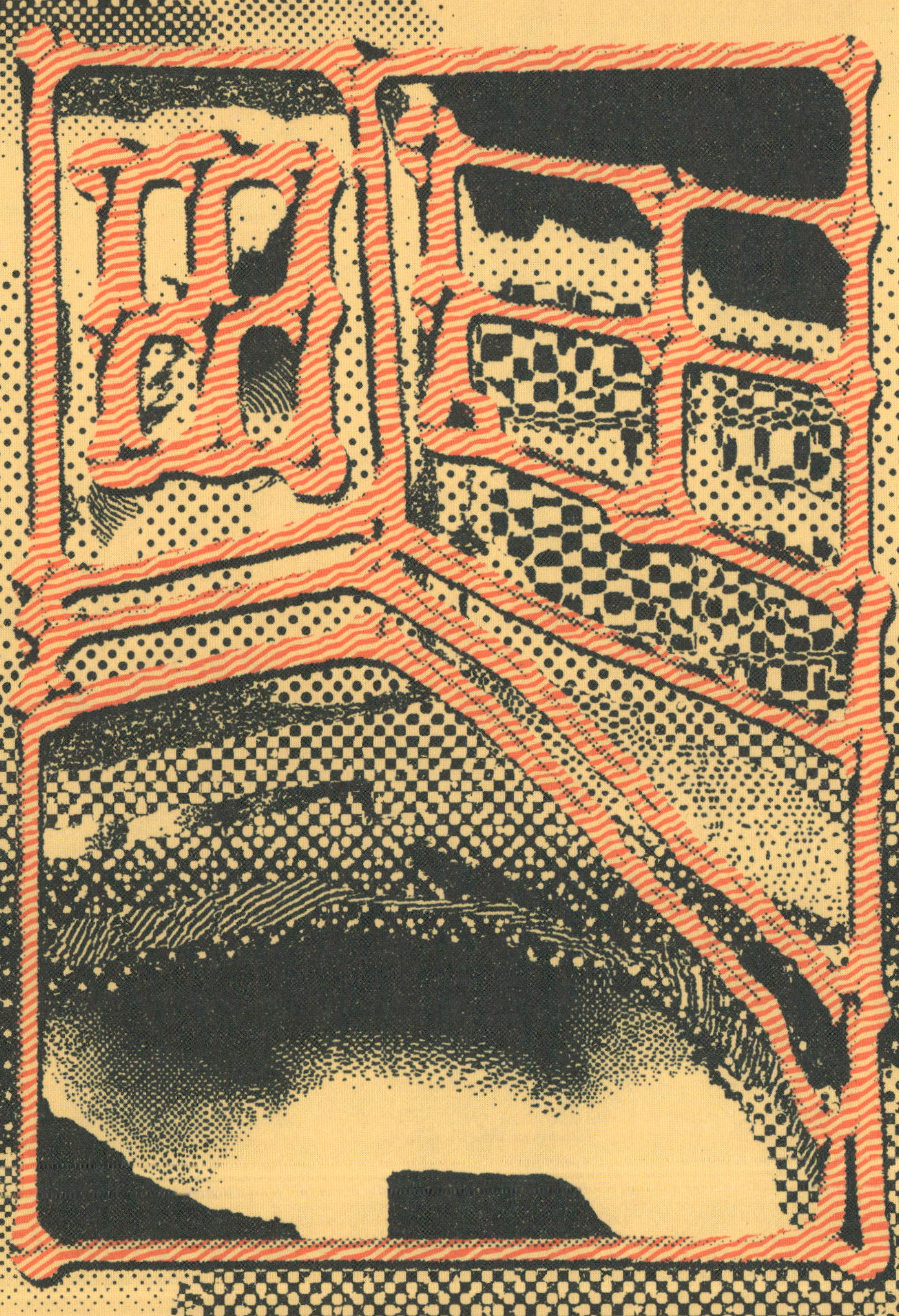

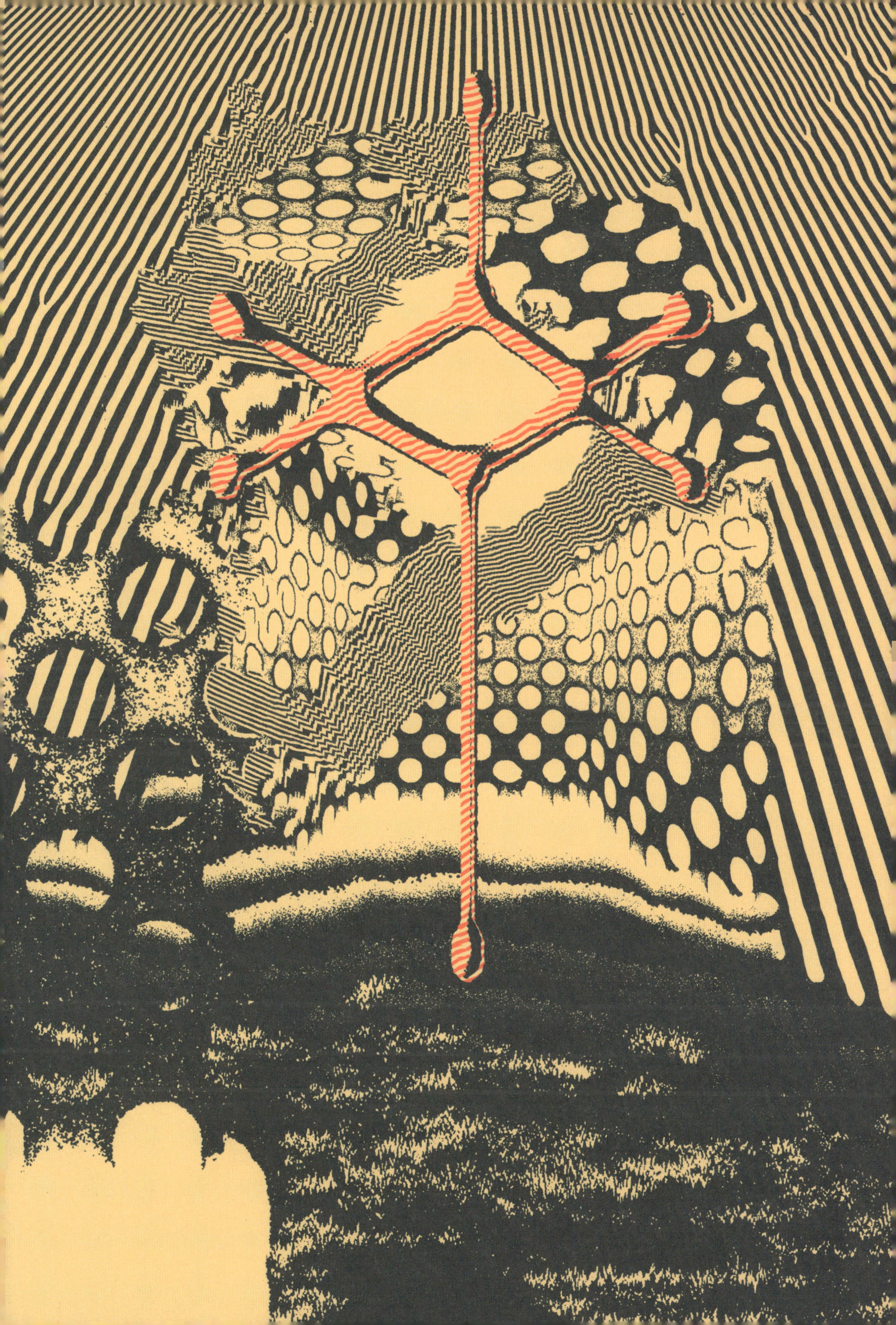

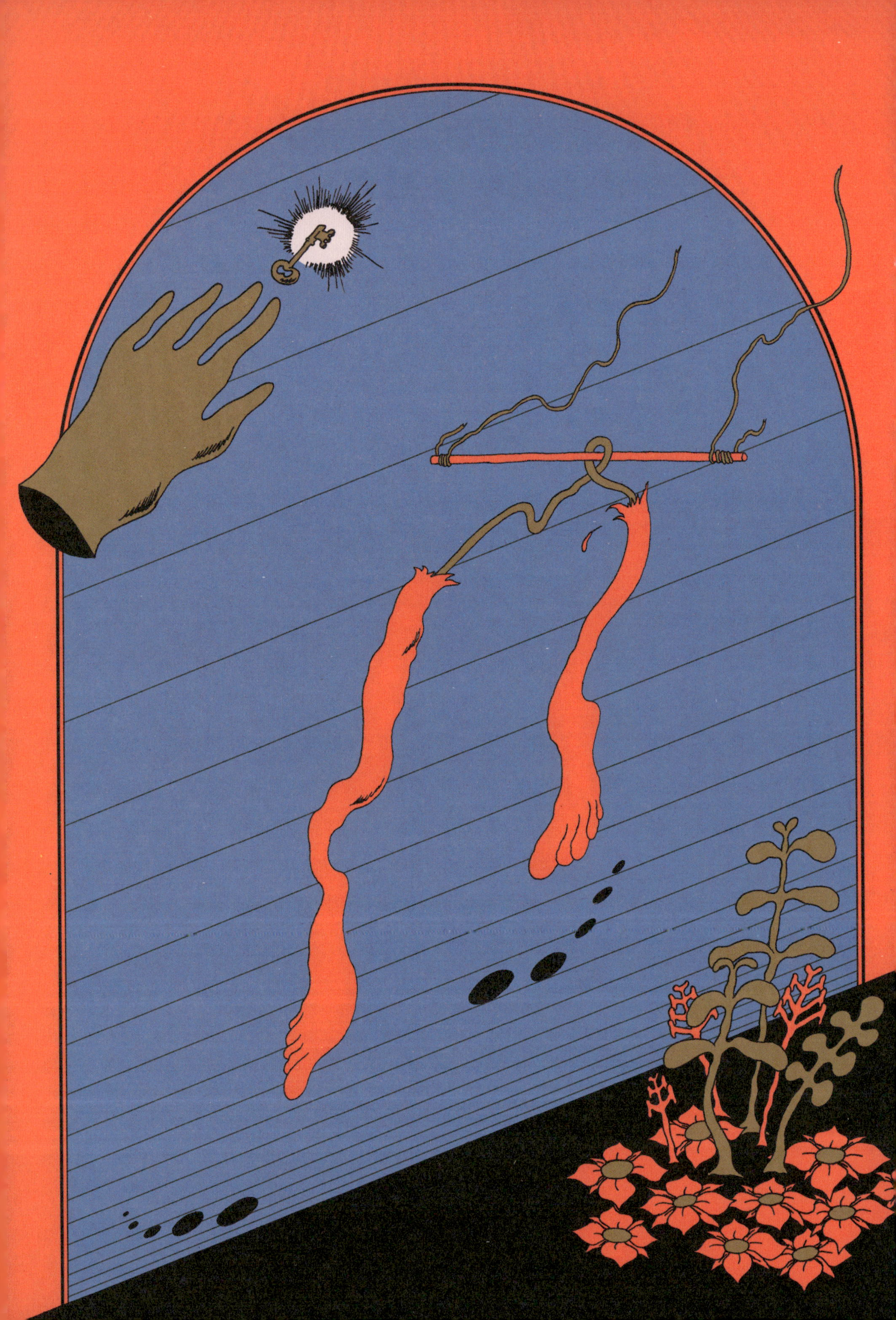

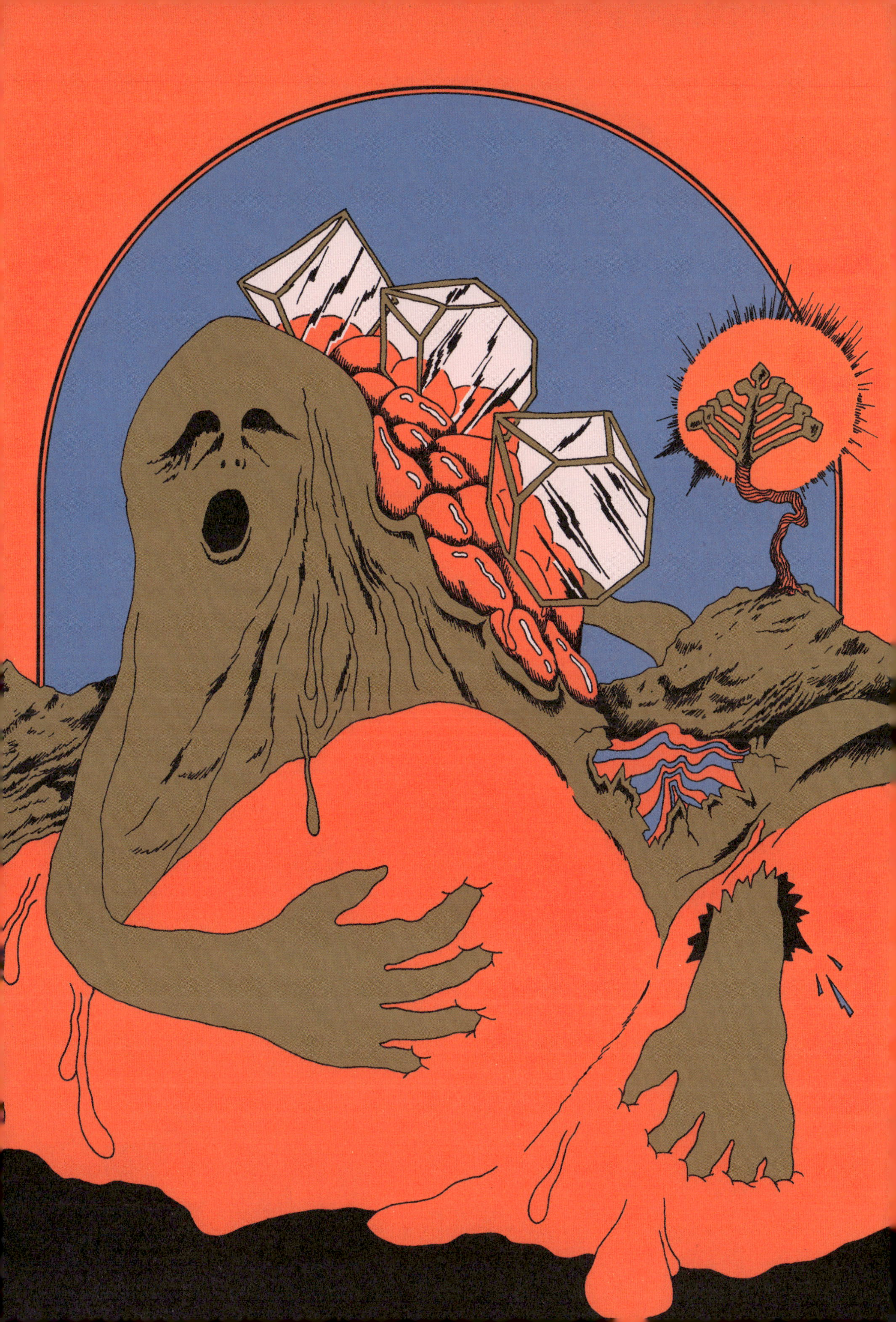

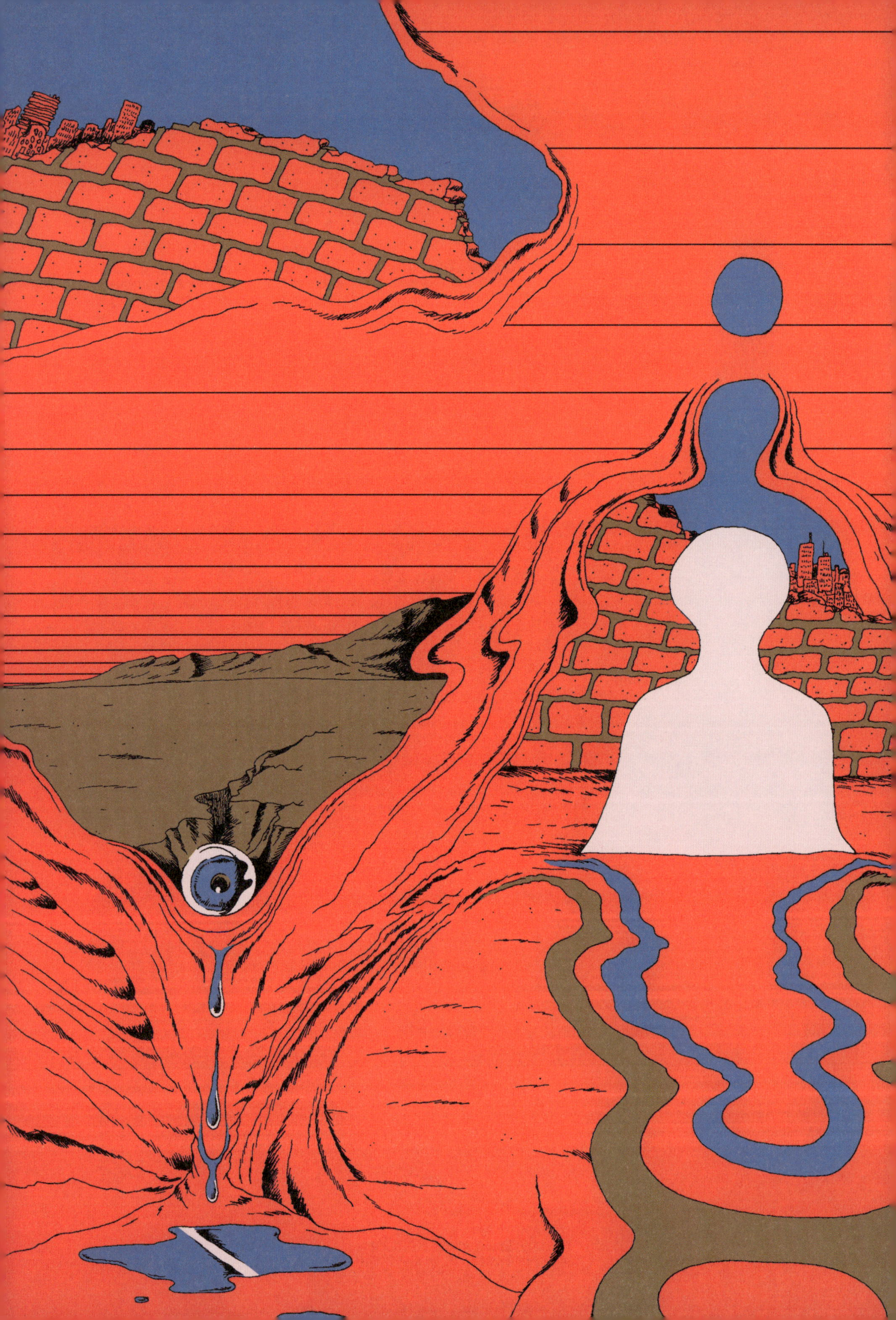

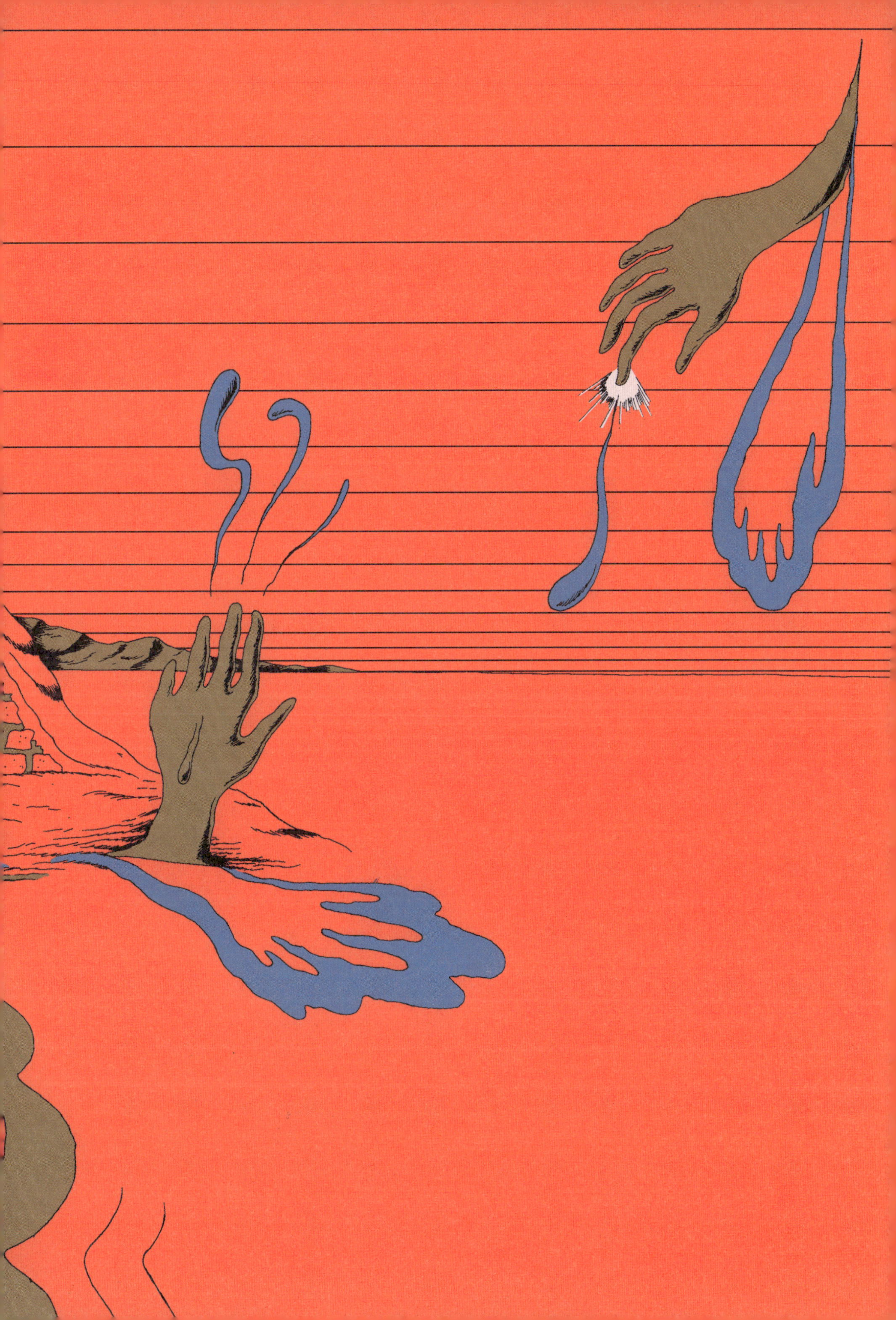

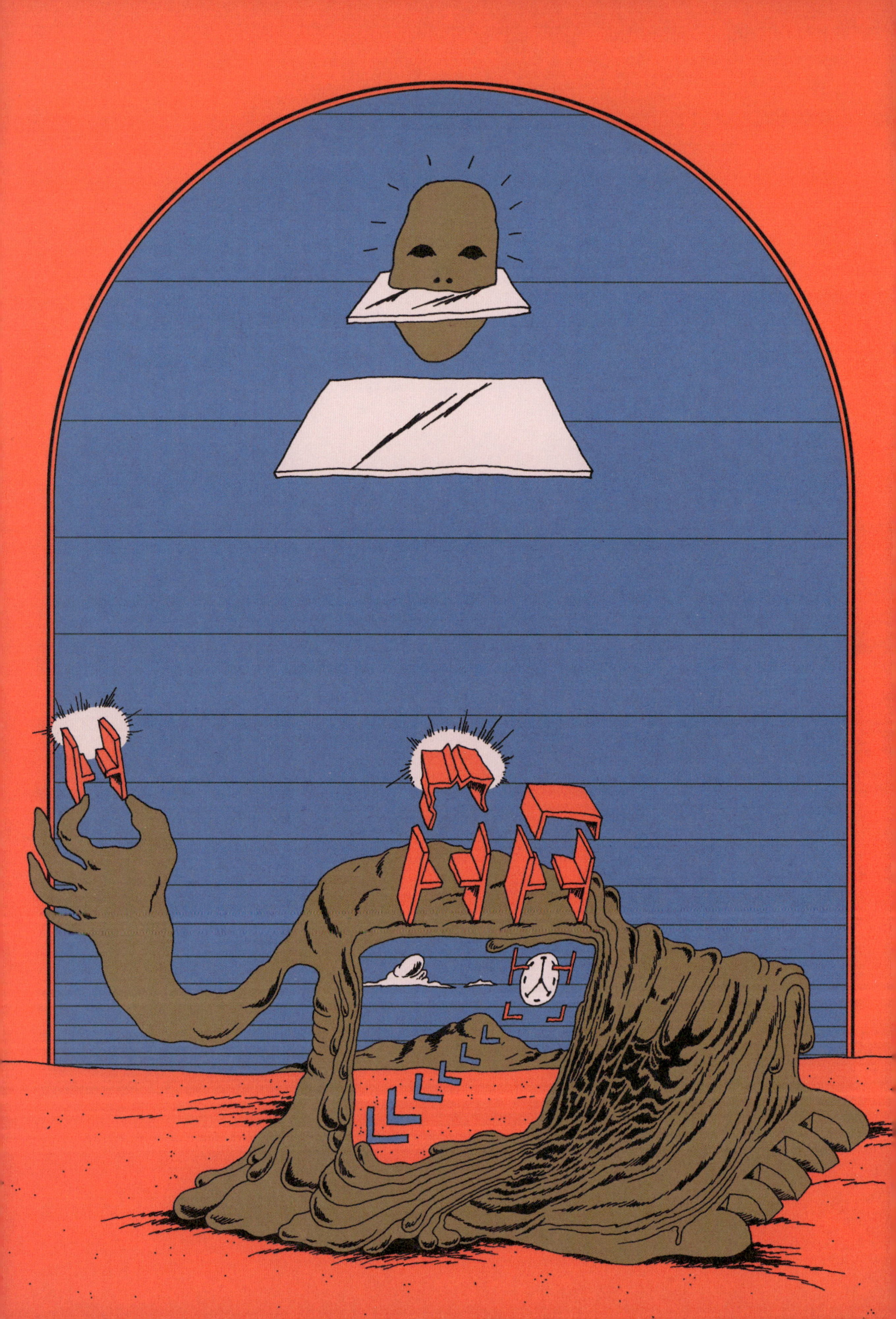

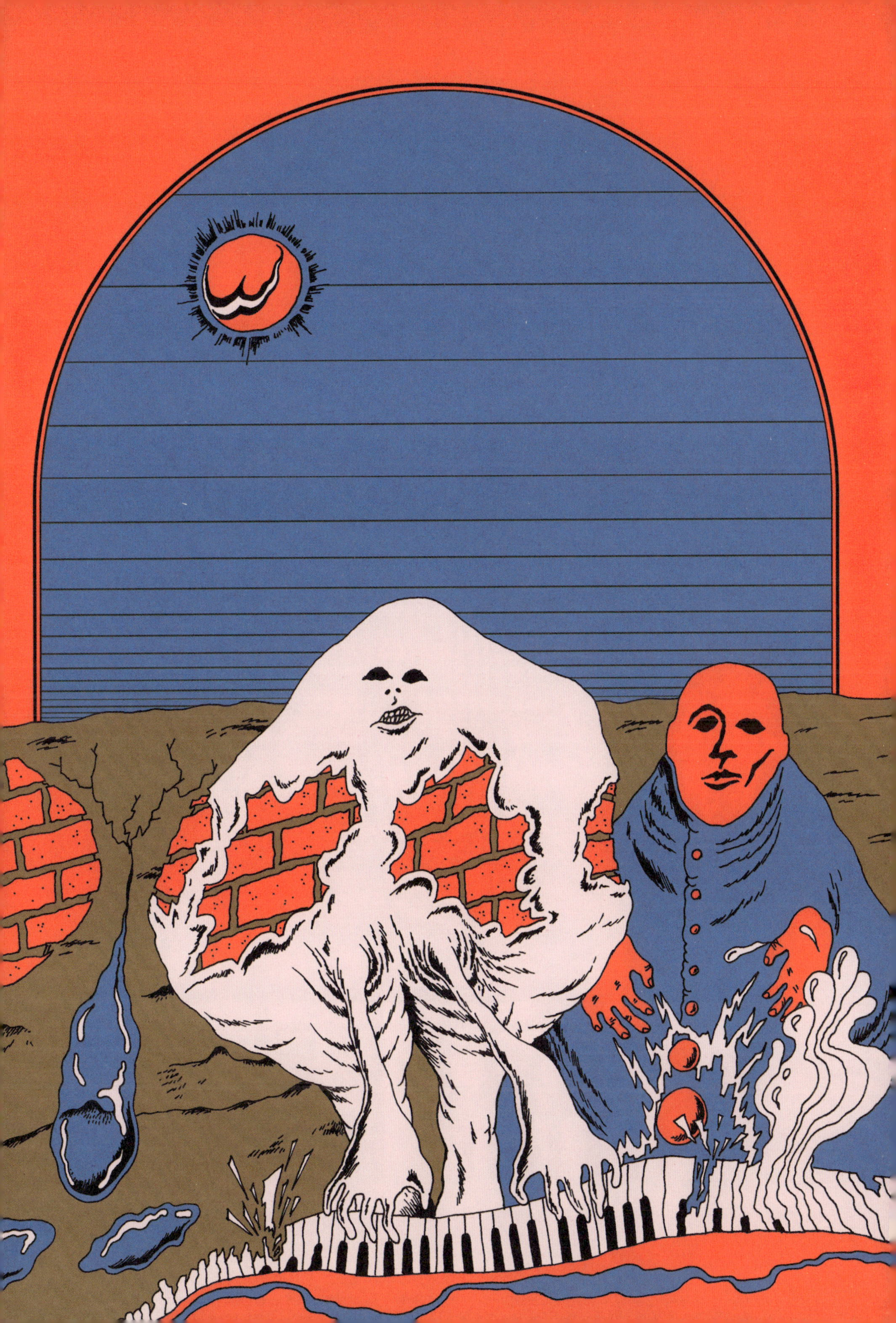

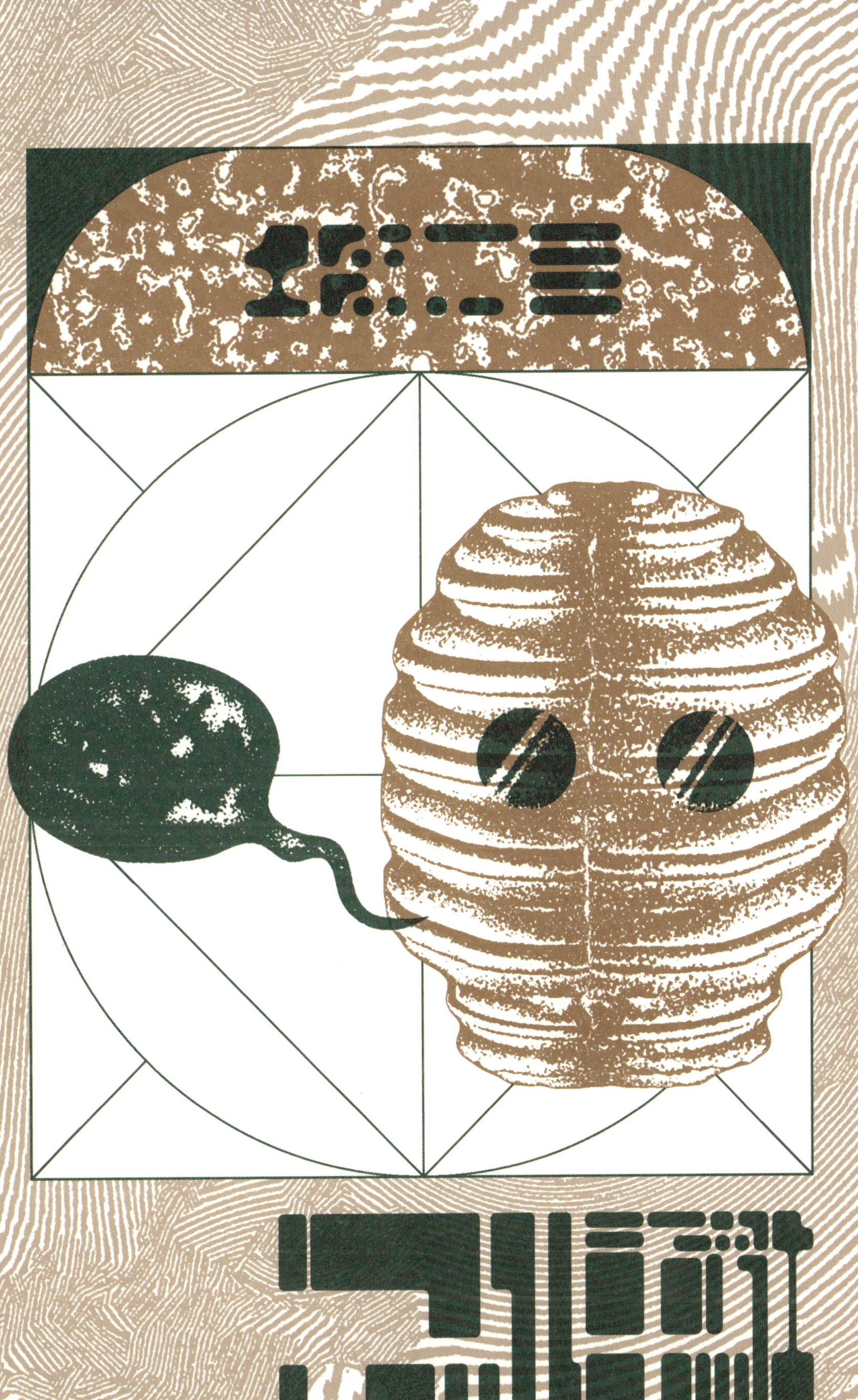

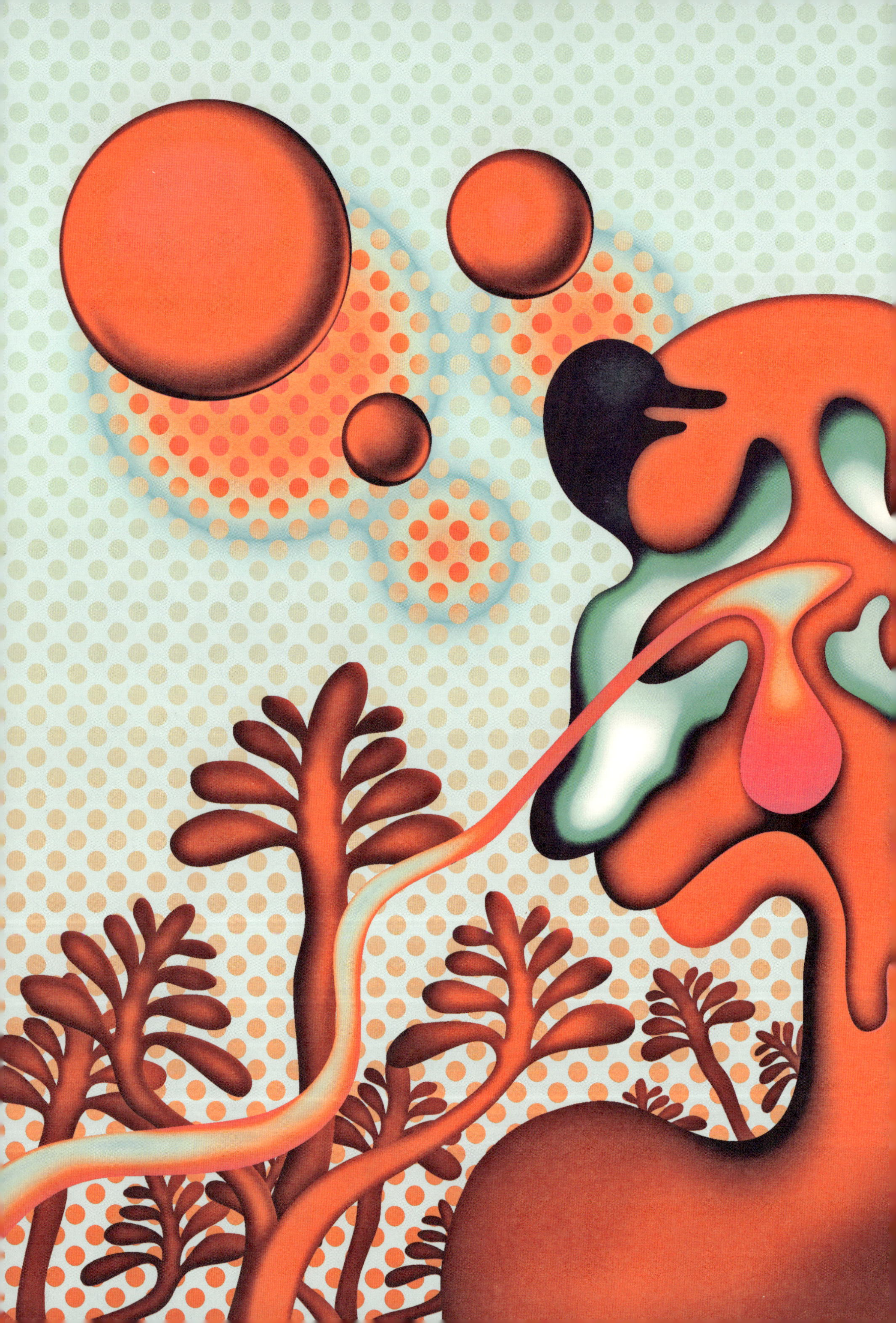

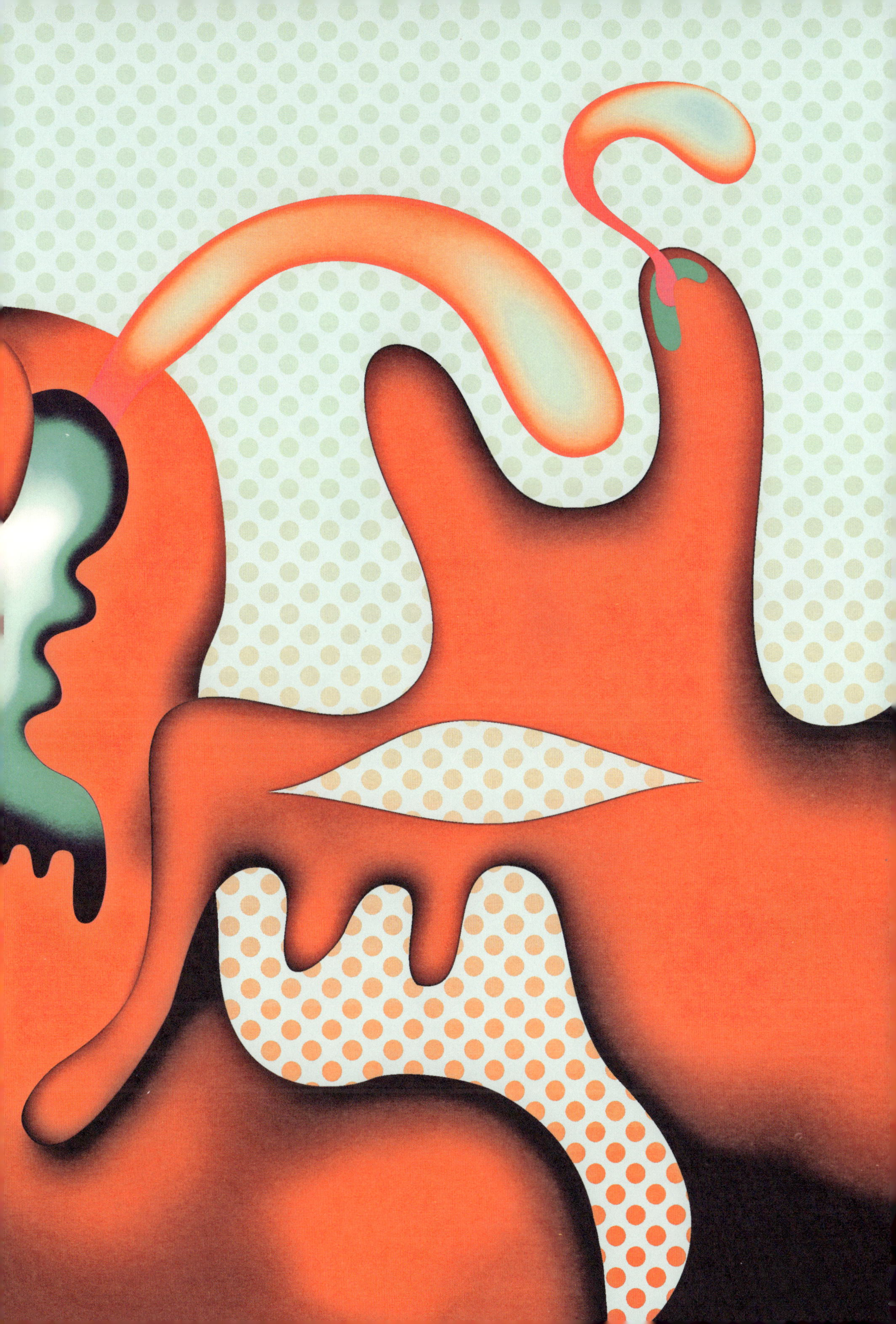

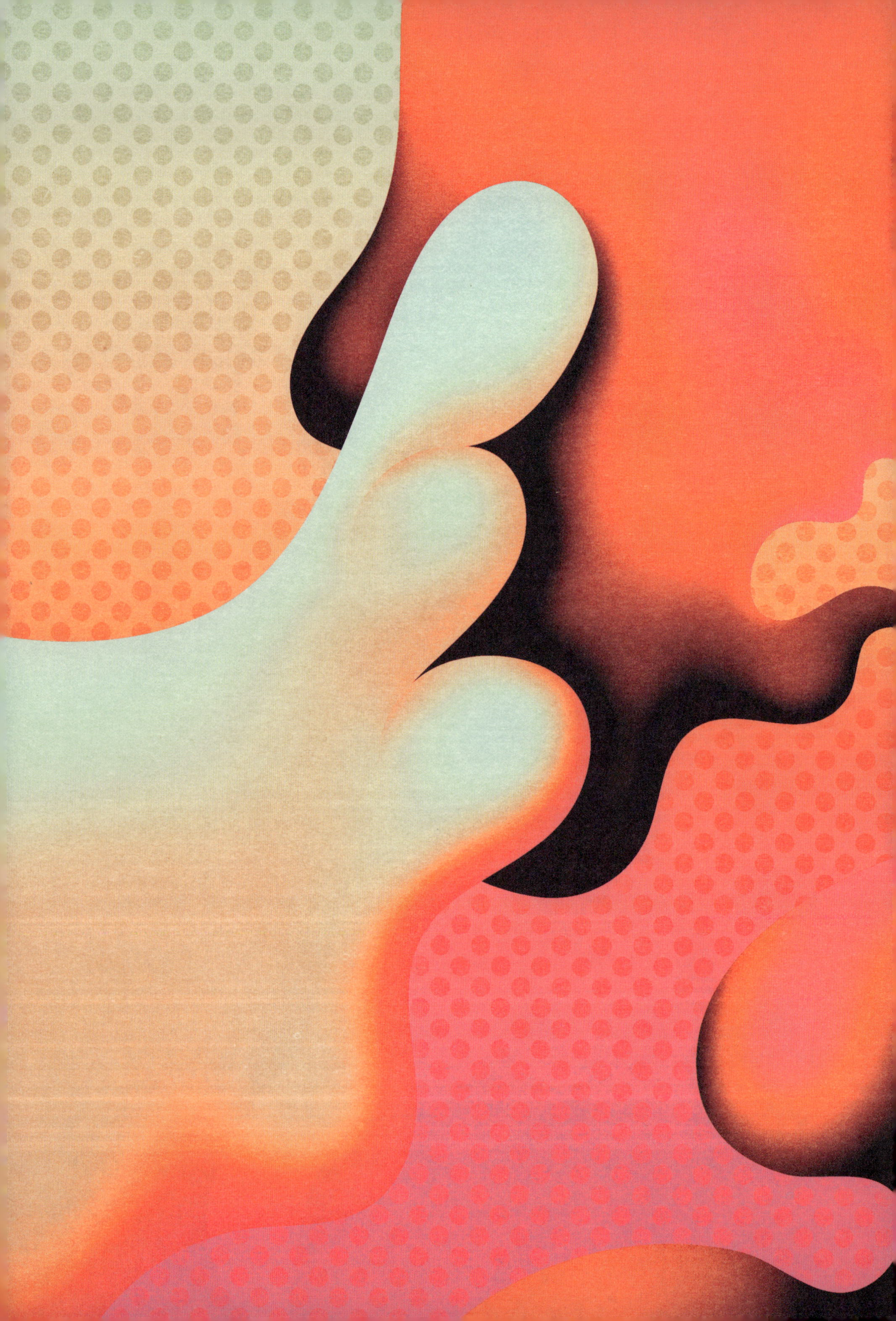

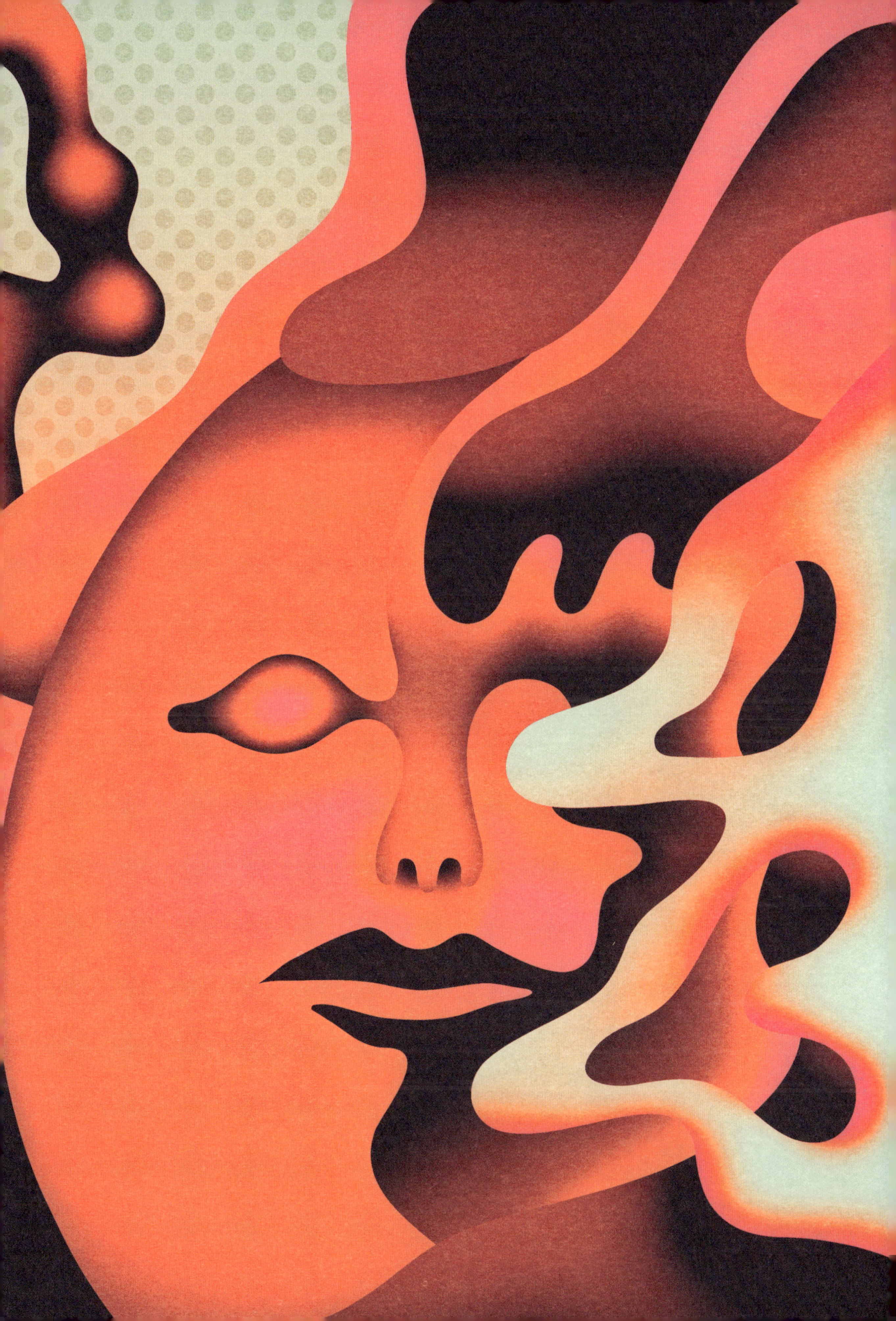

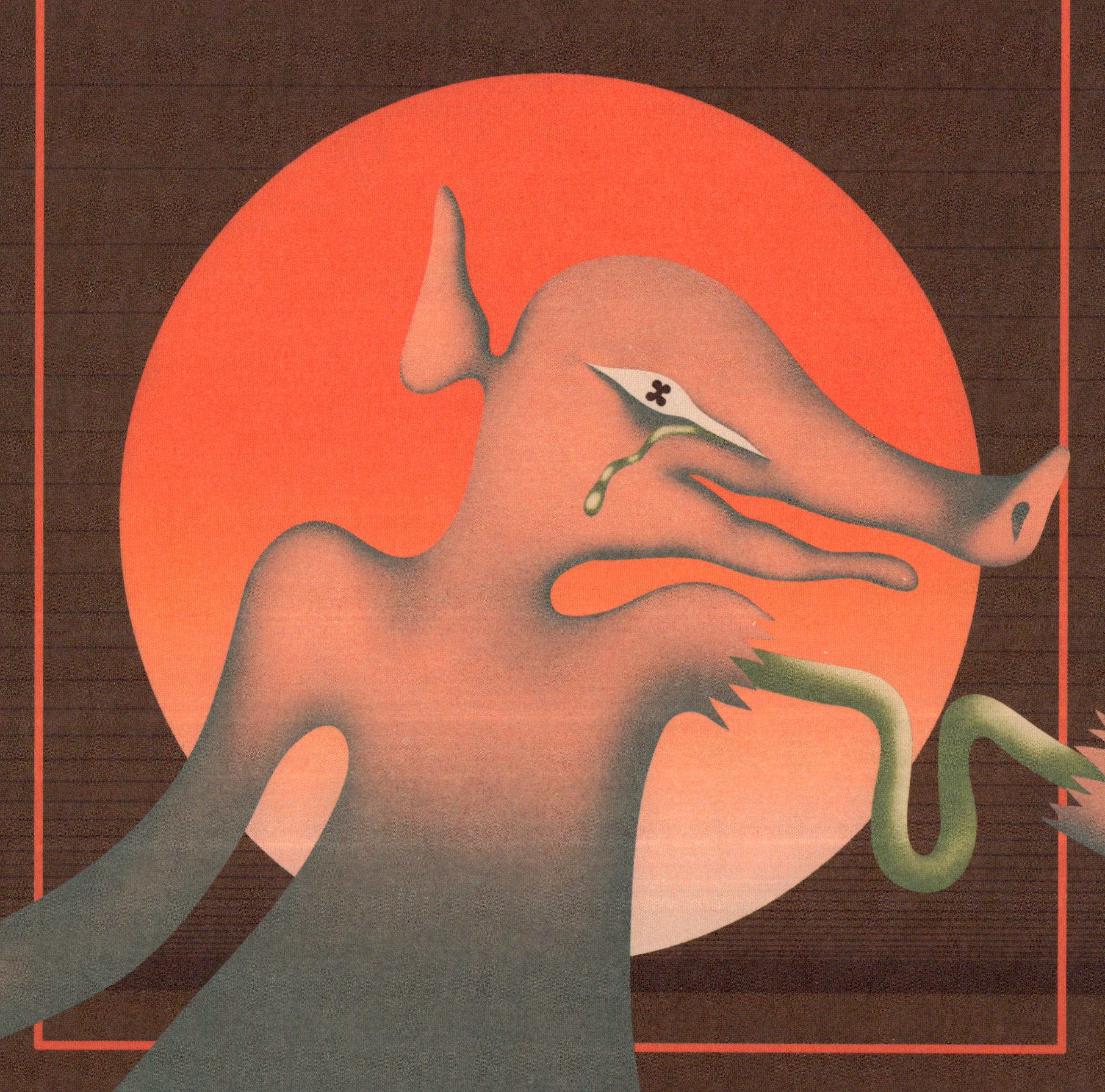

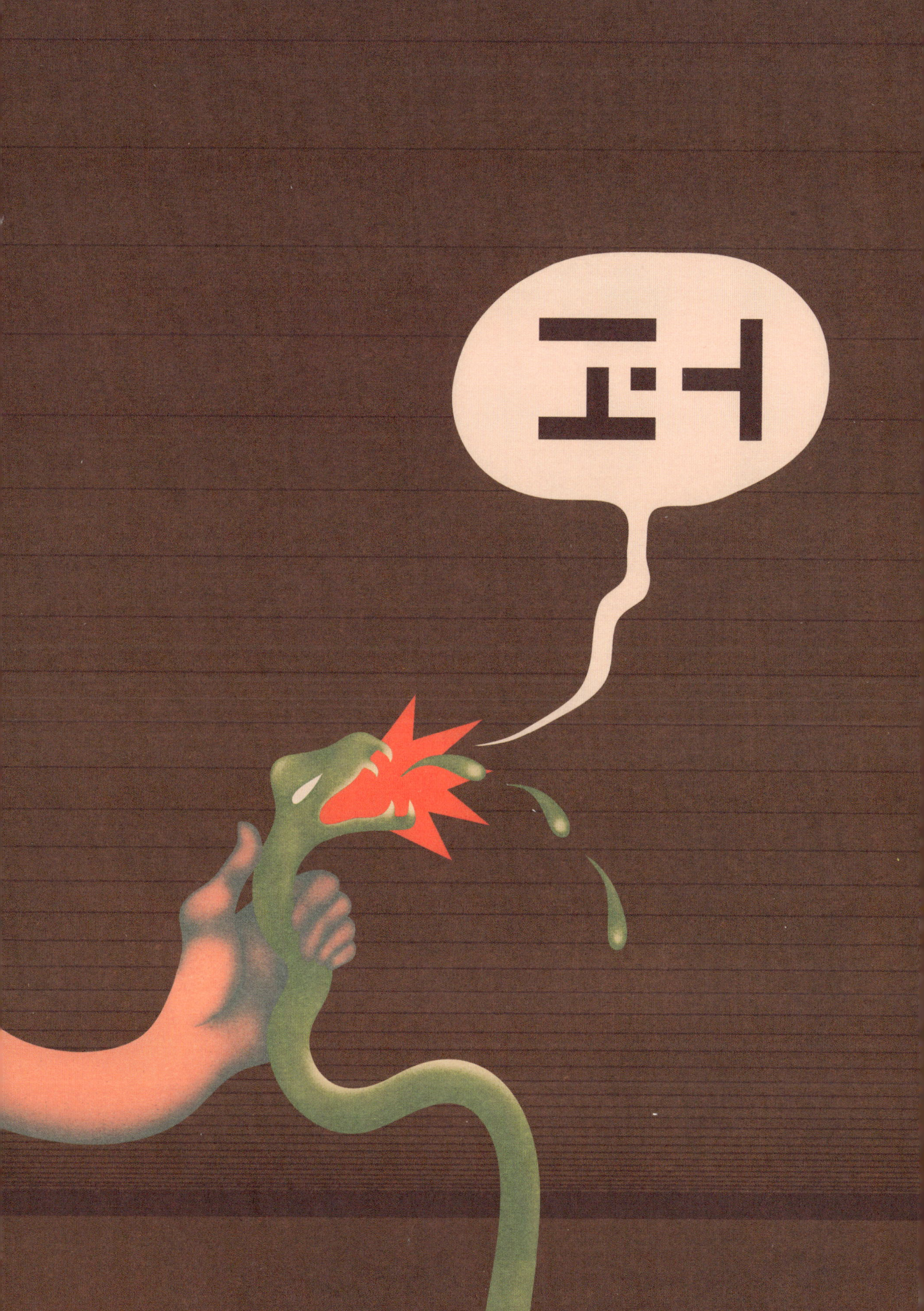

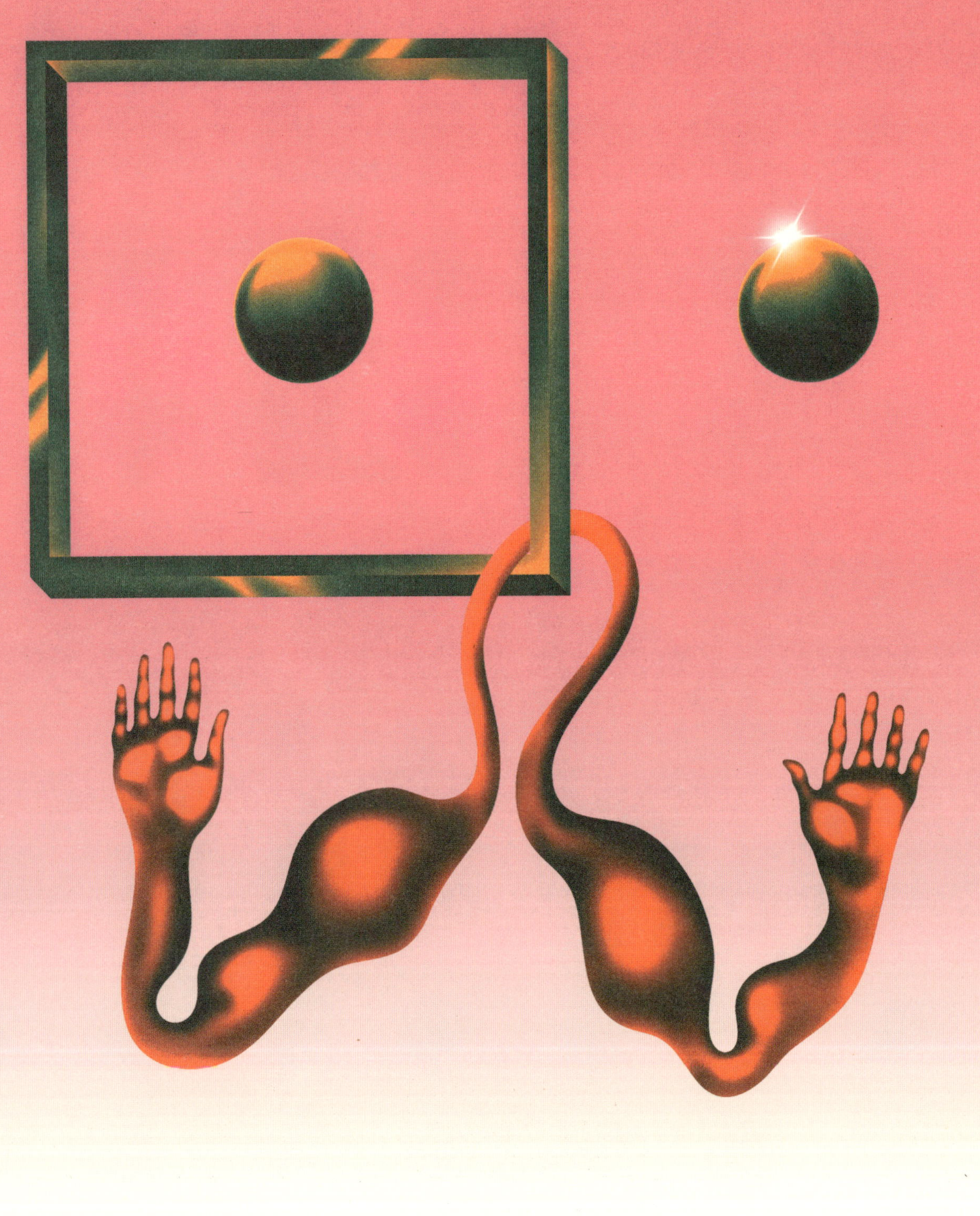

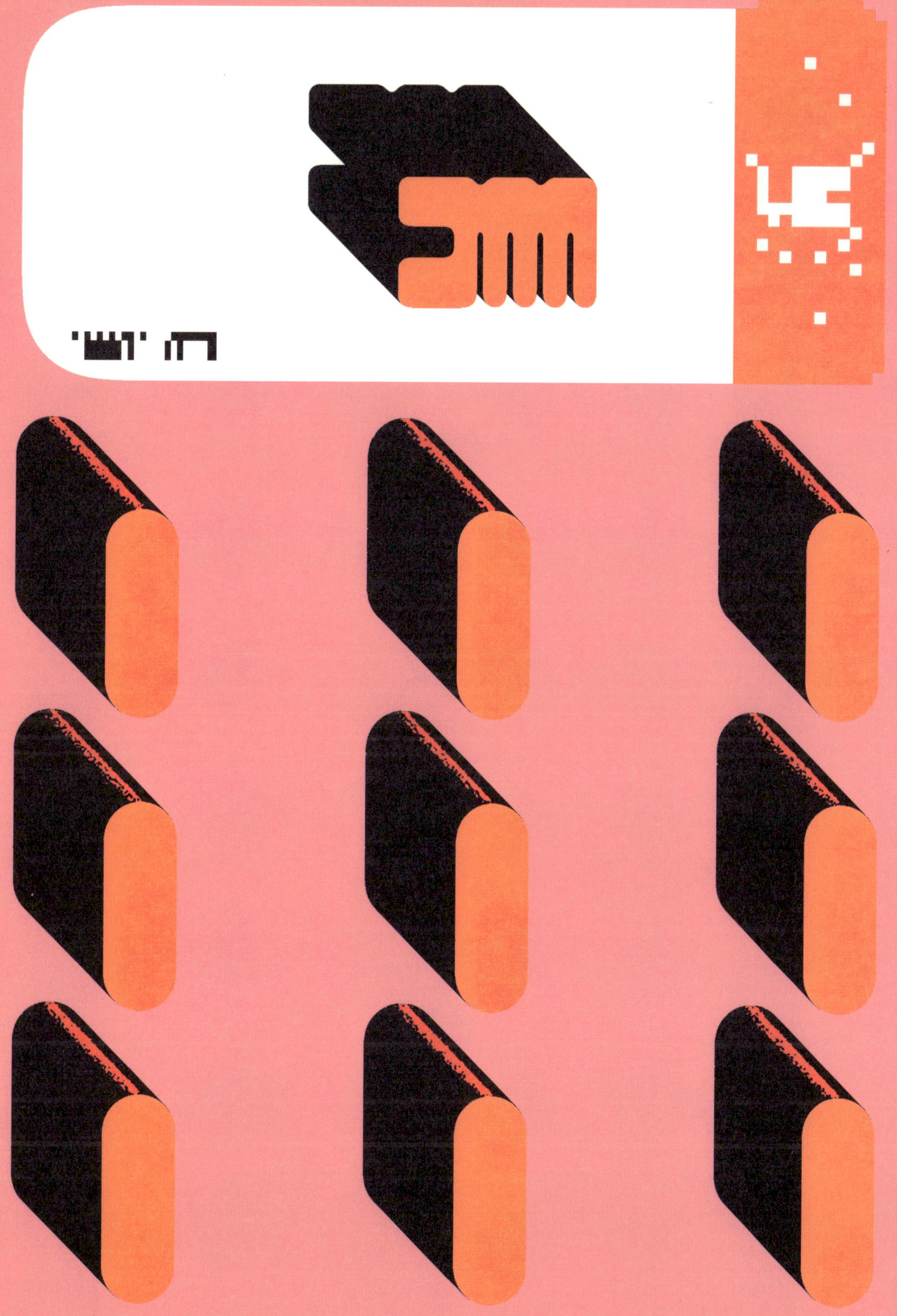

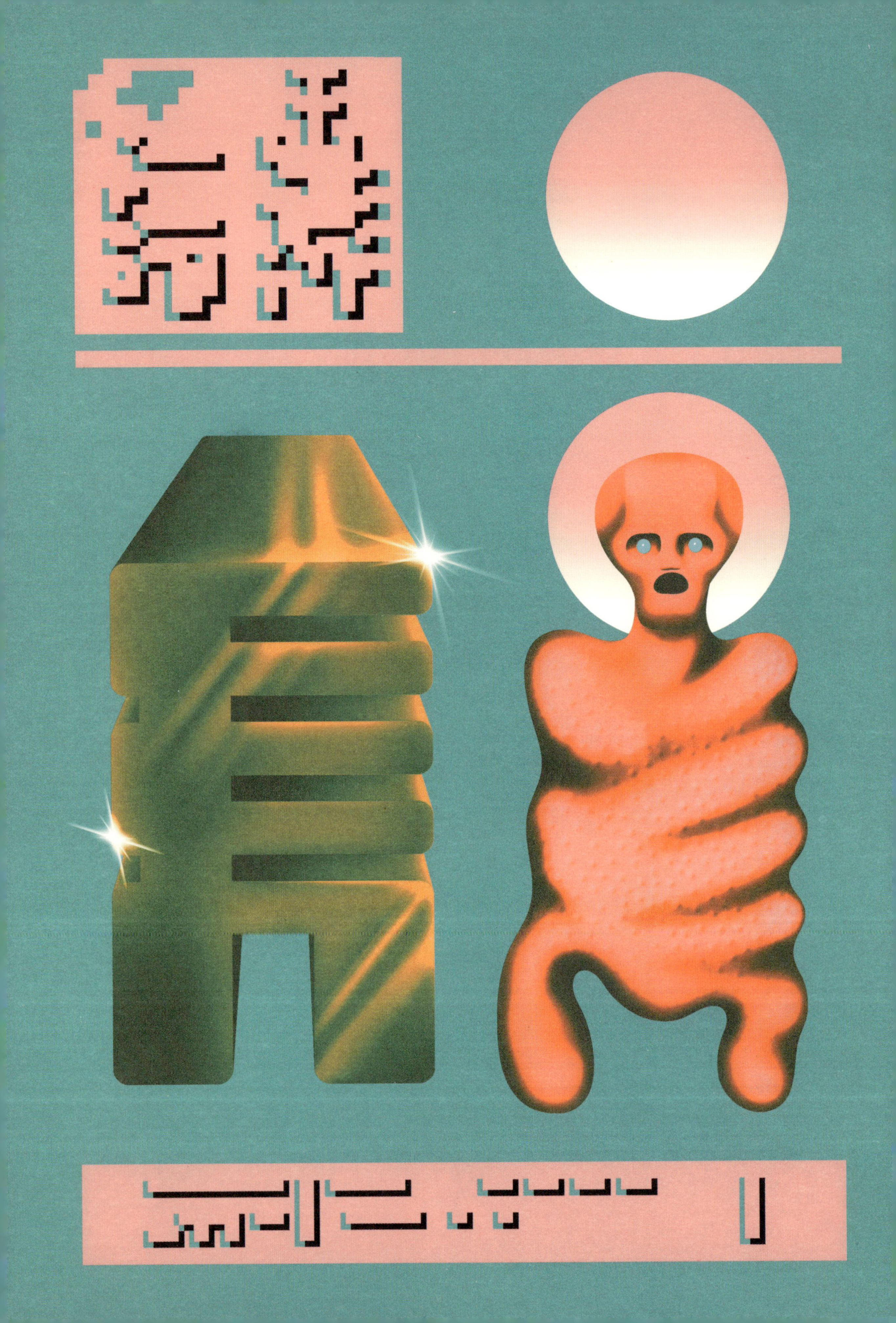

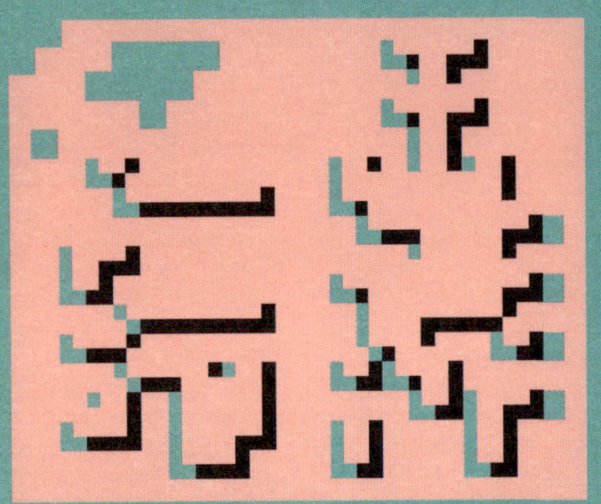

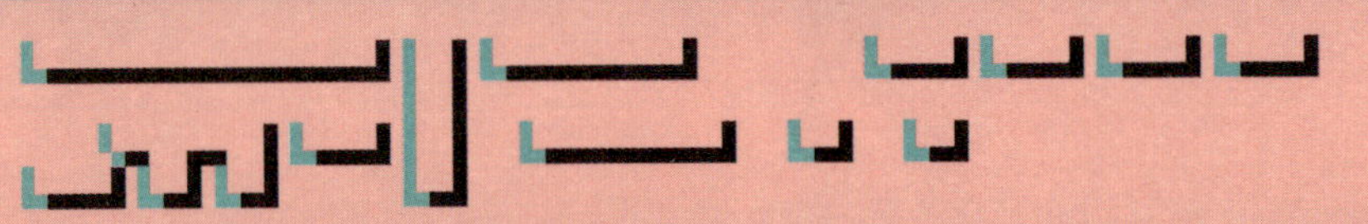

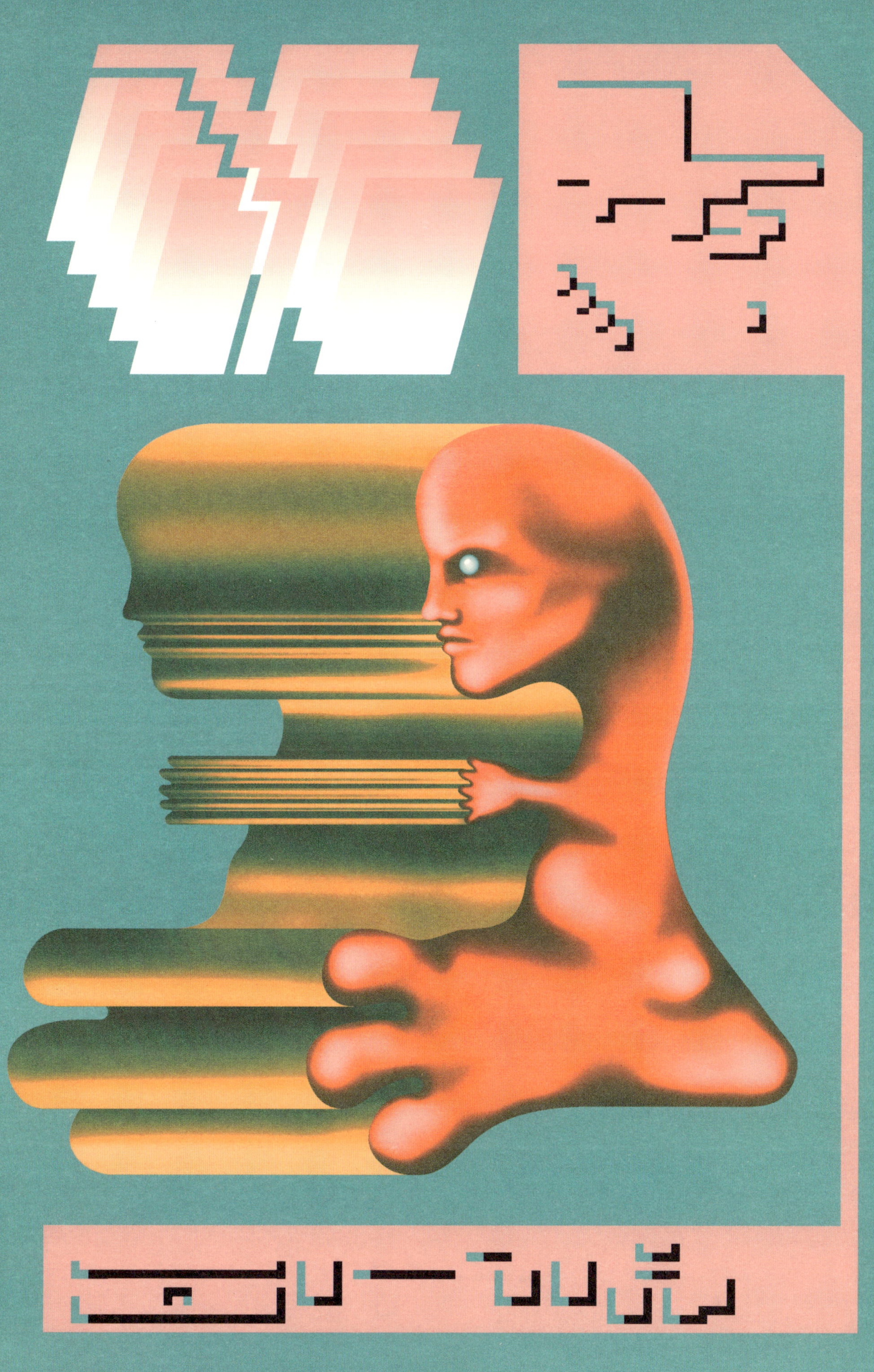

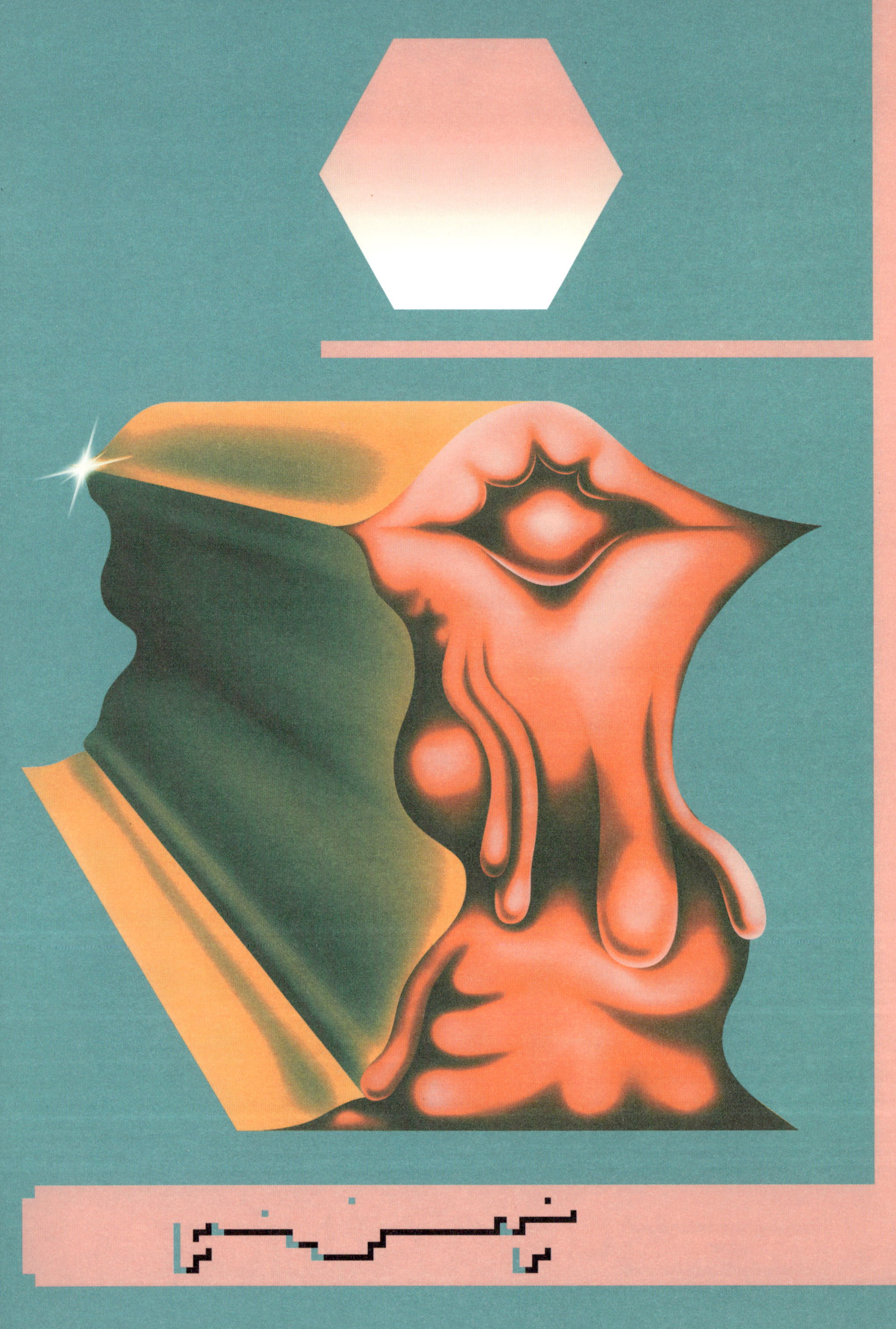

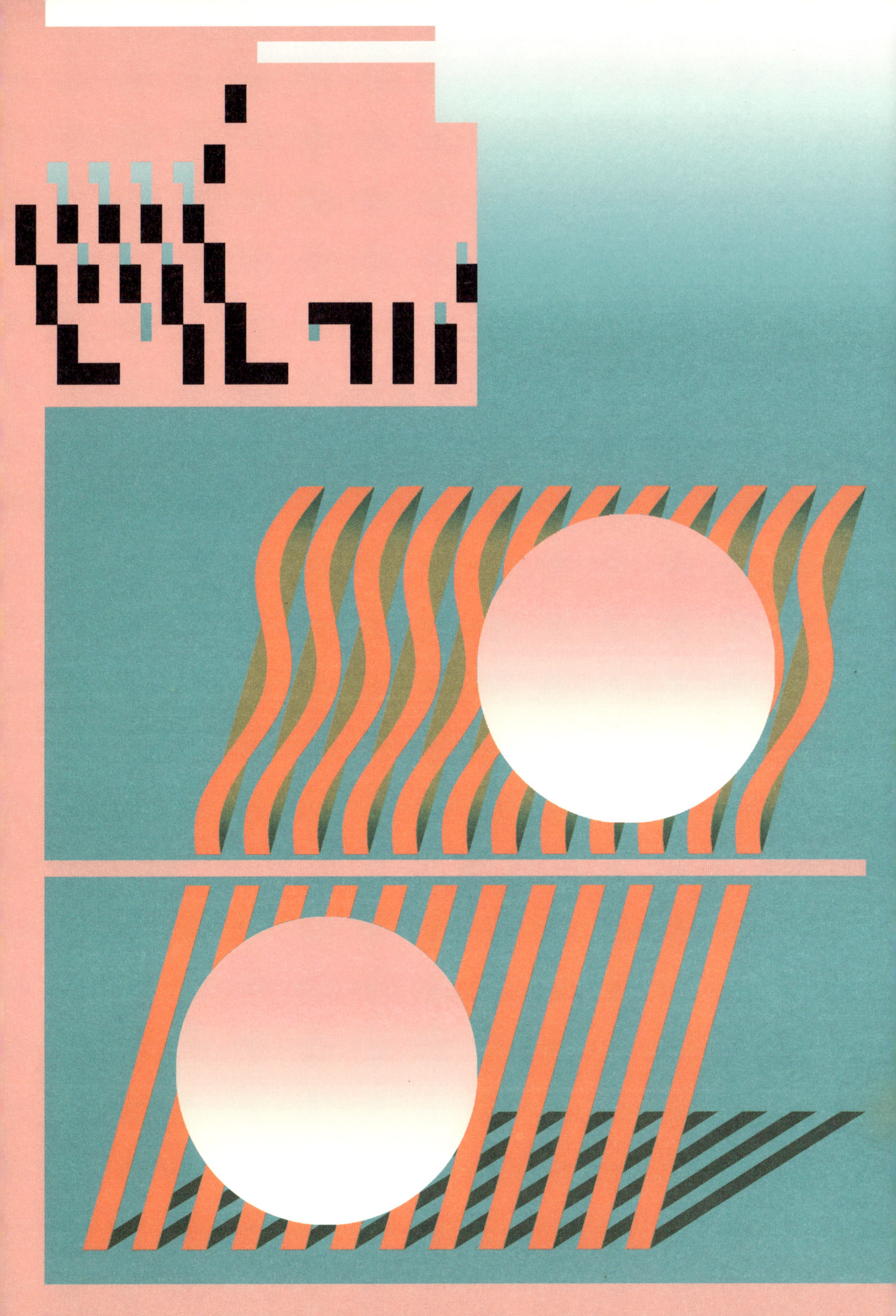

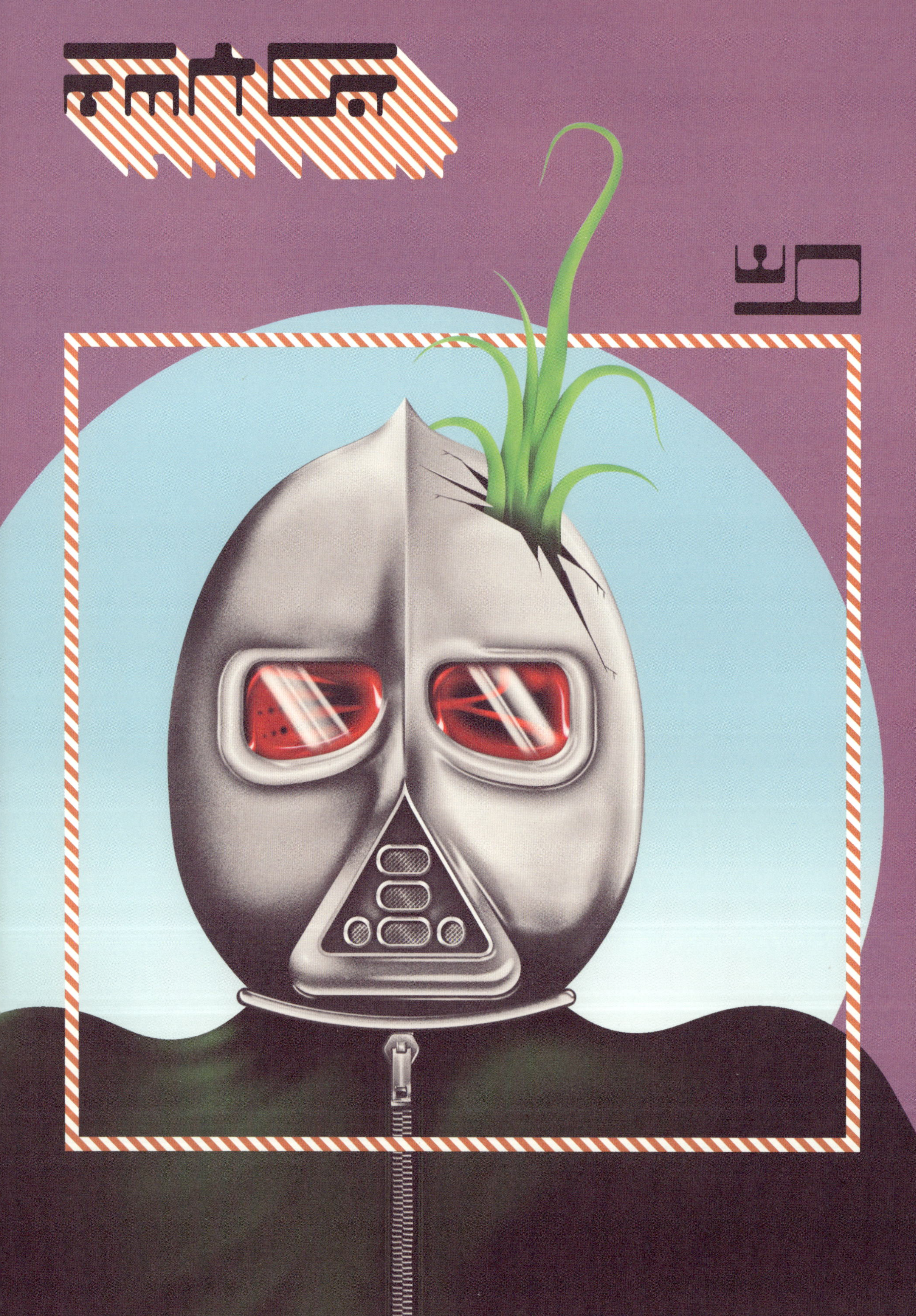

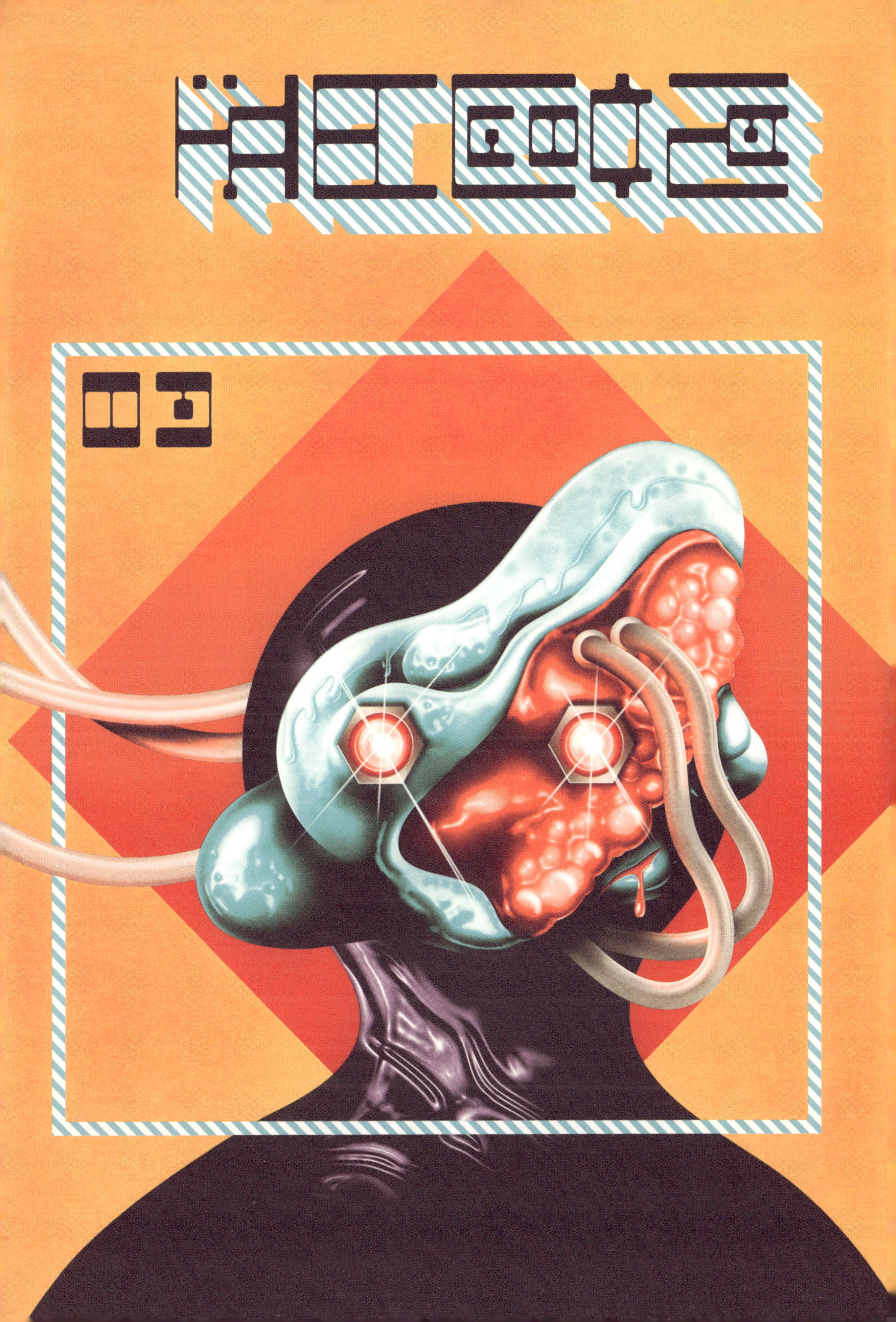

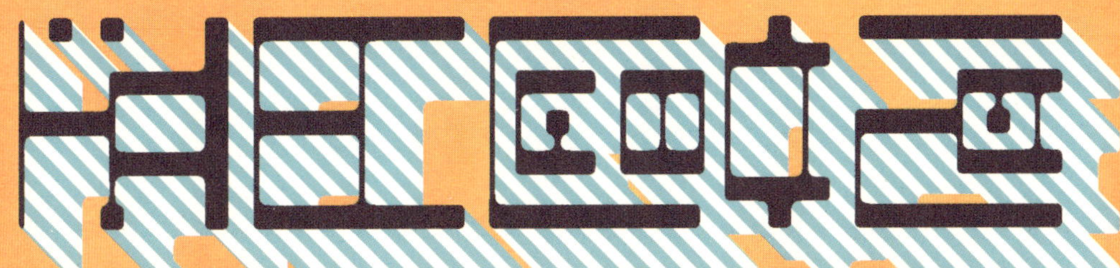

03

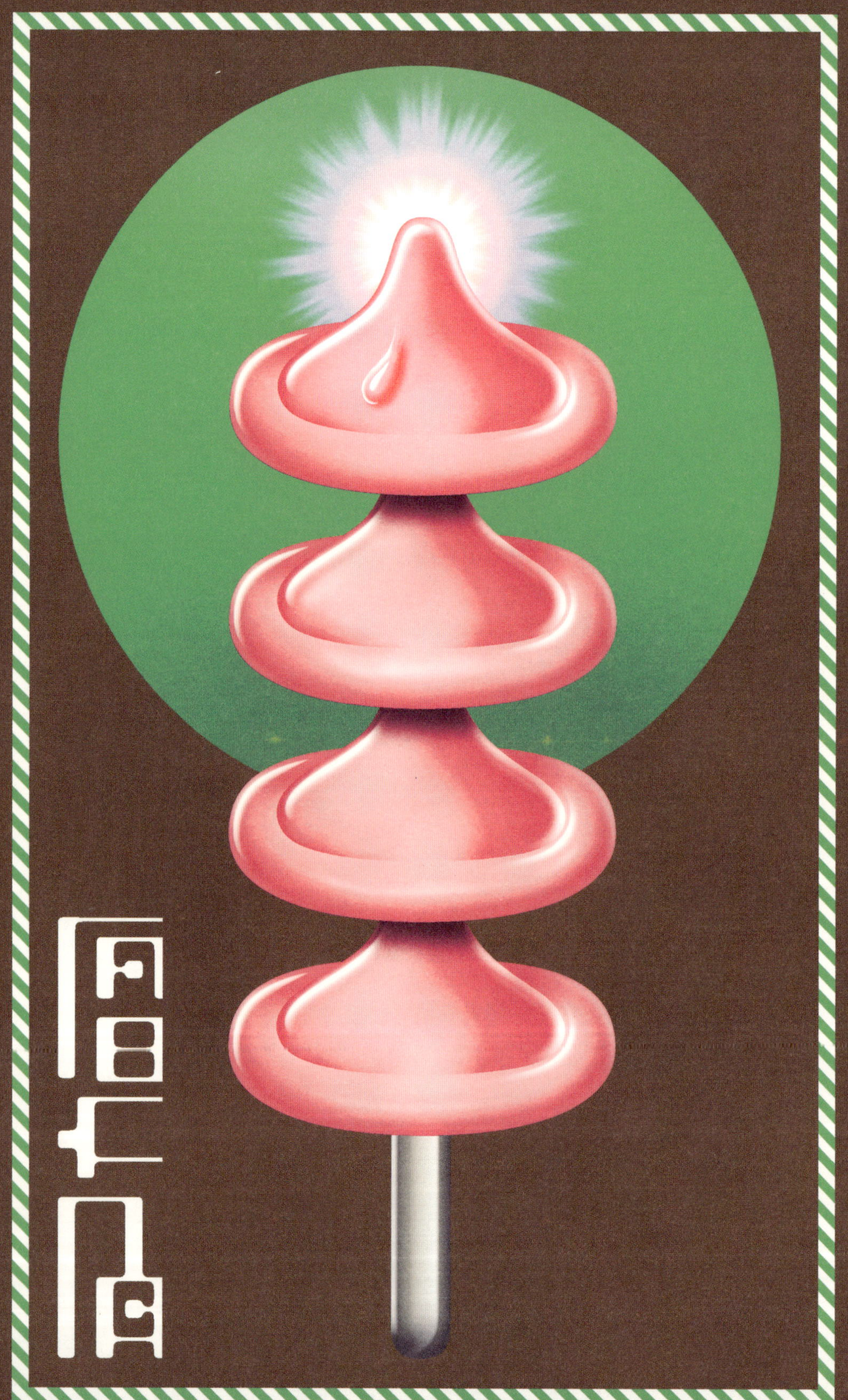

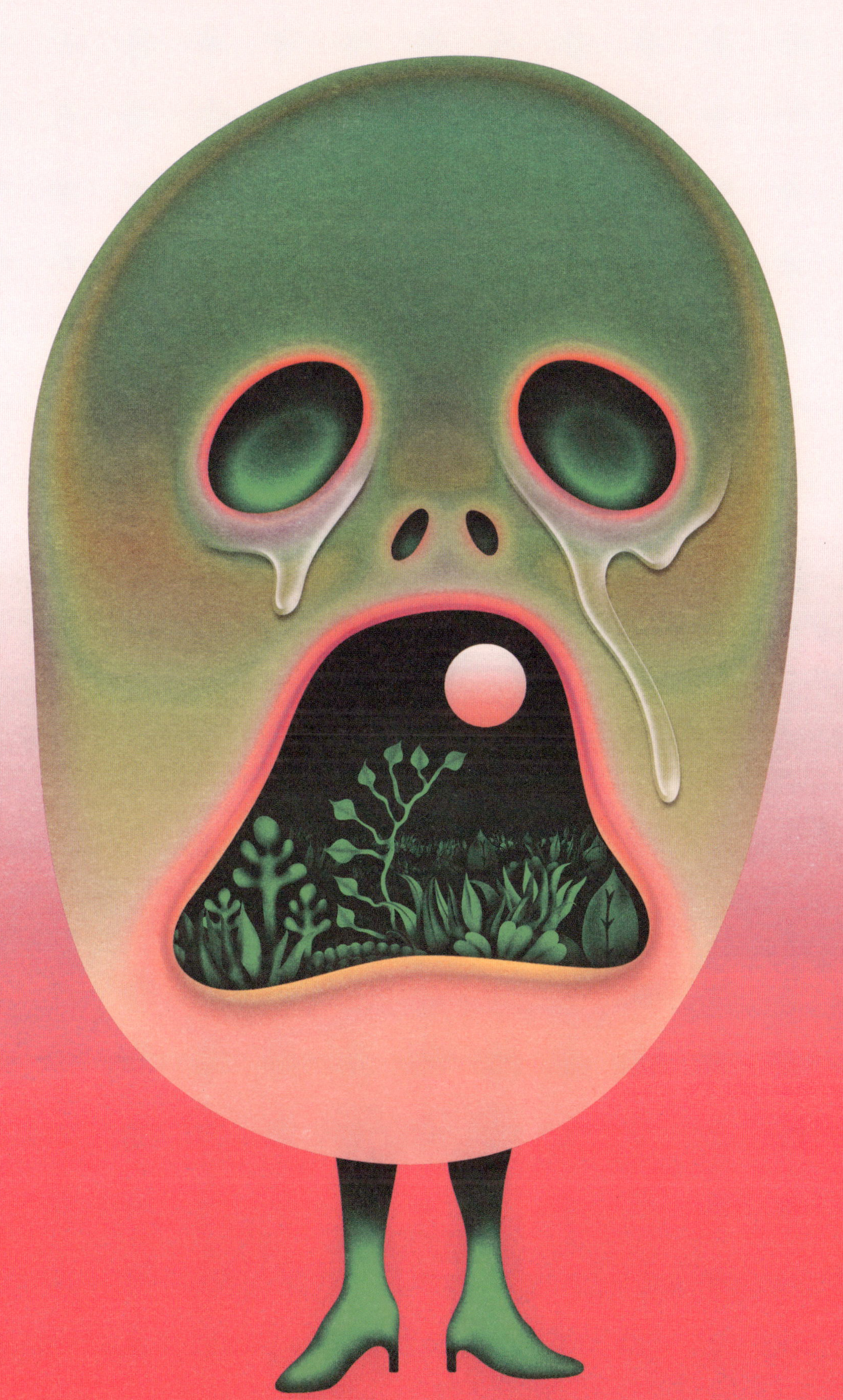

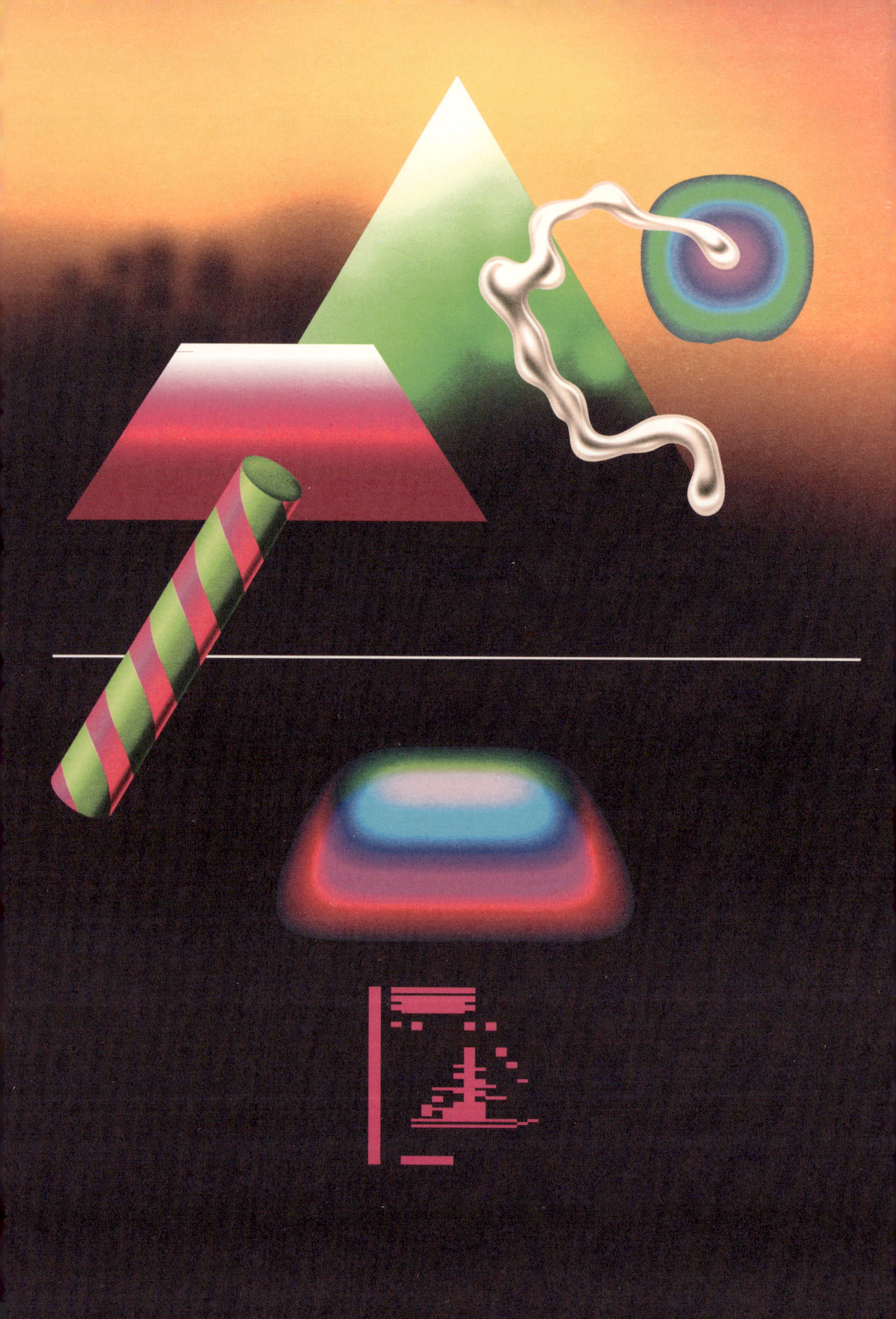

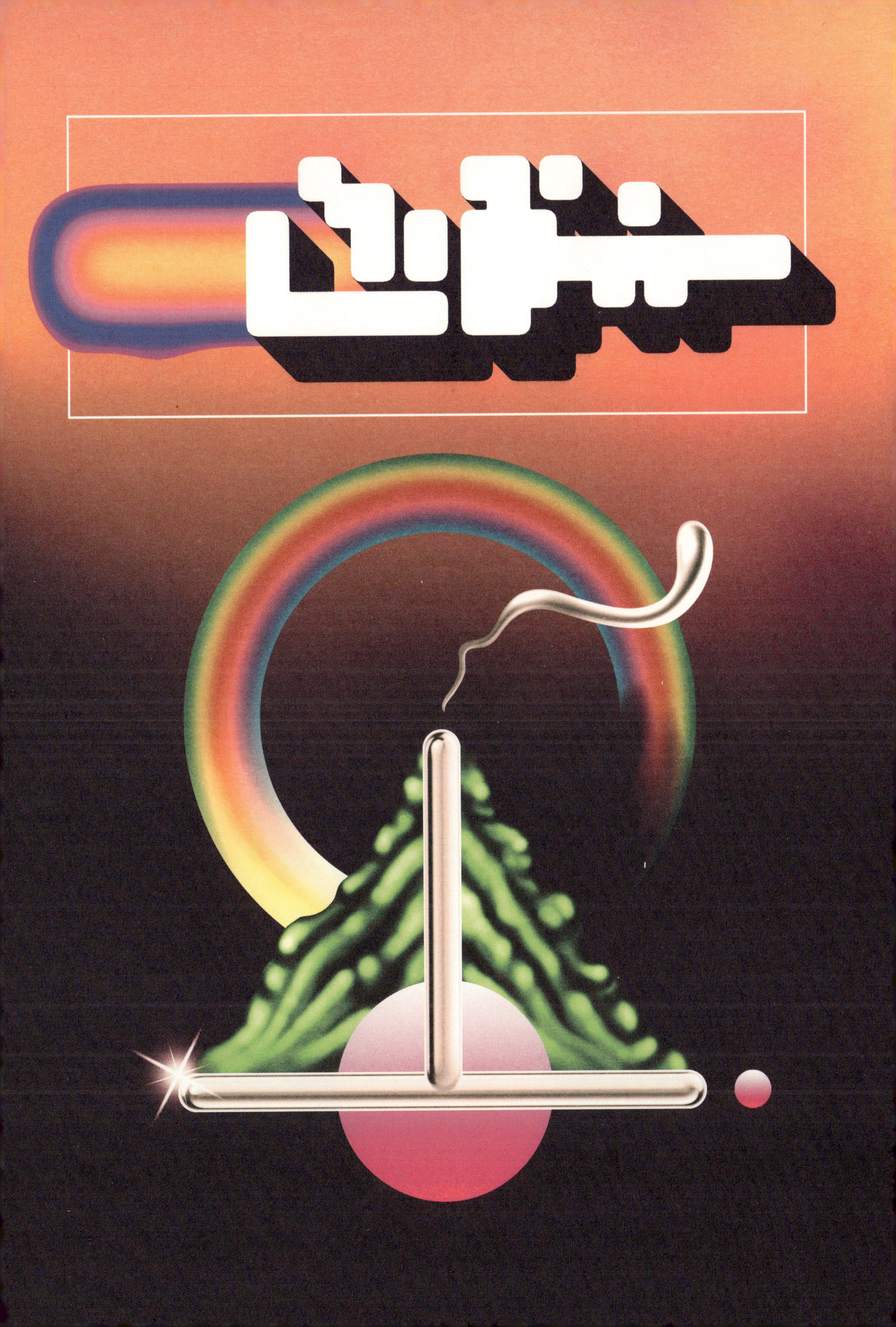

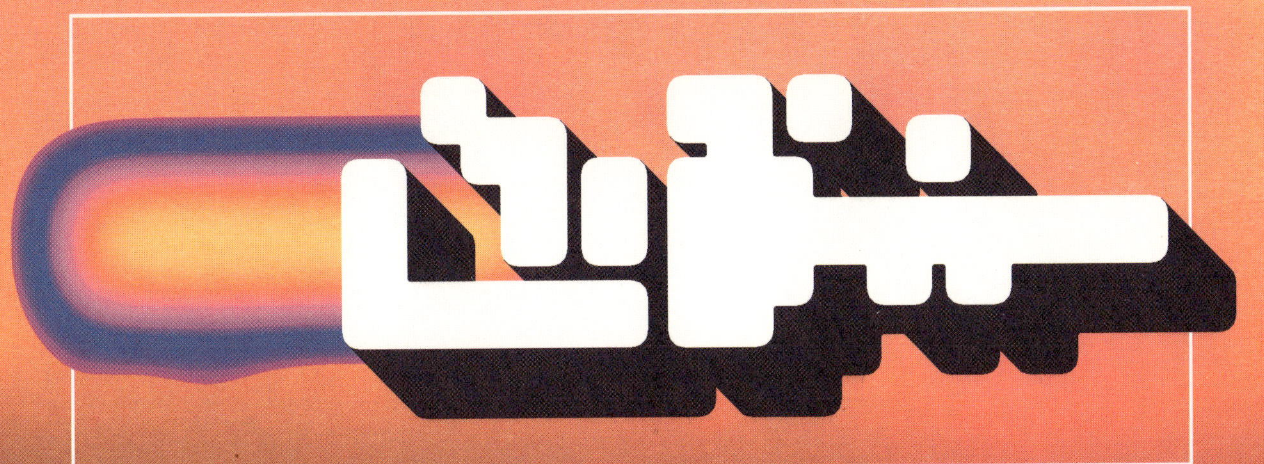

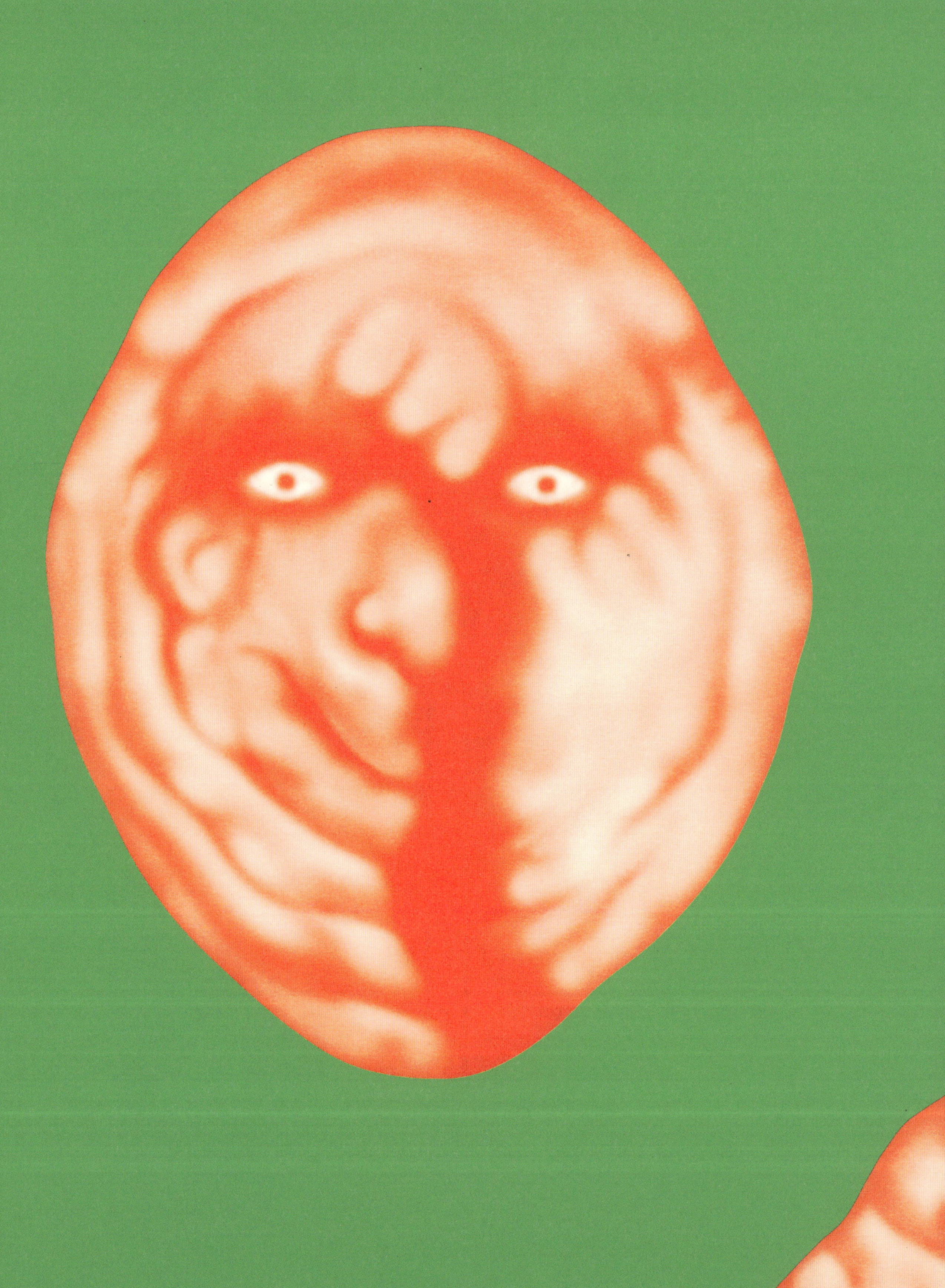

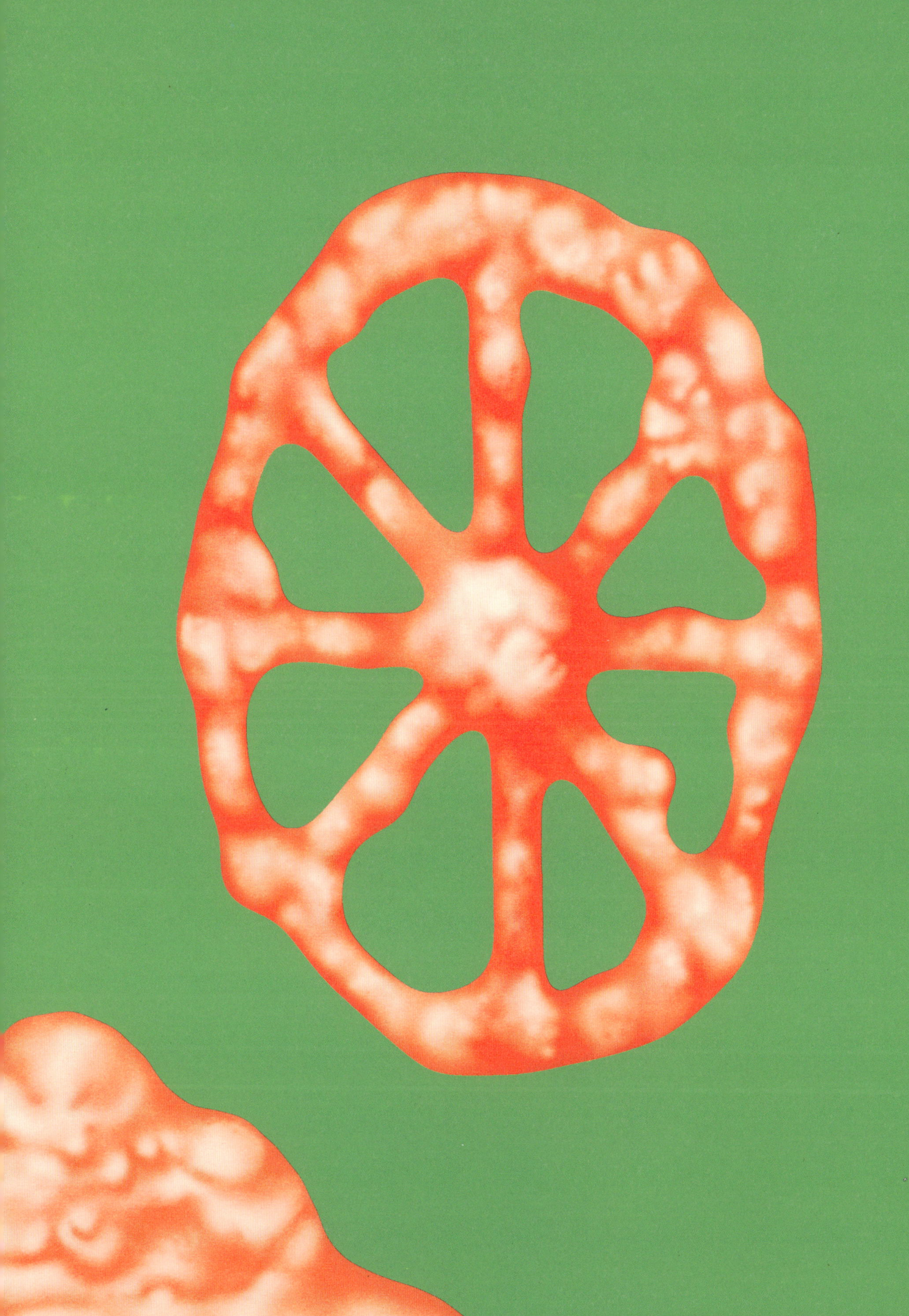

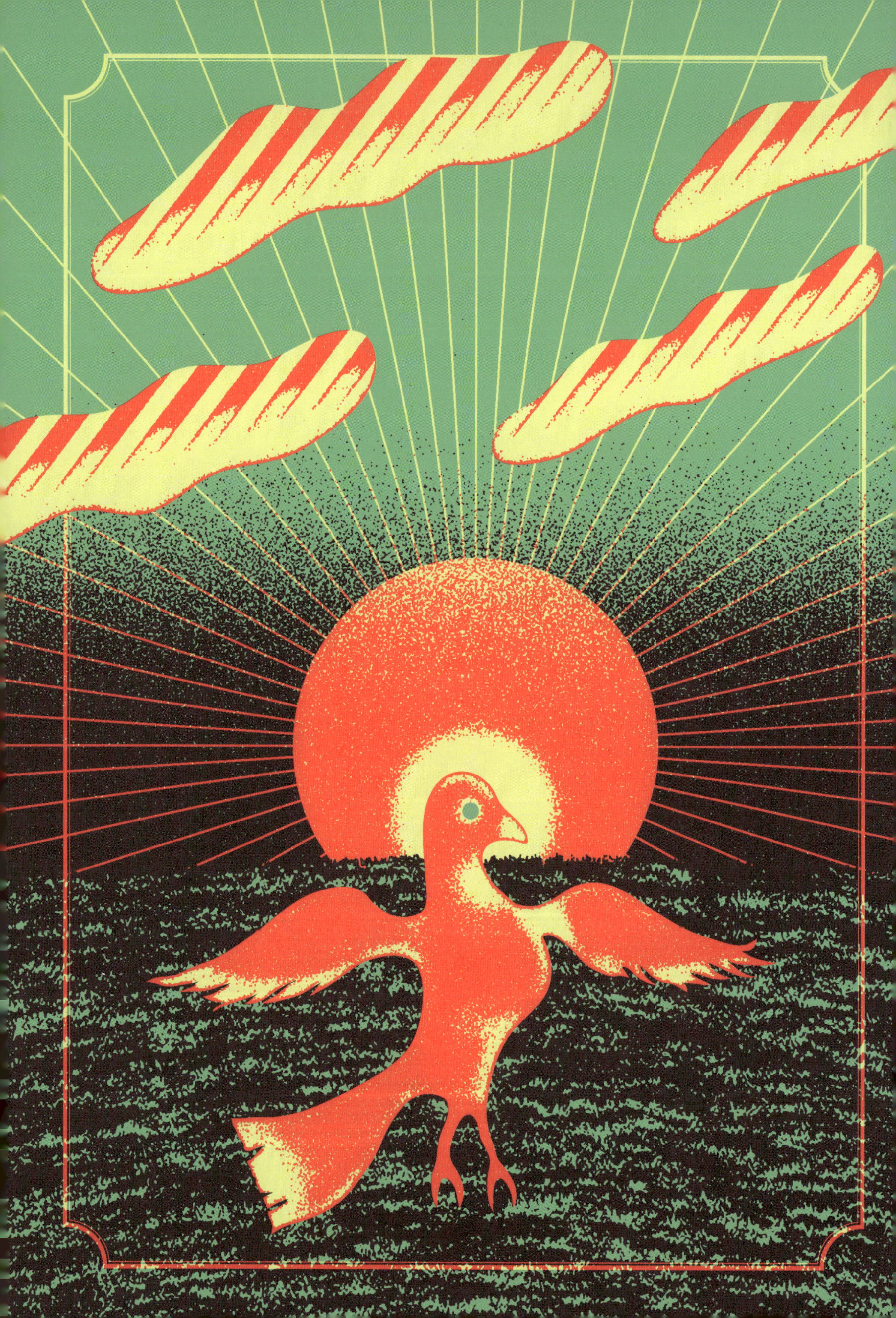

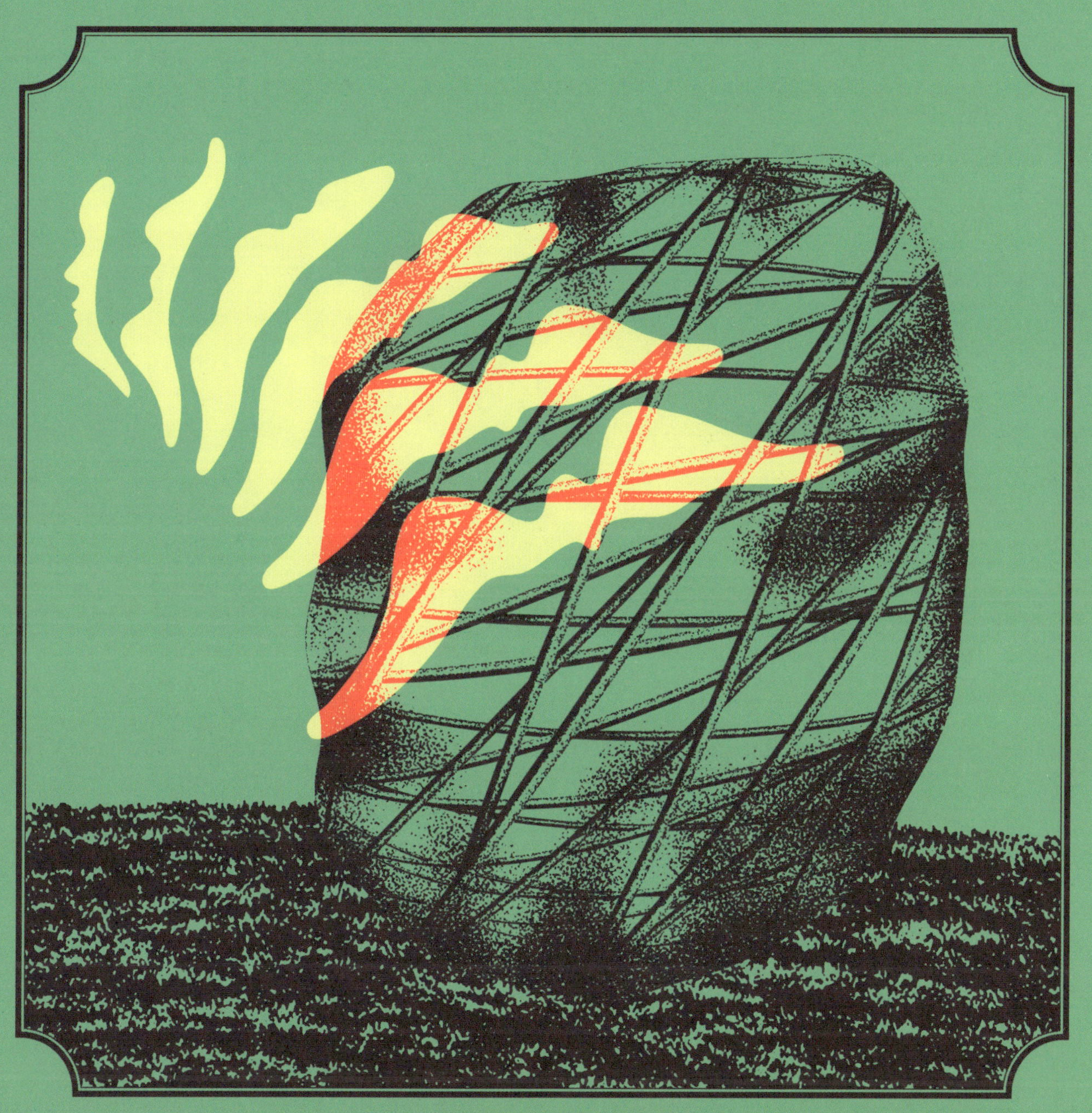

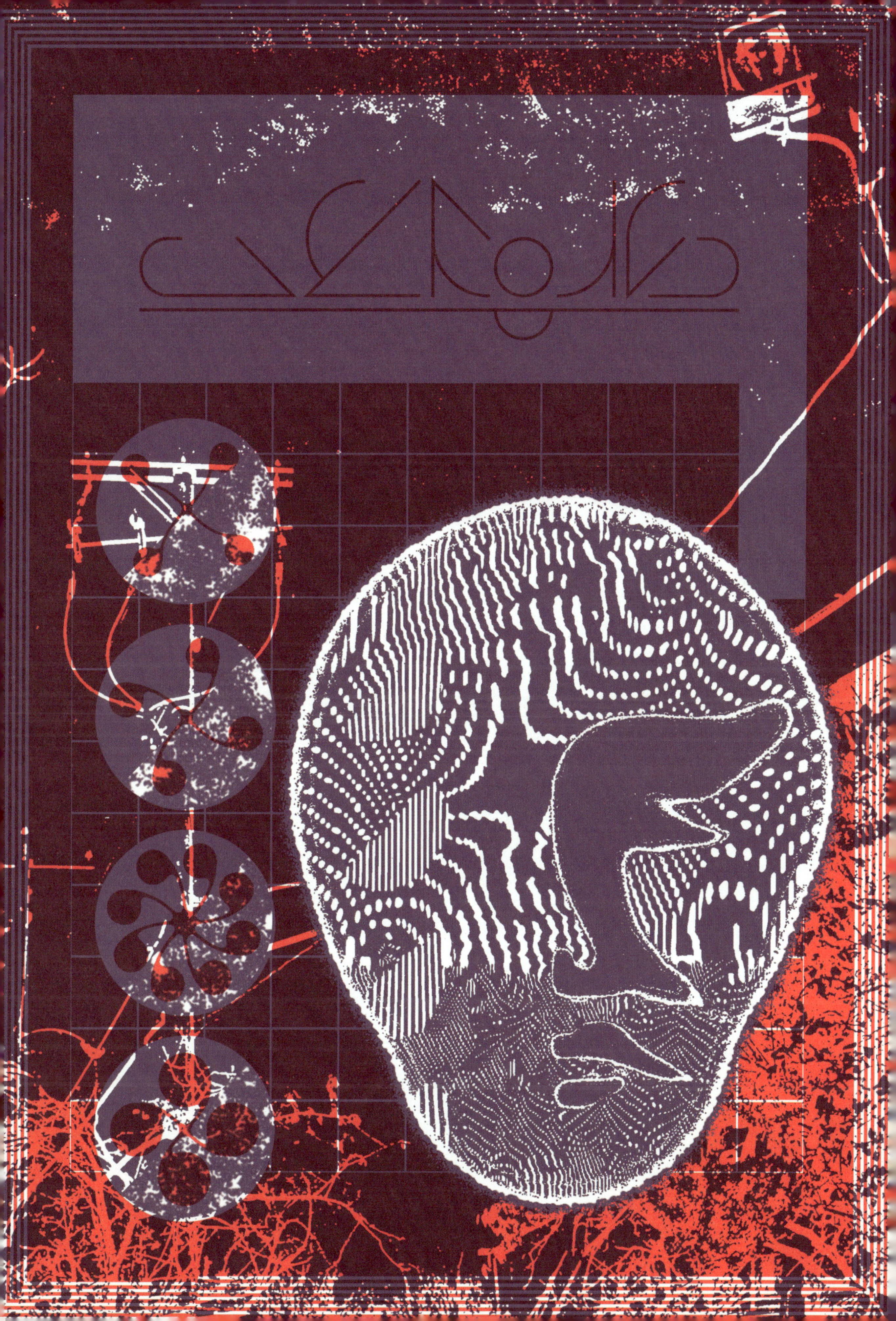

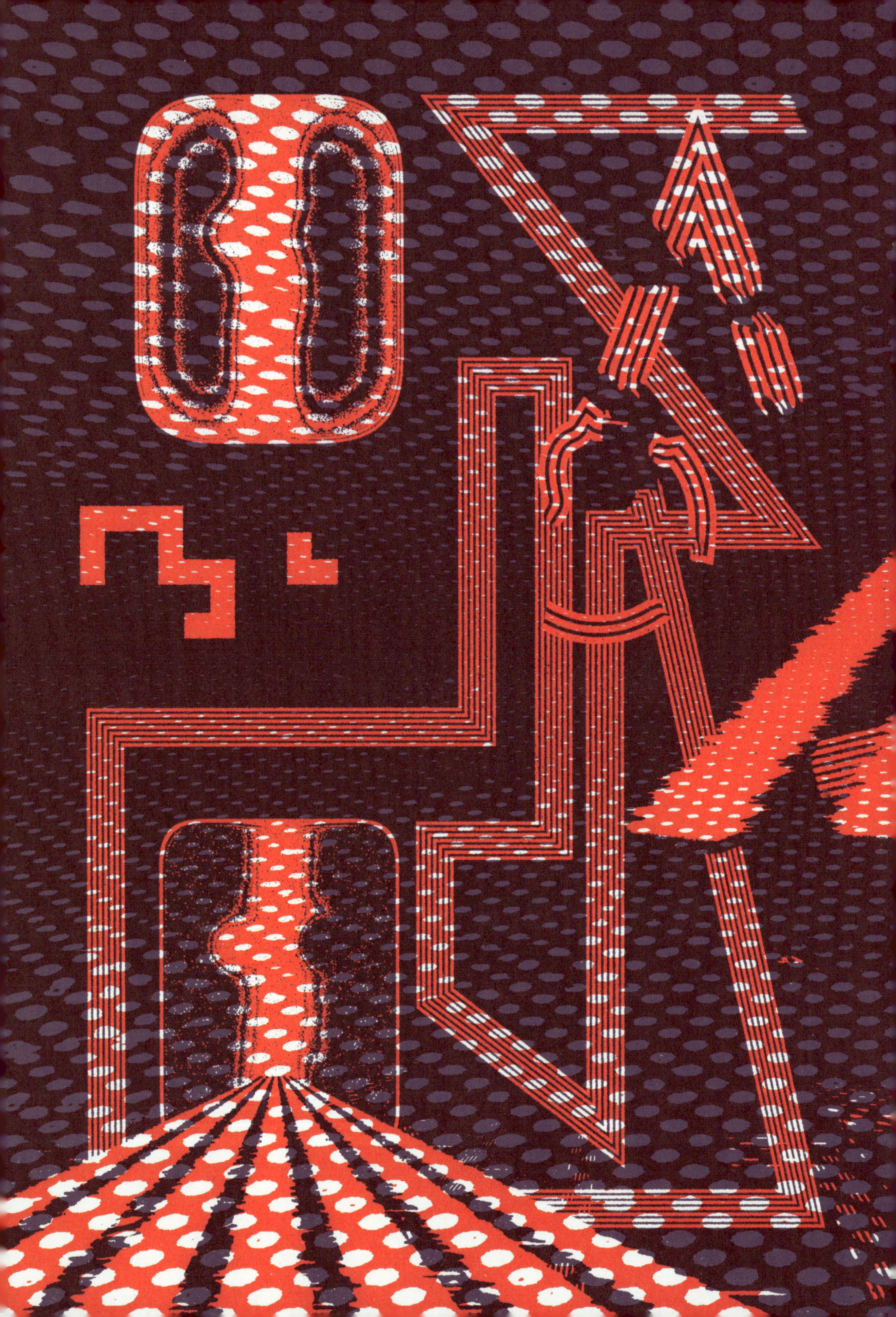

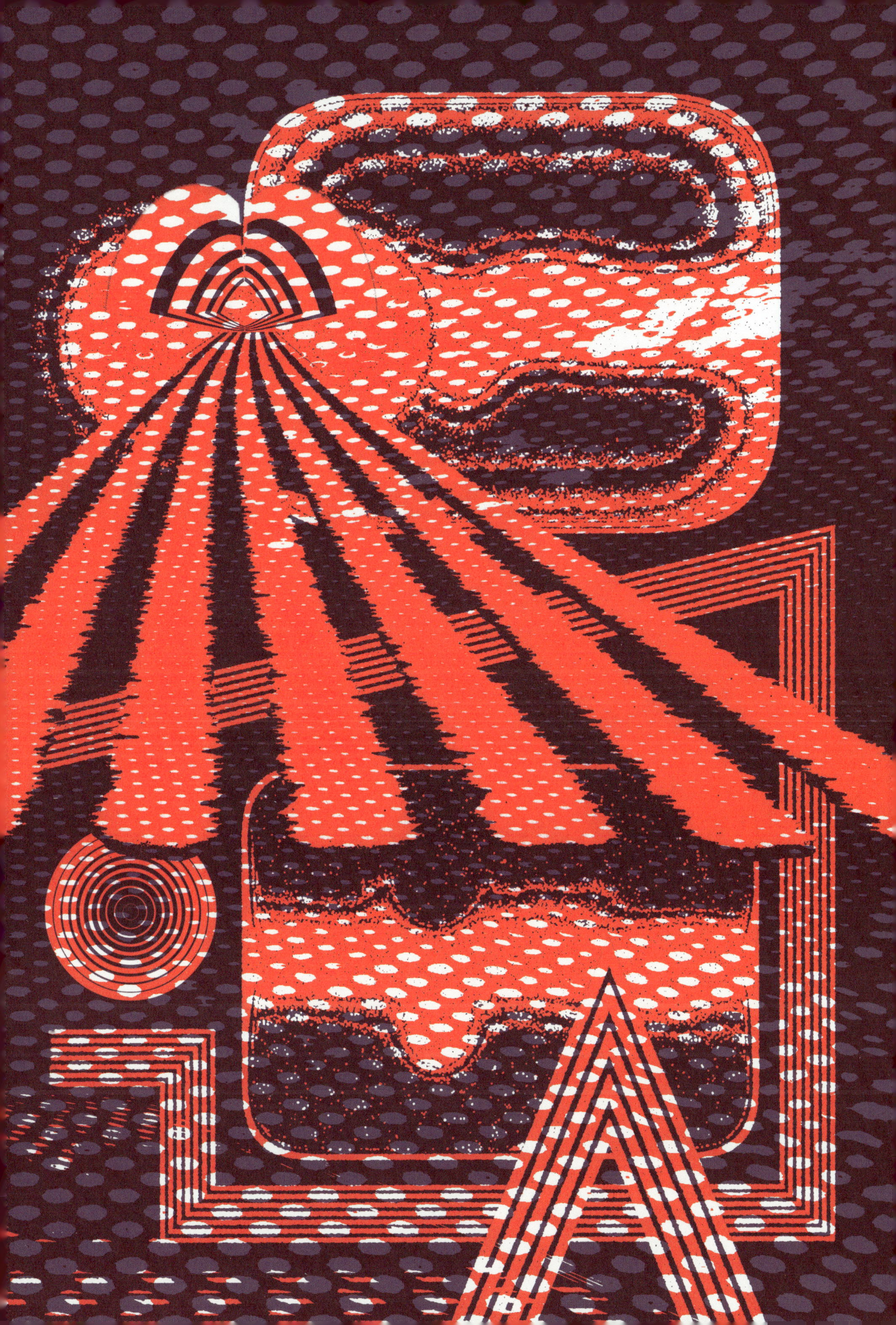

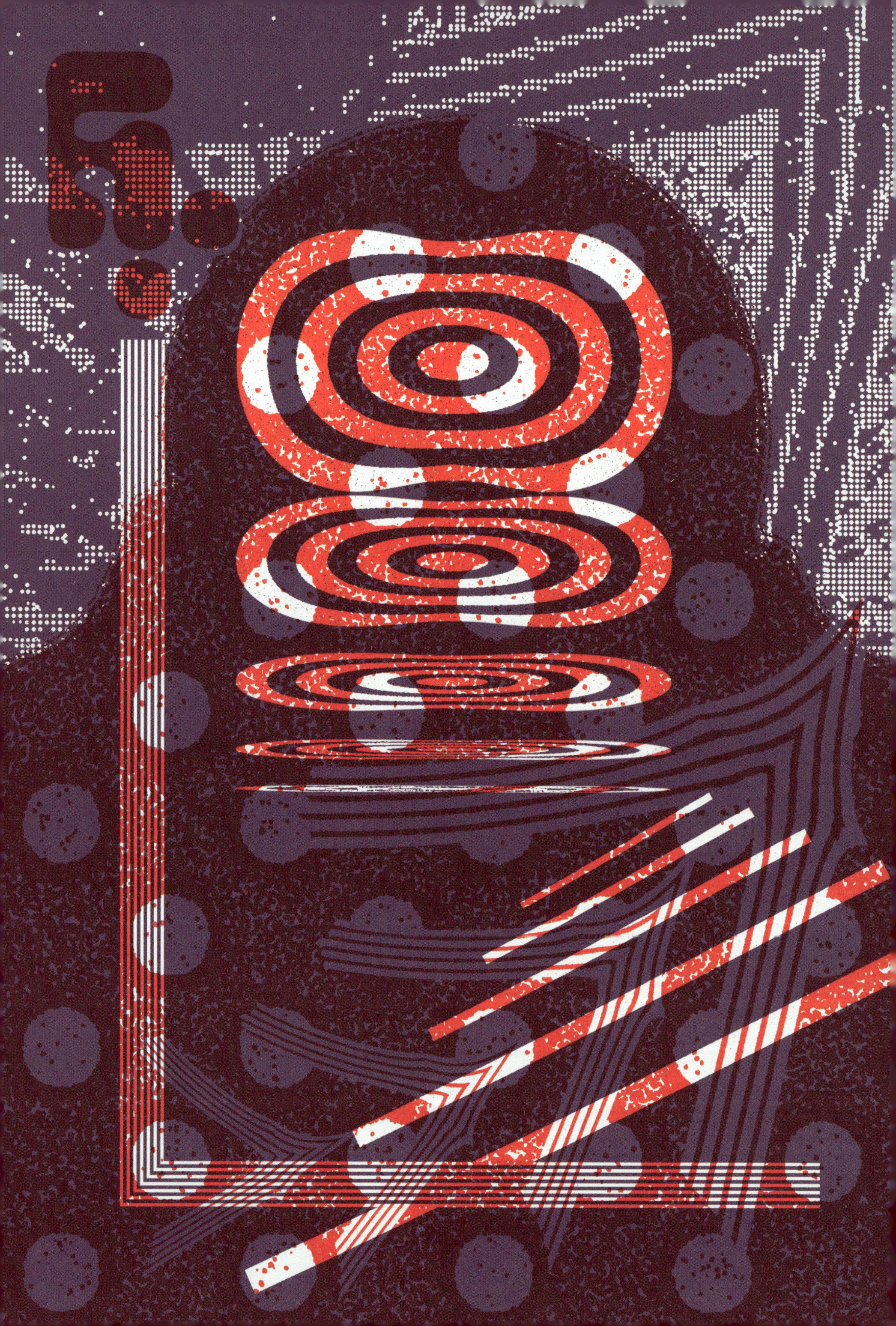

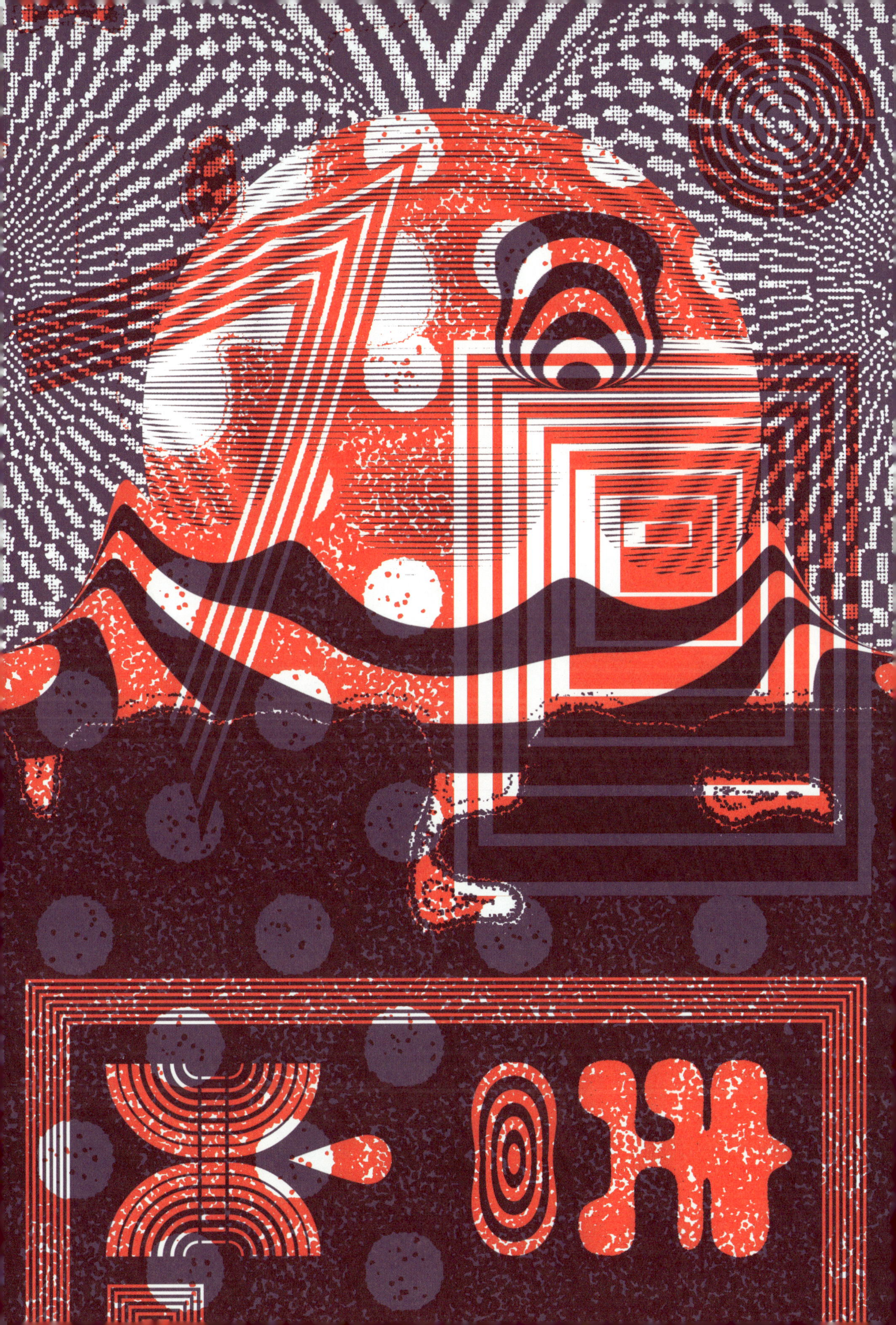

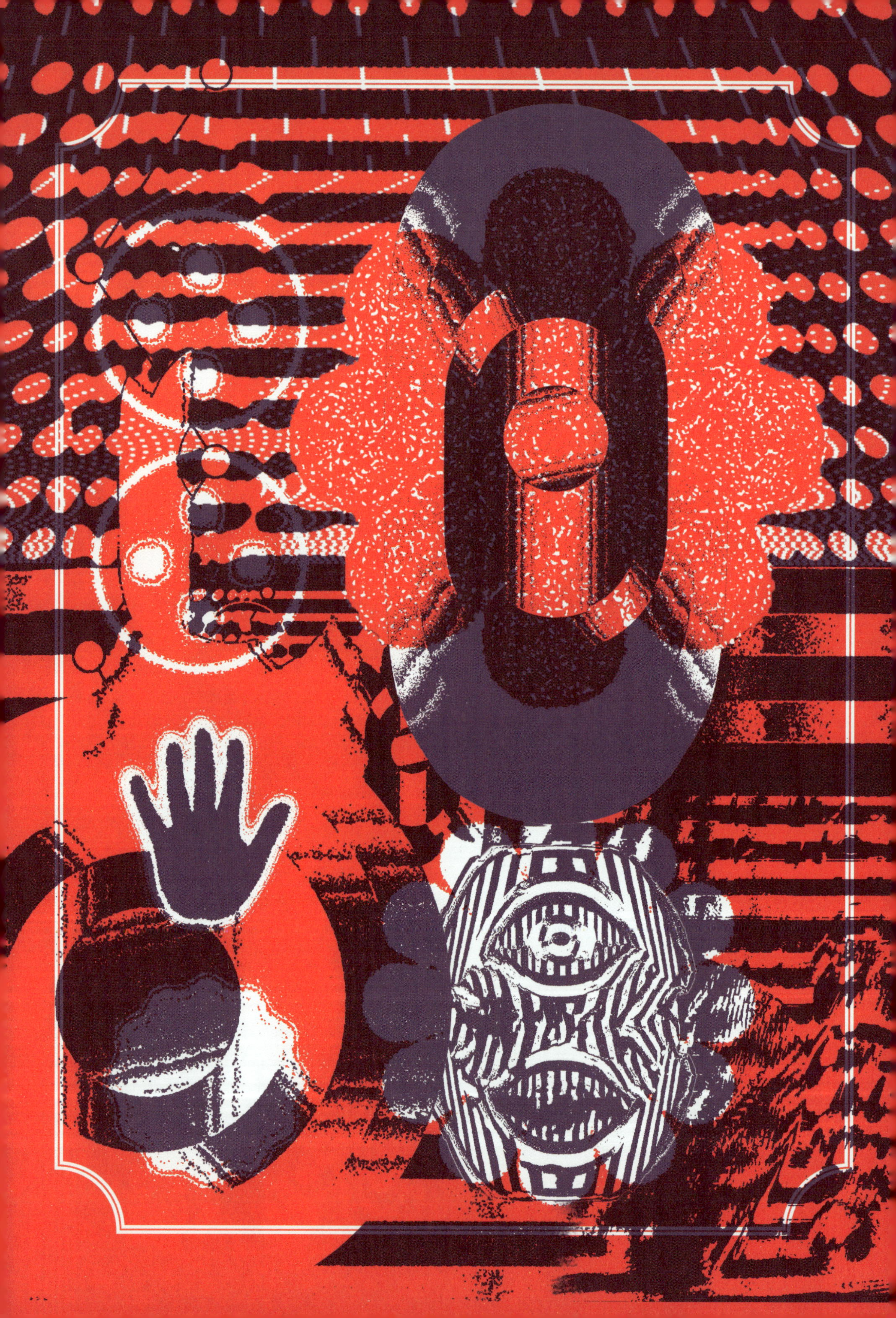

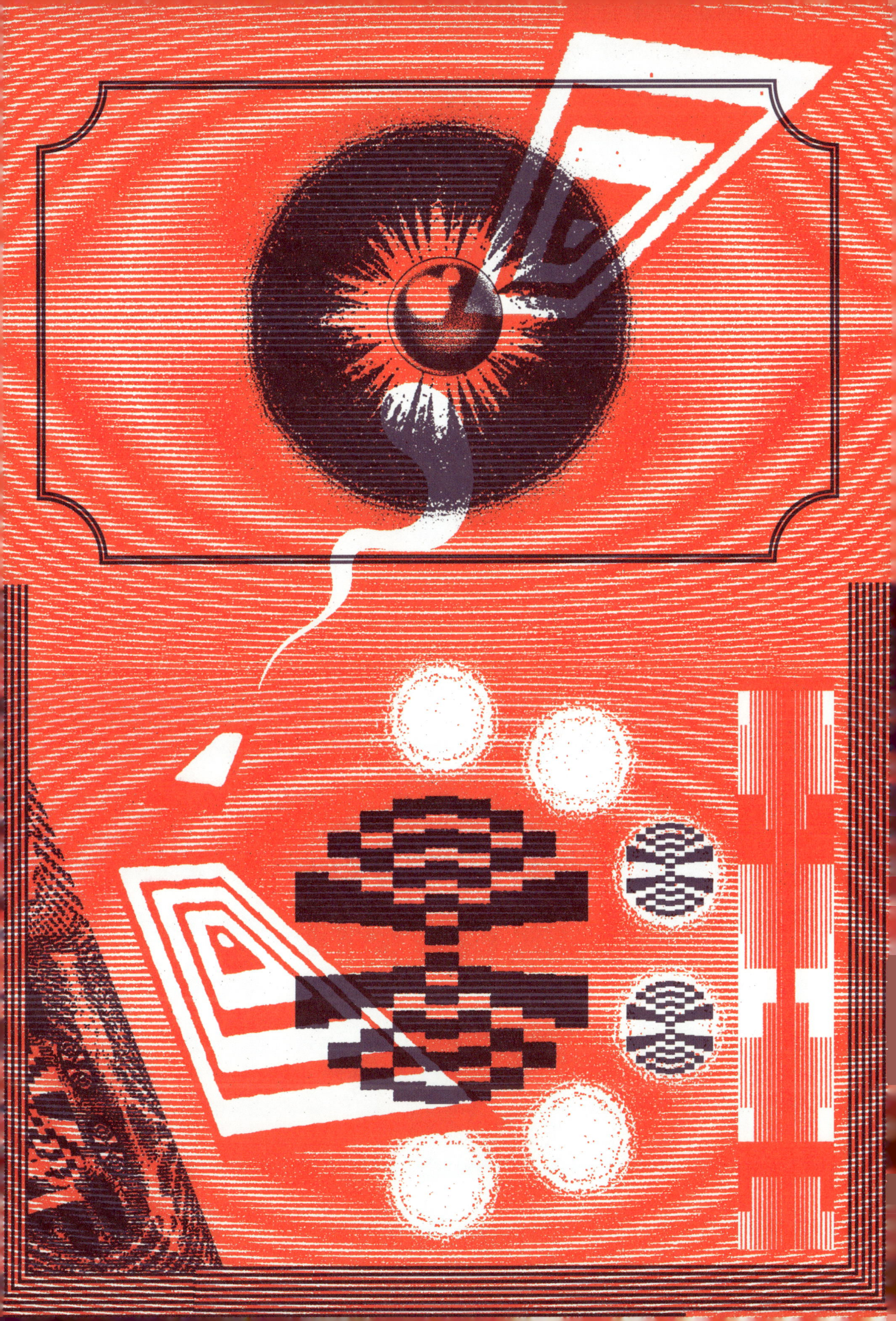

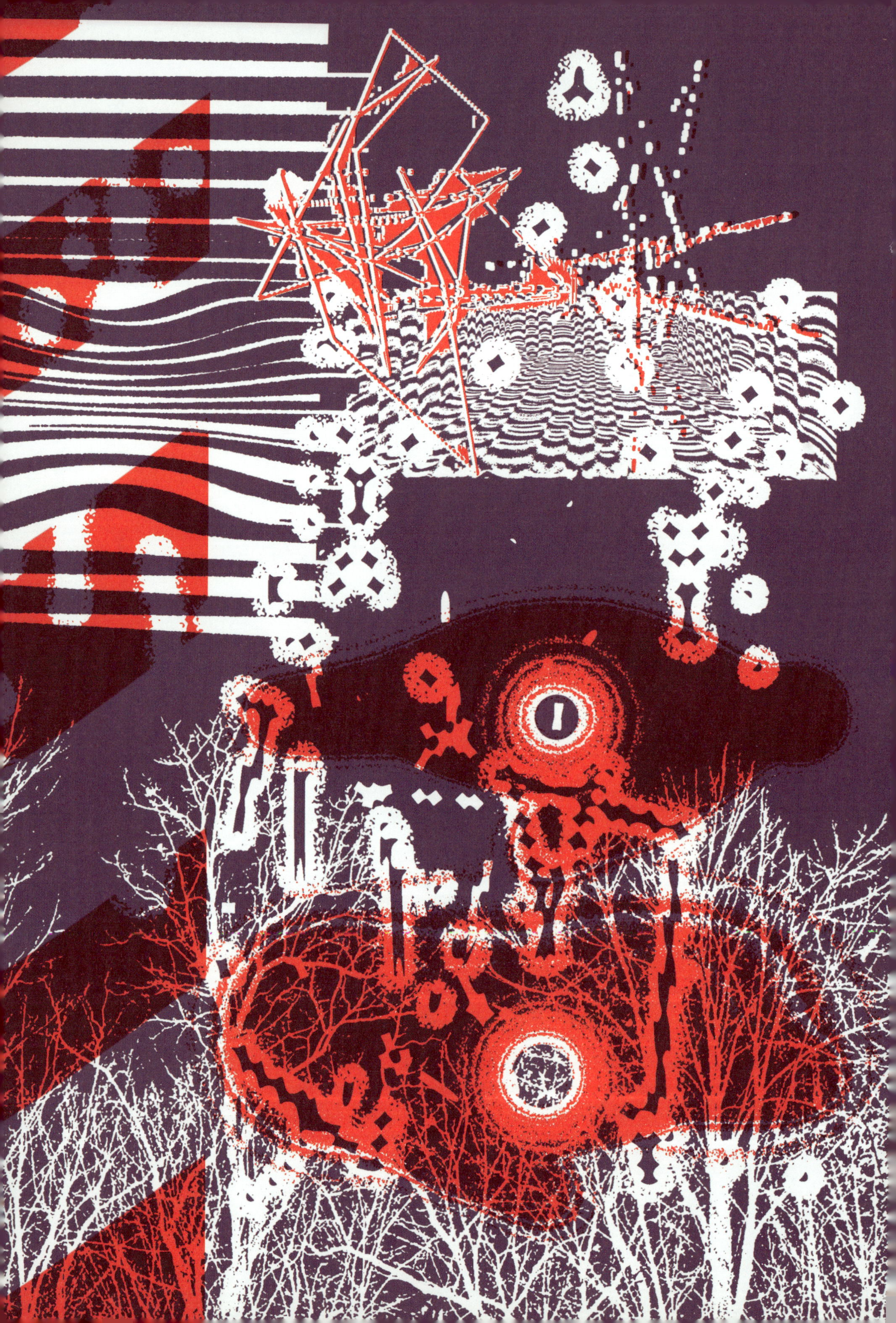

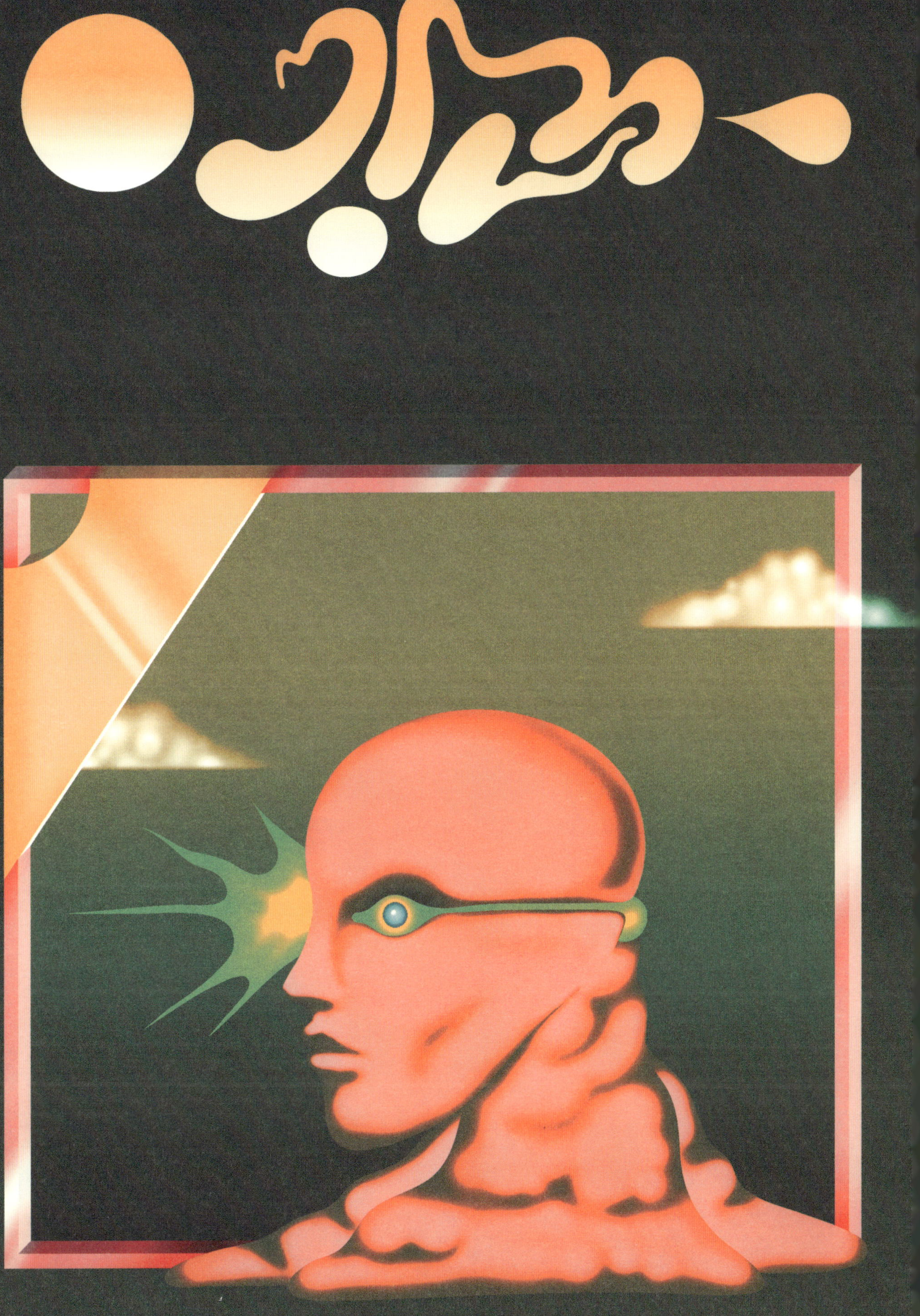

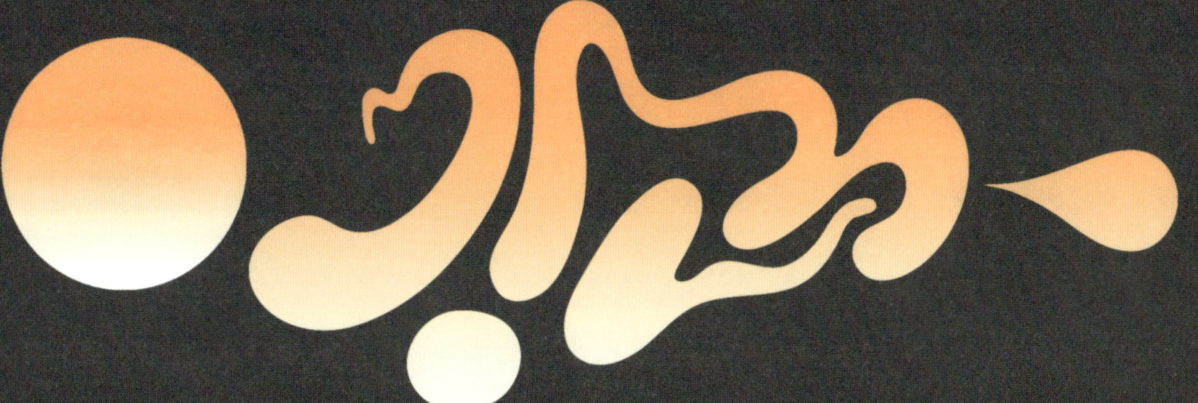

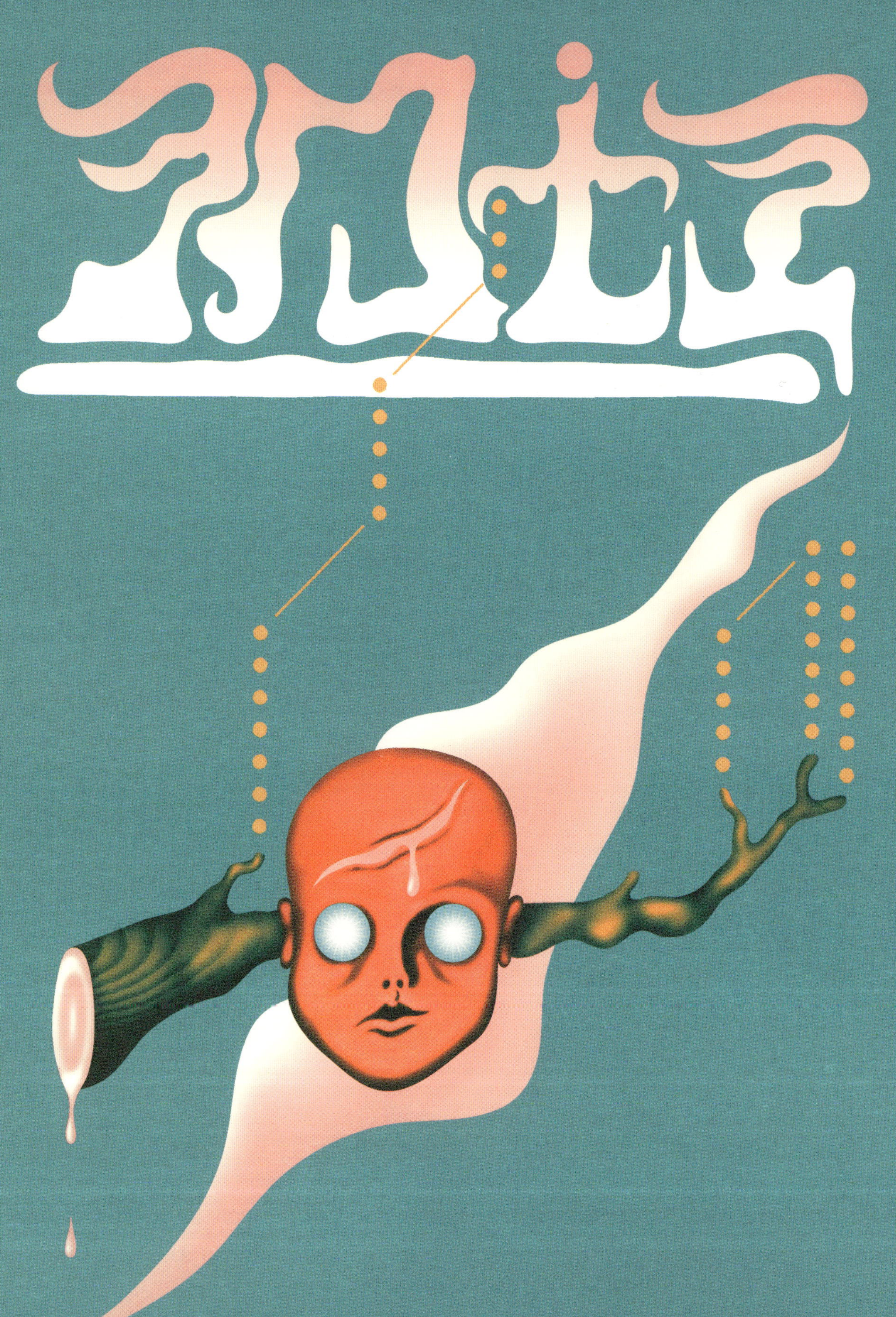

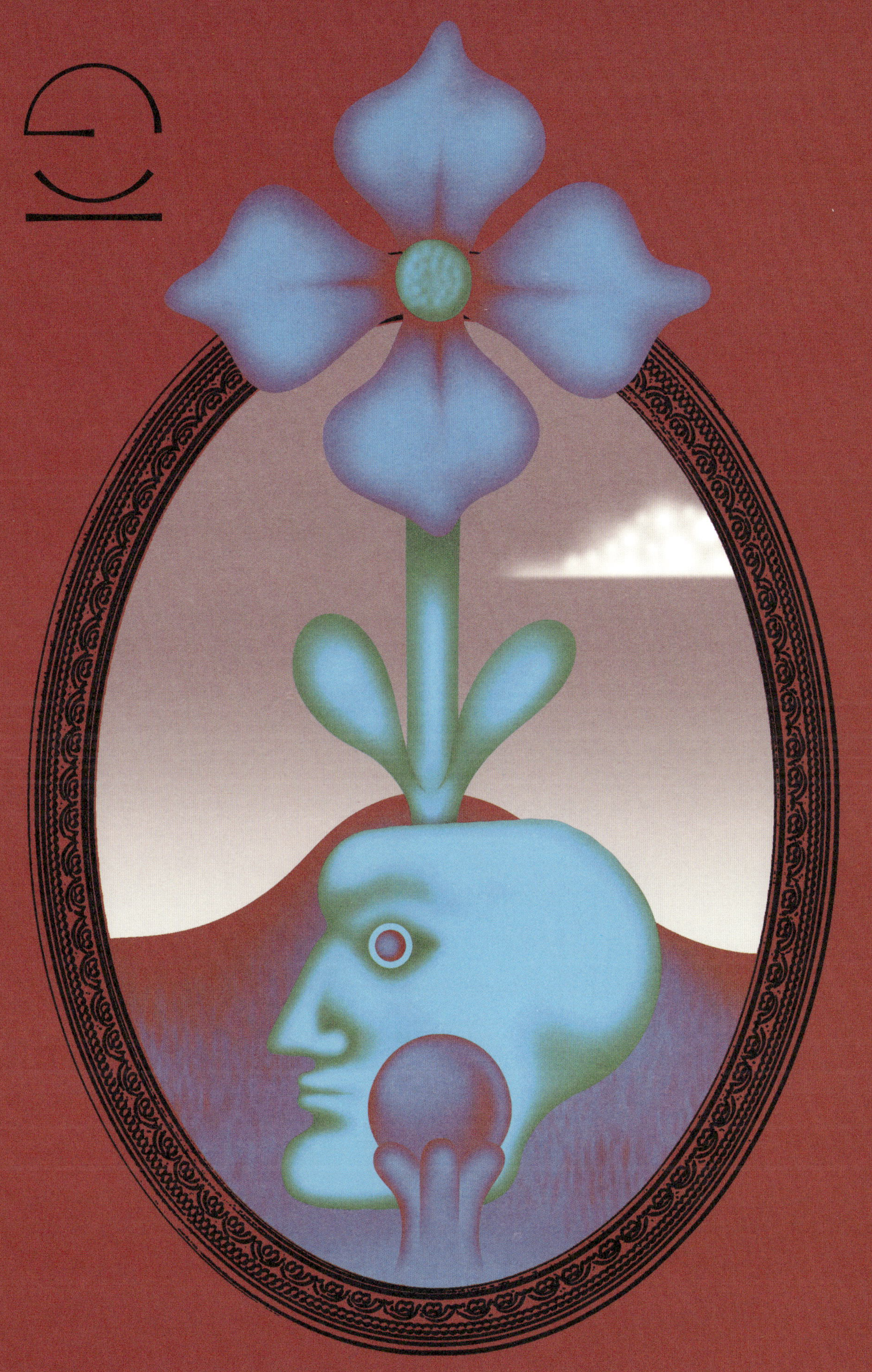

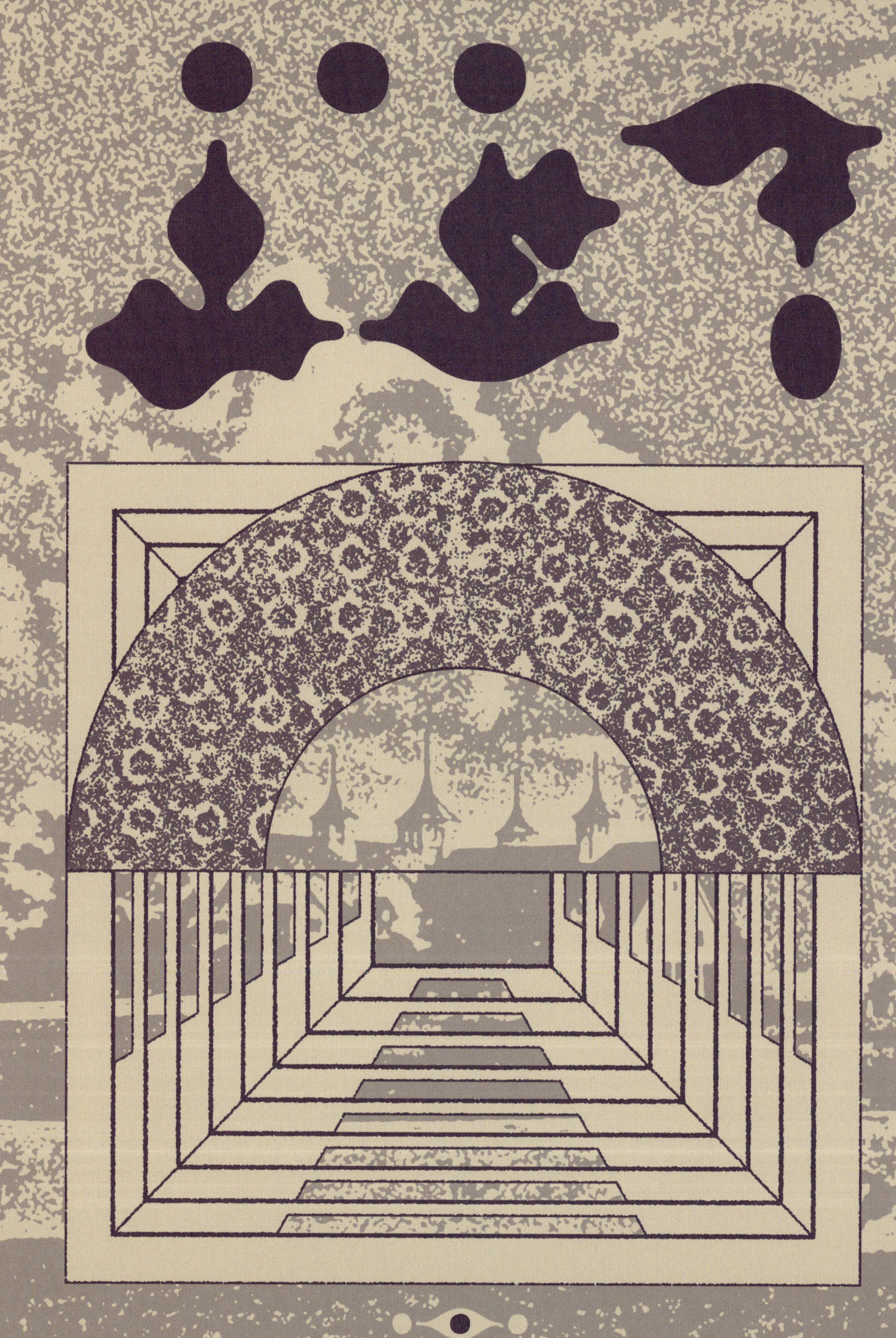

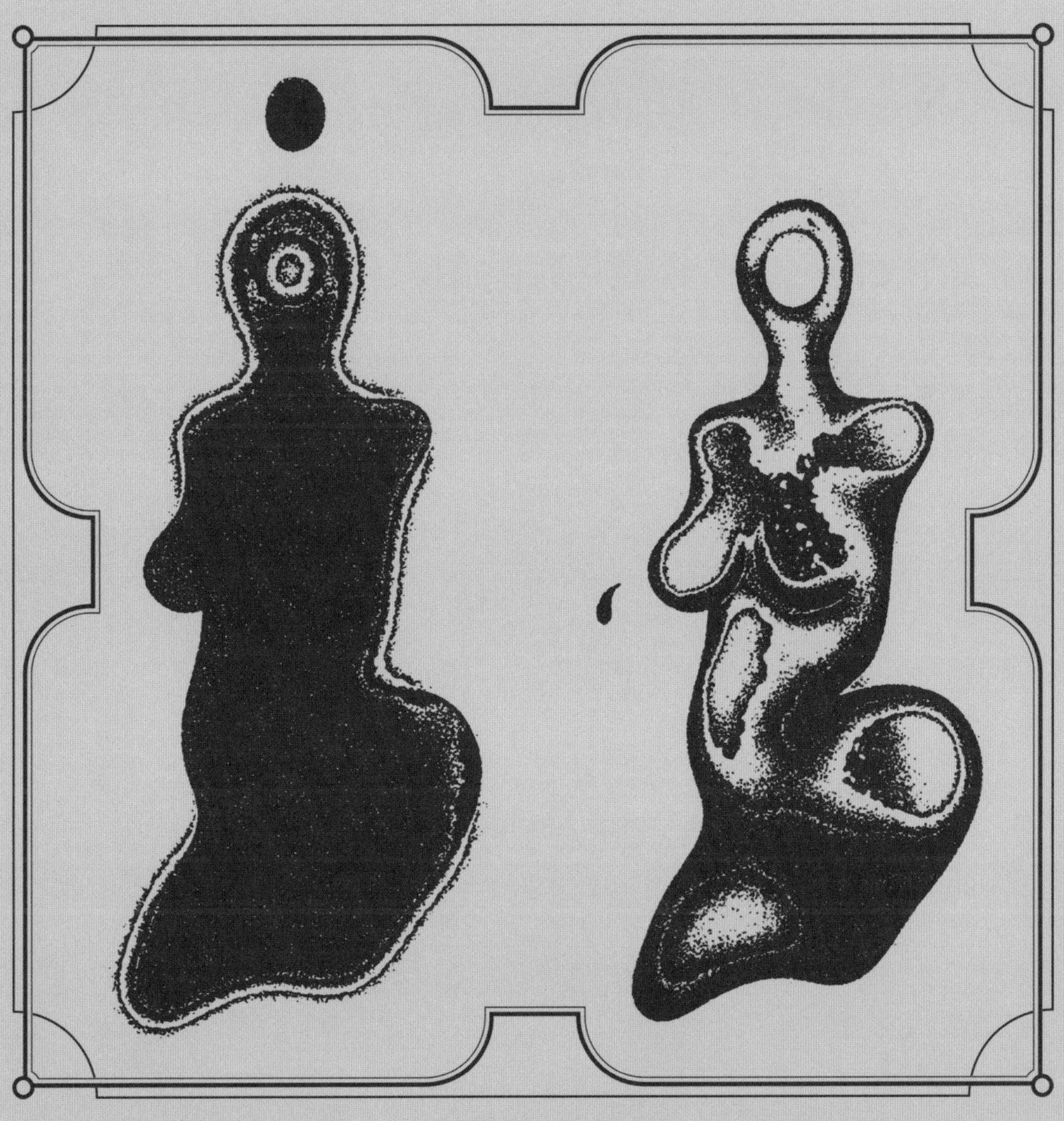

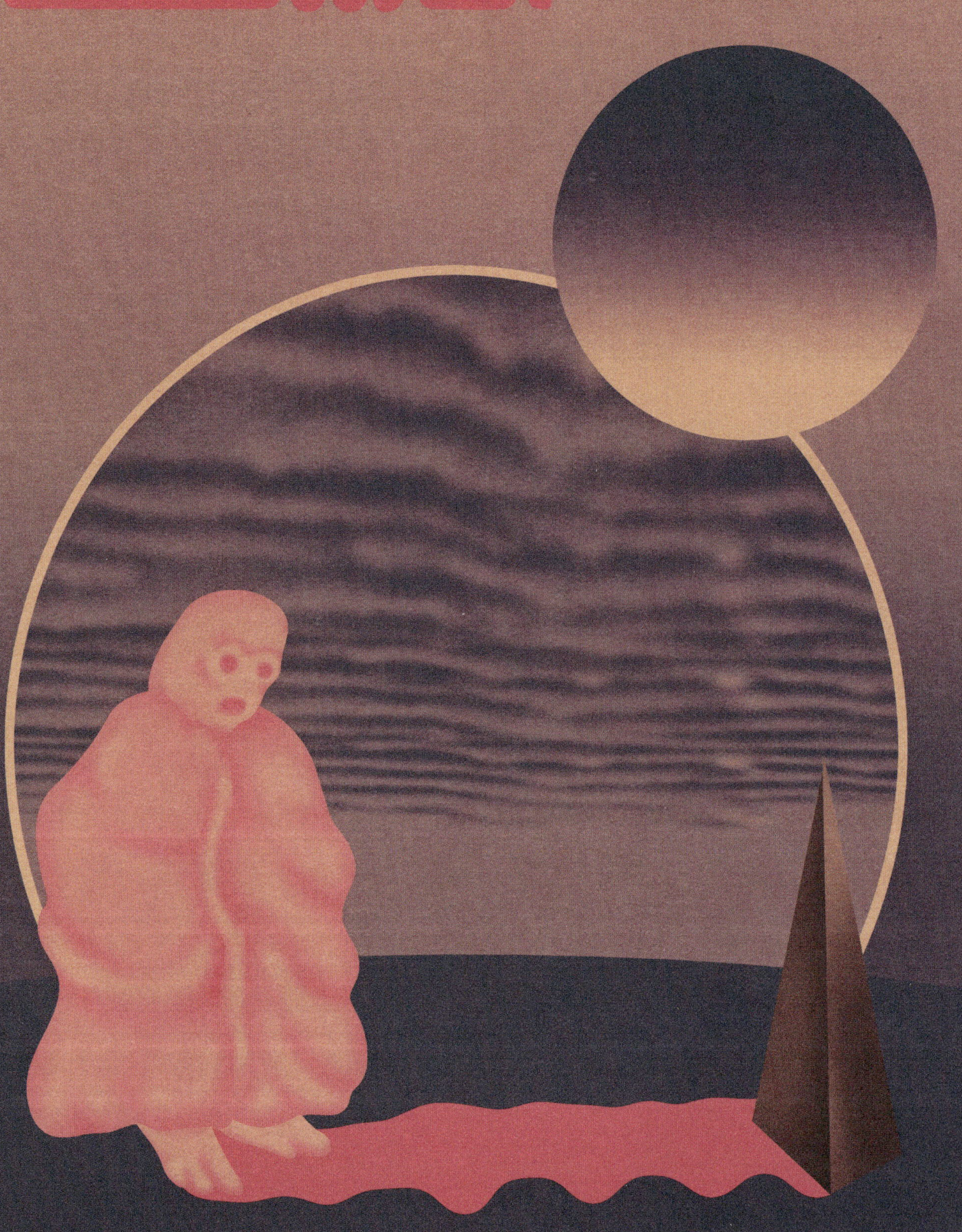

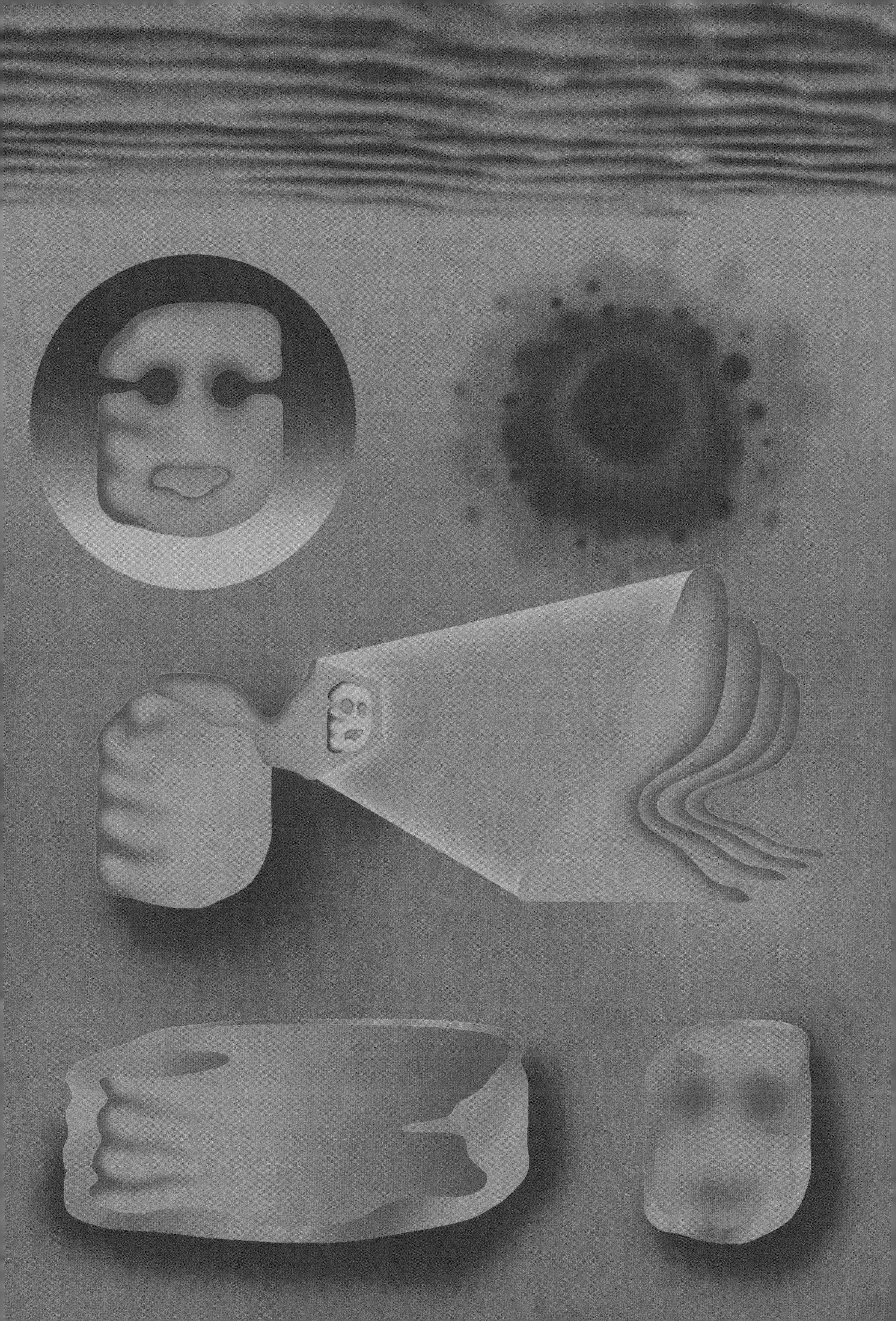

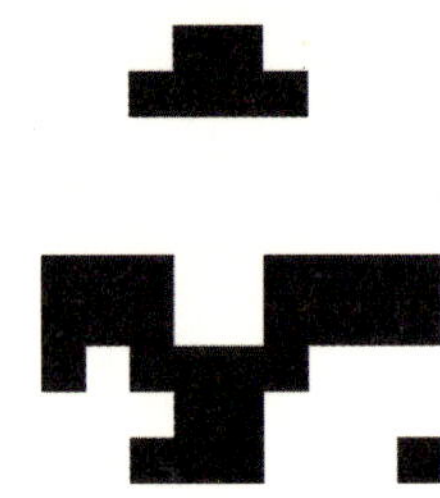

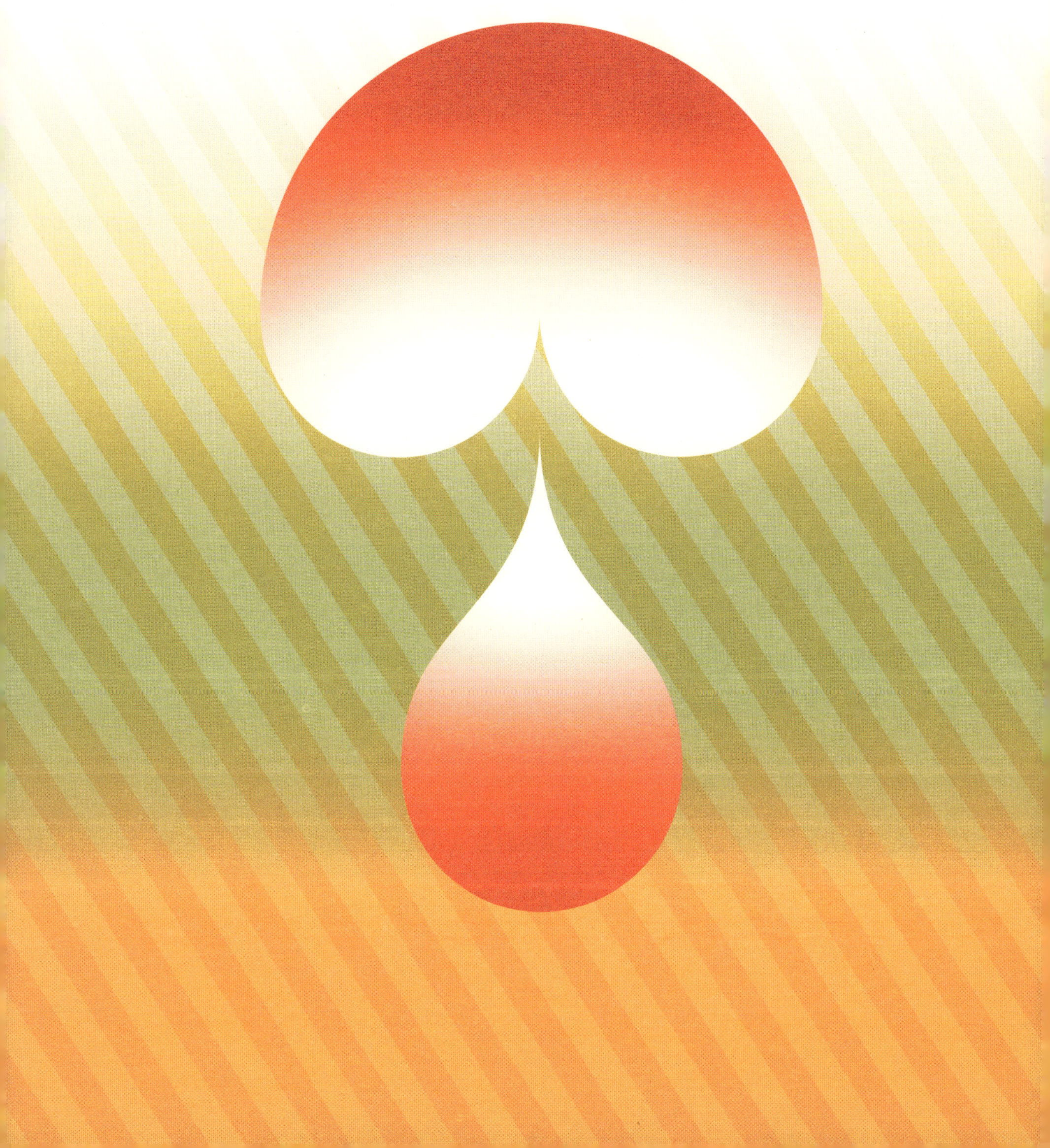

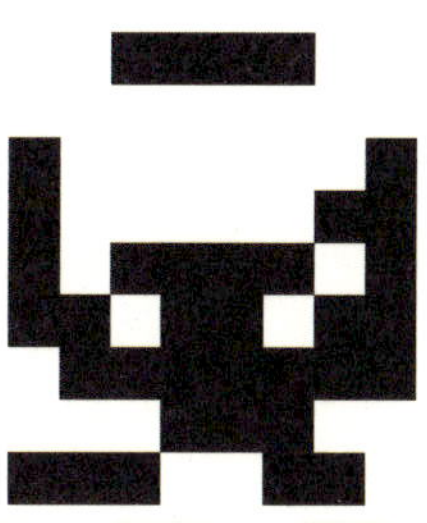

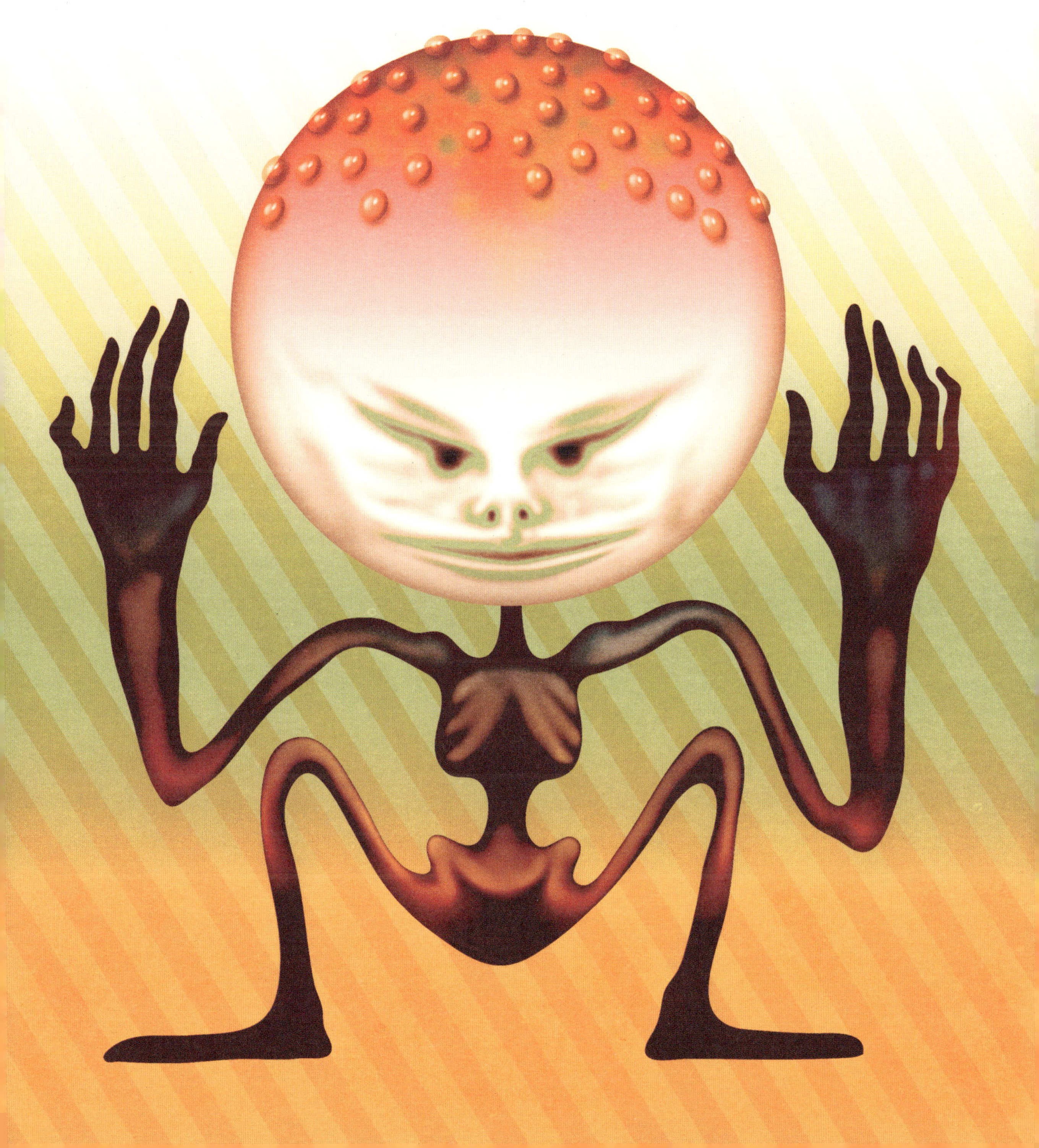

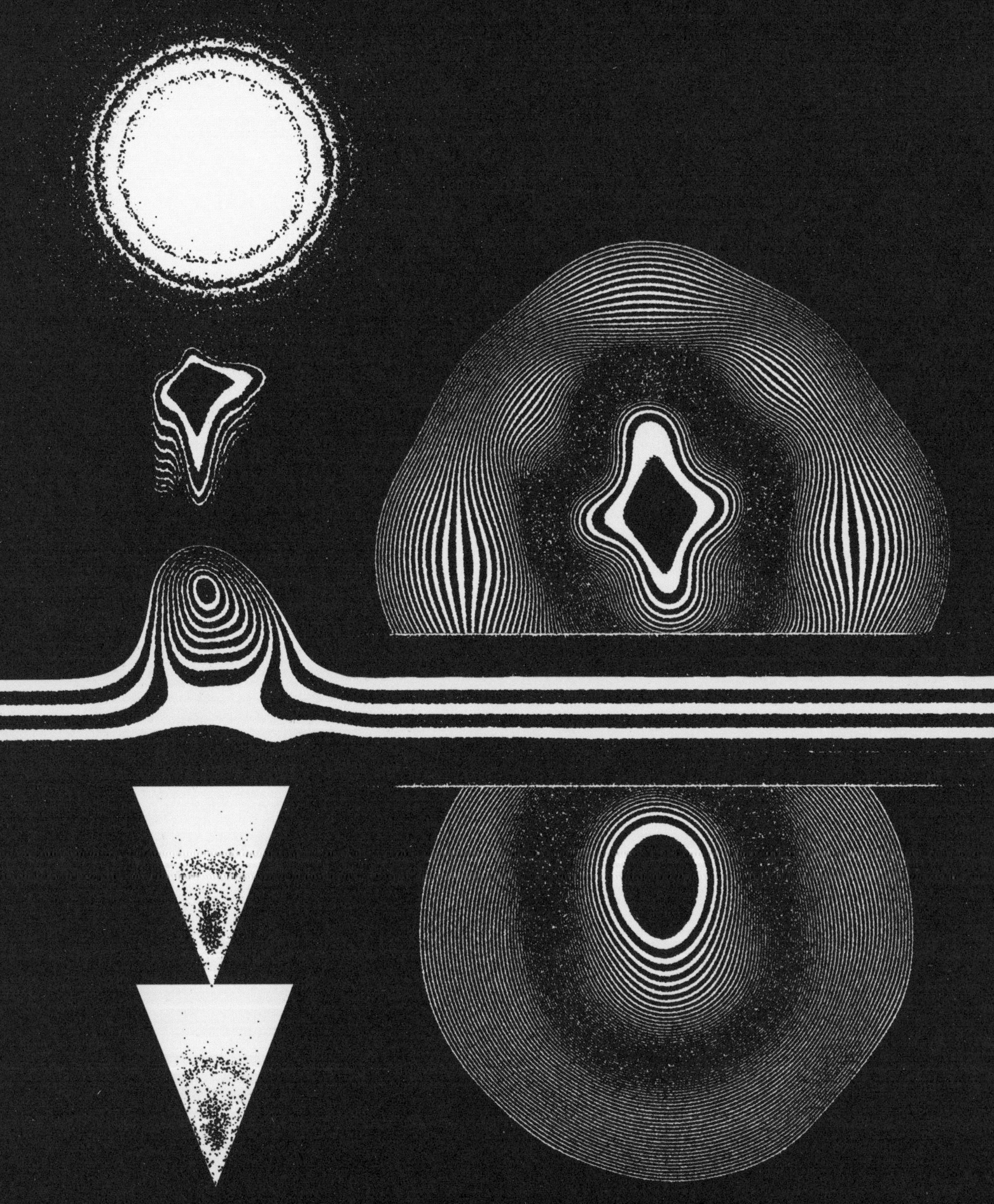

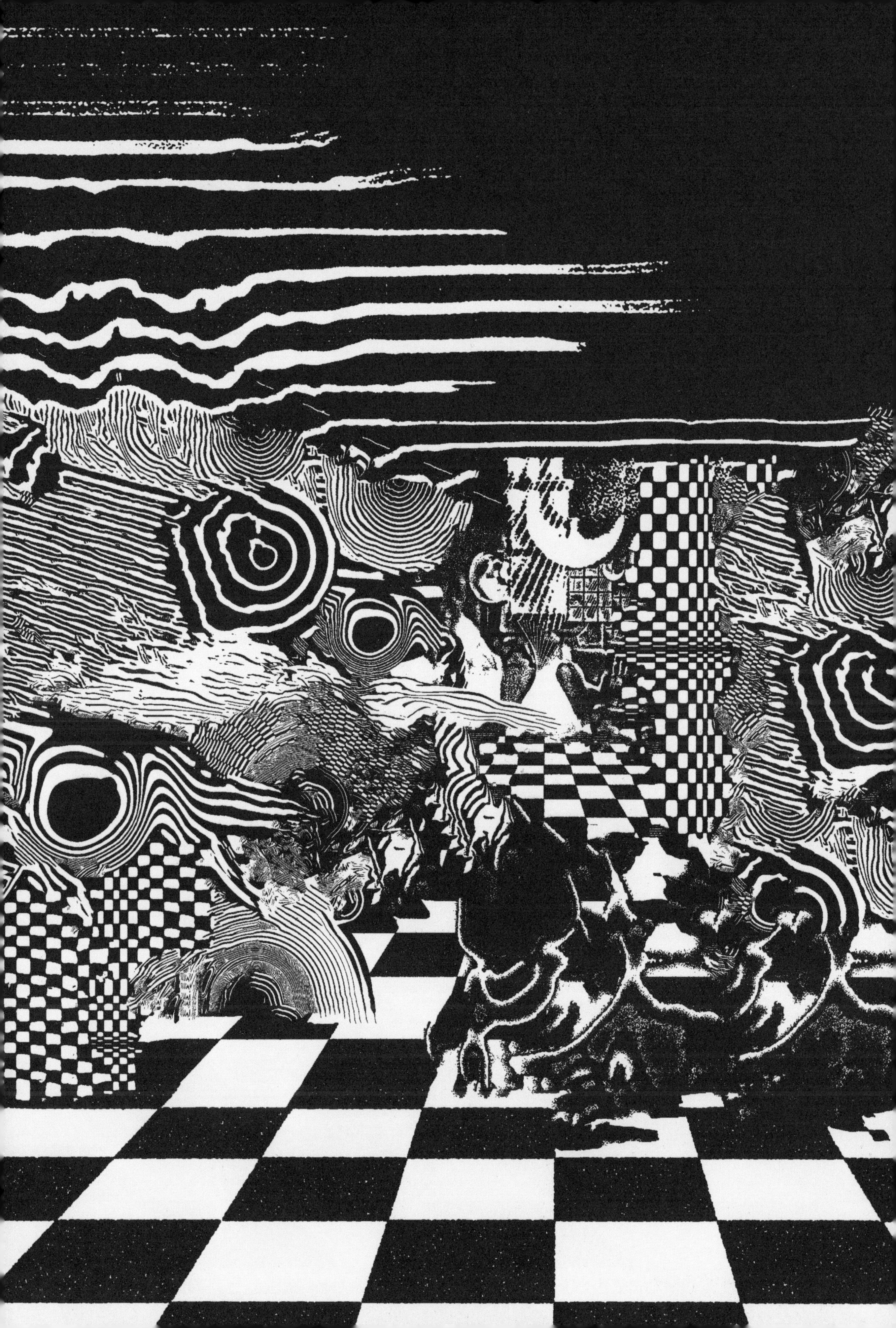

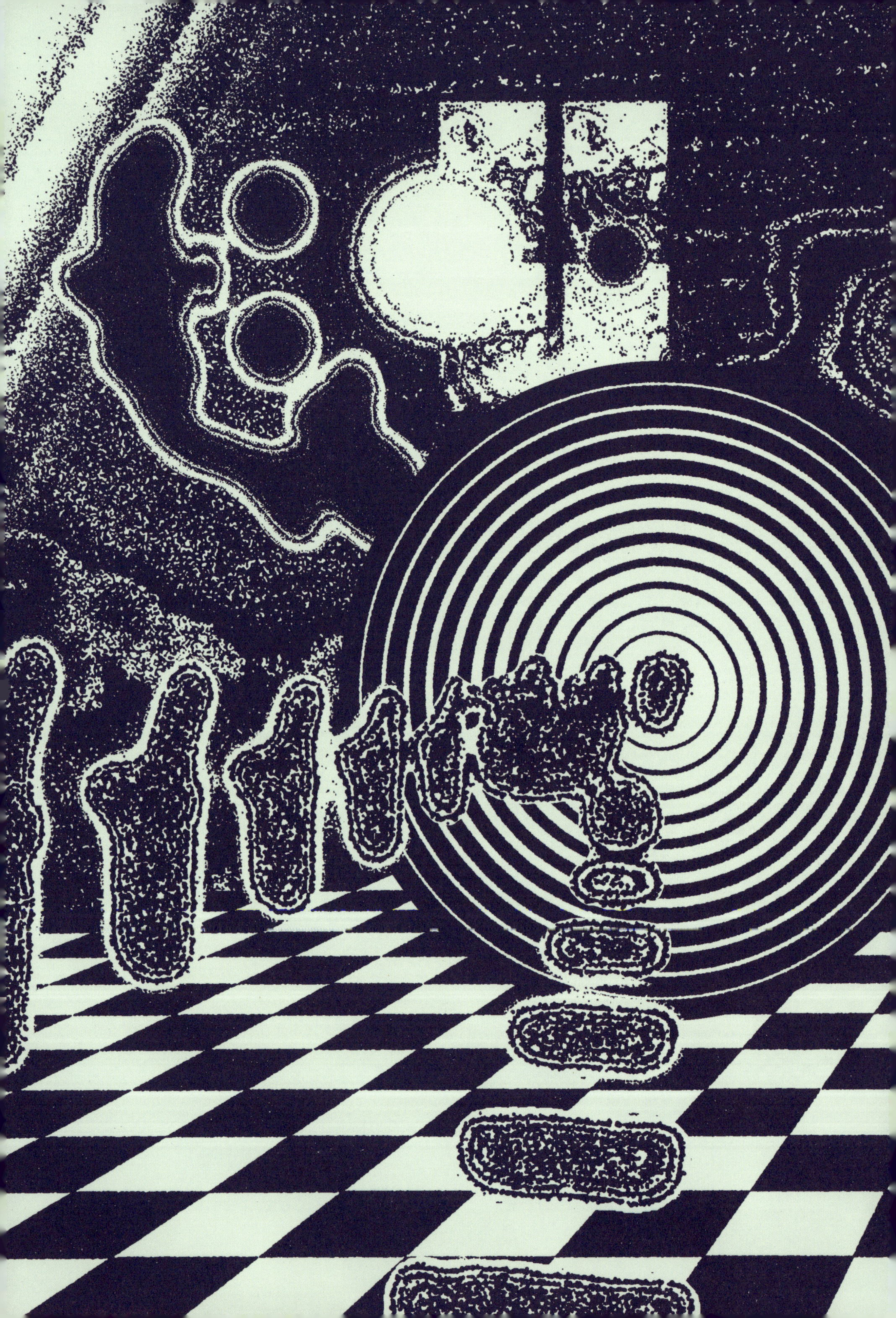

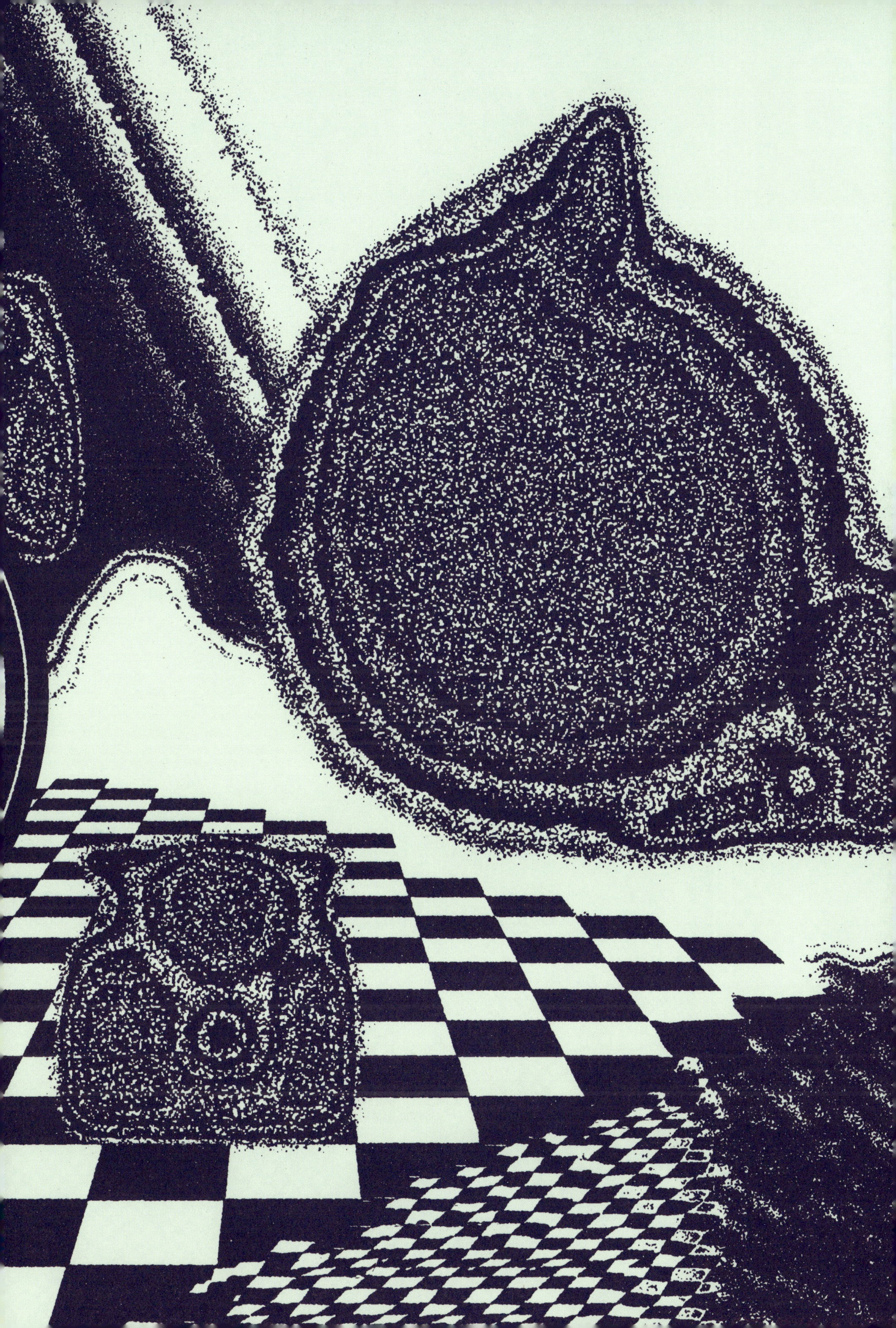

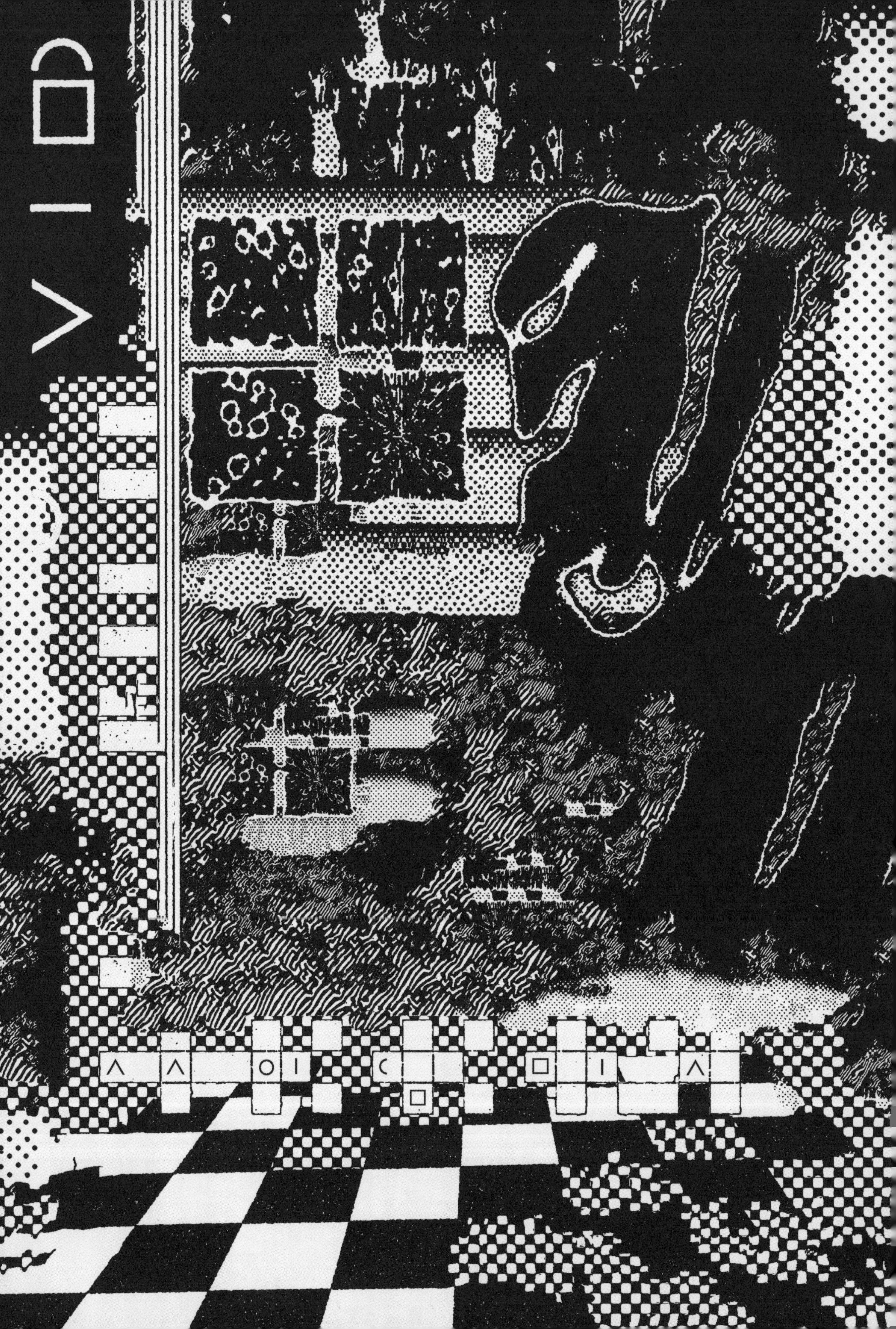

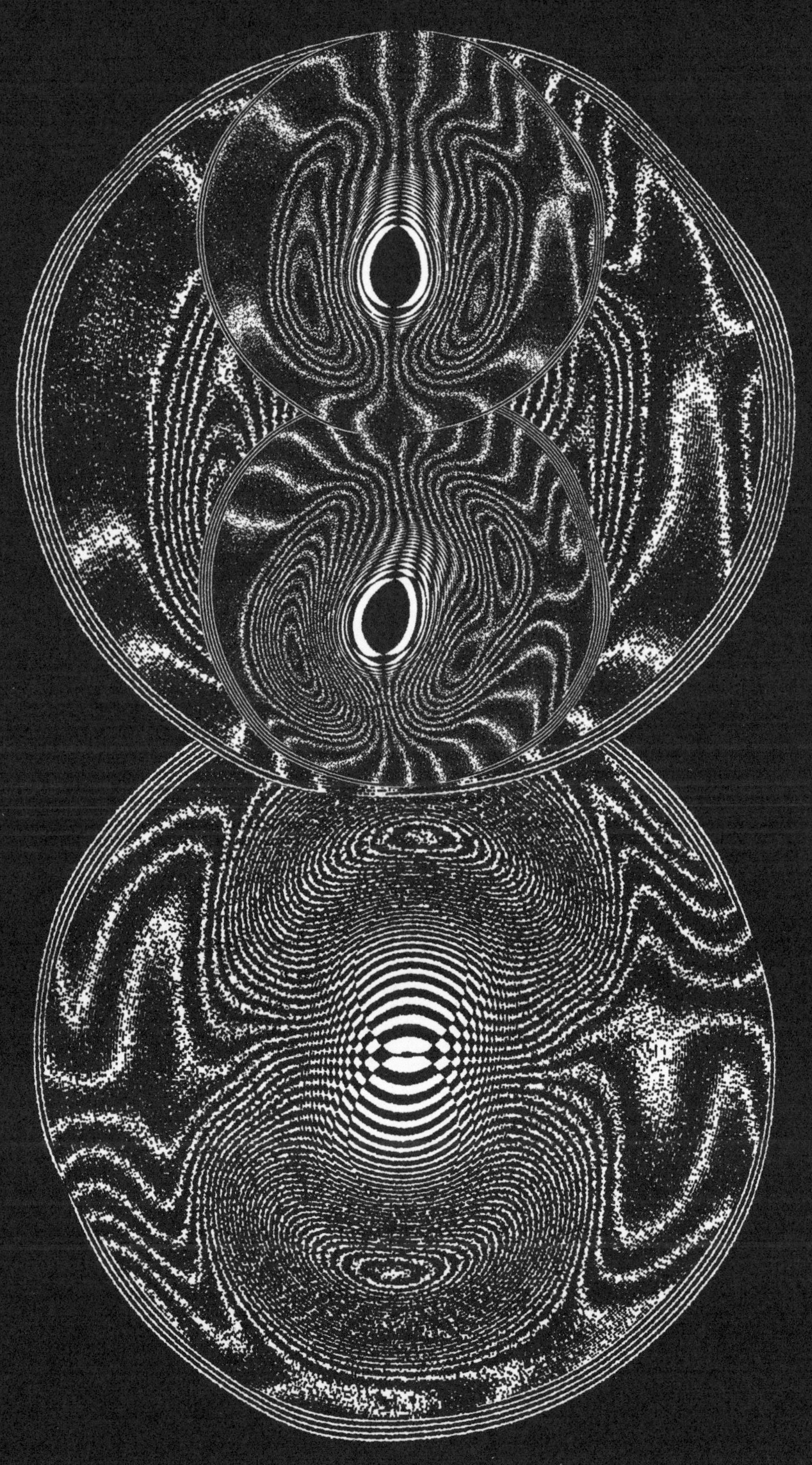

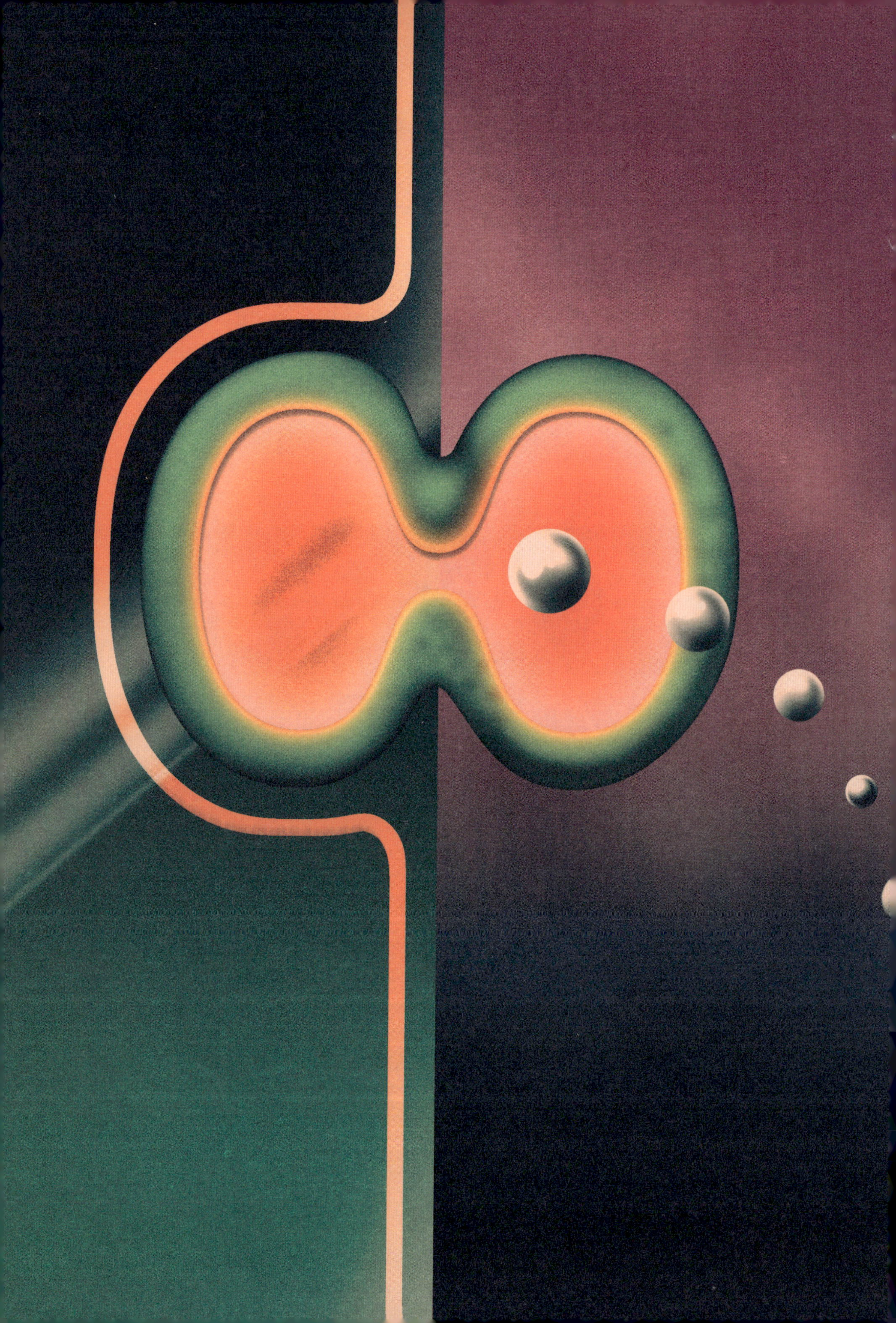

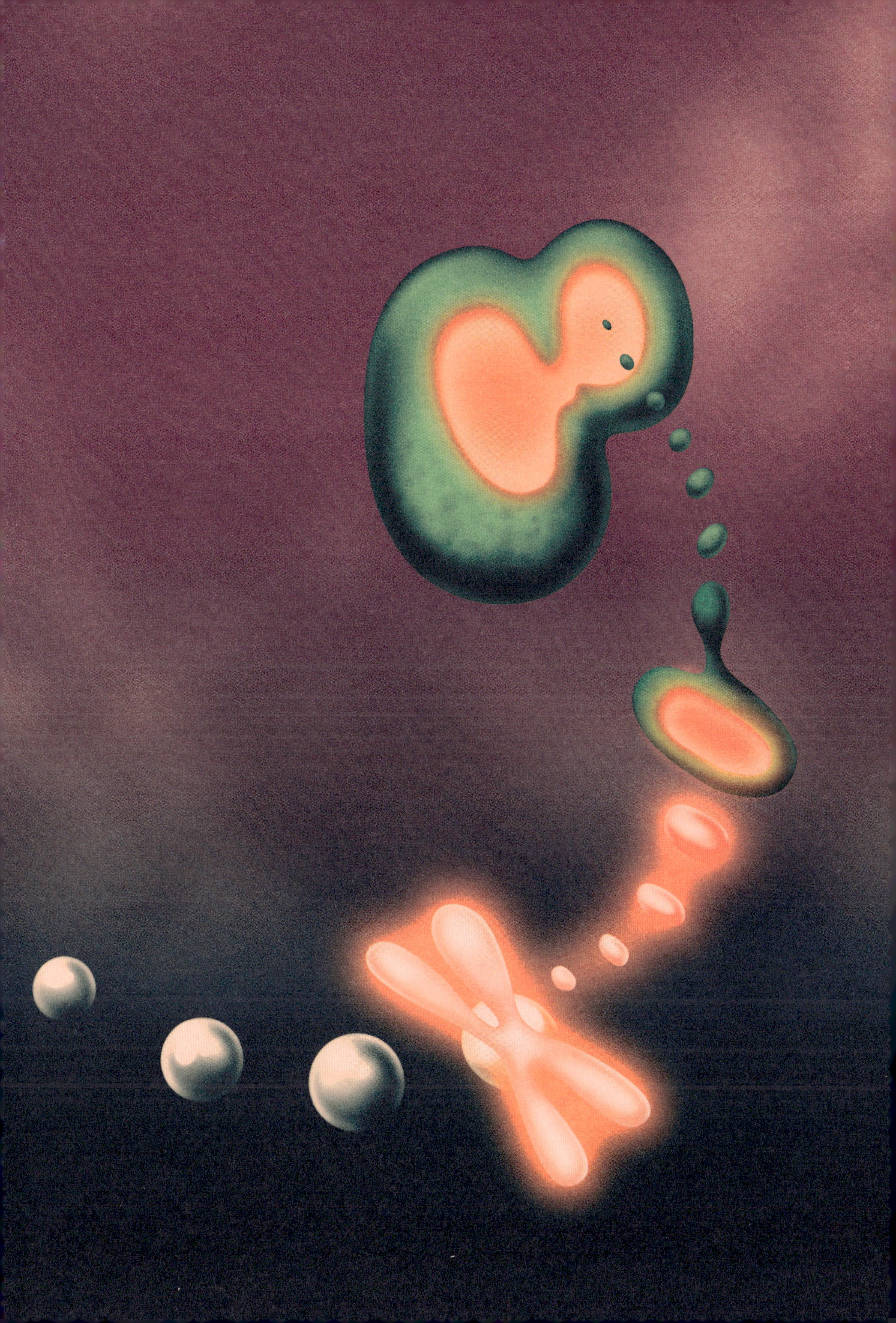

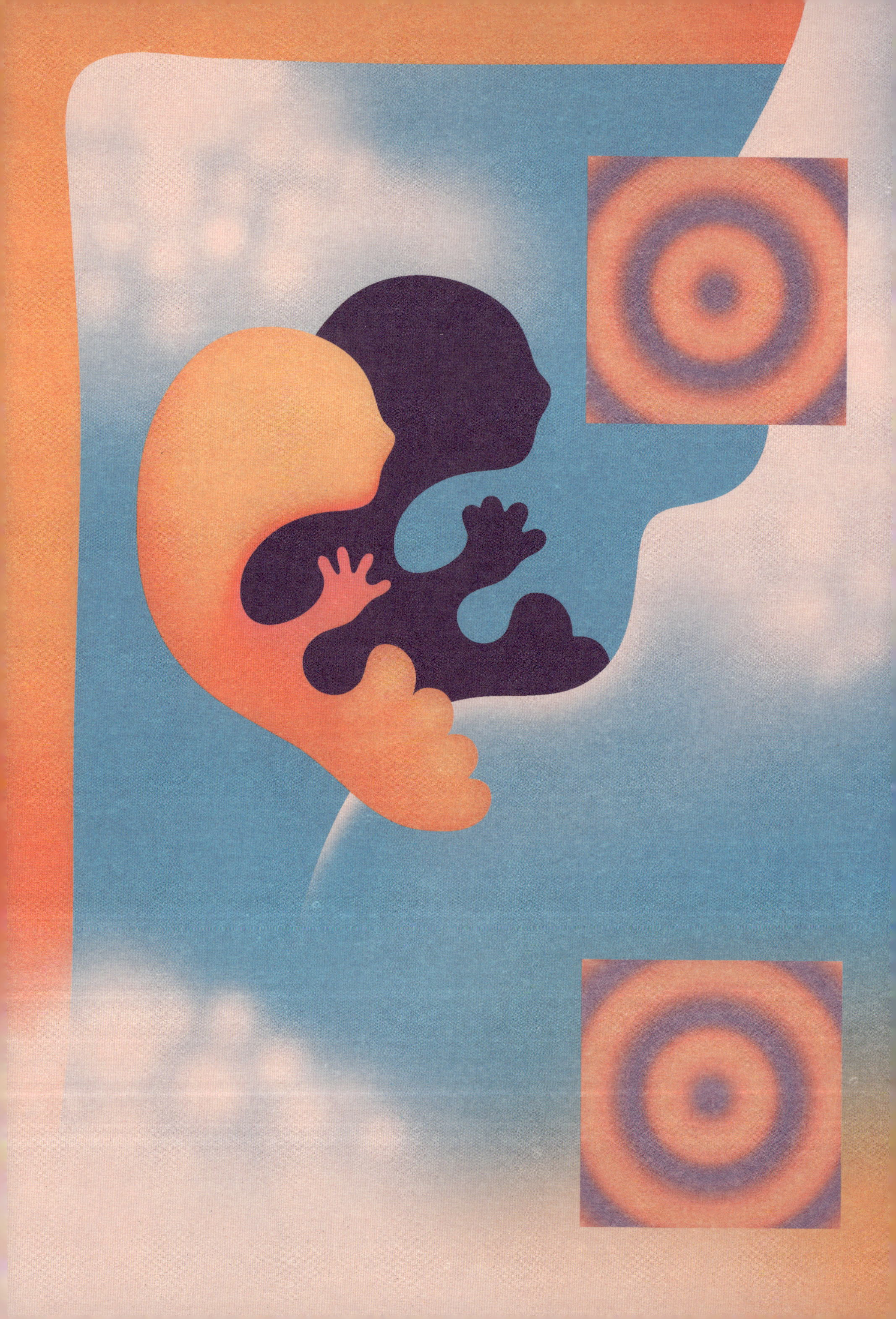

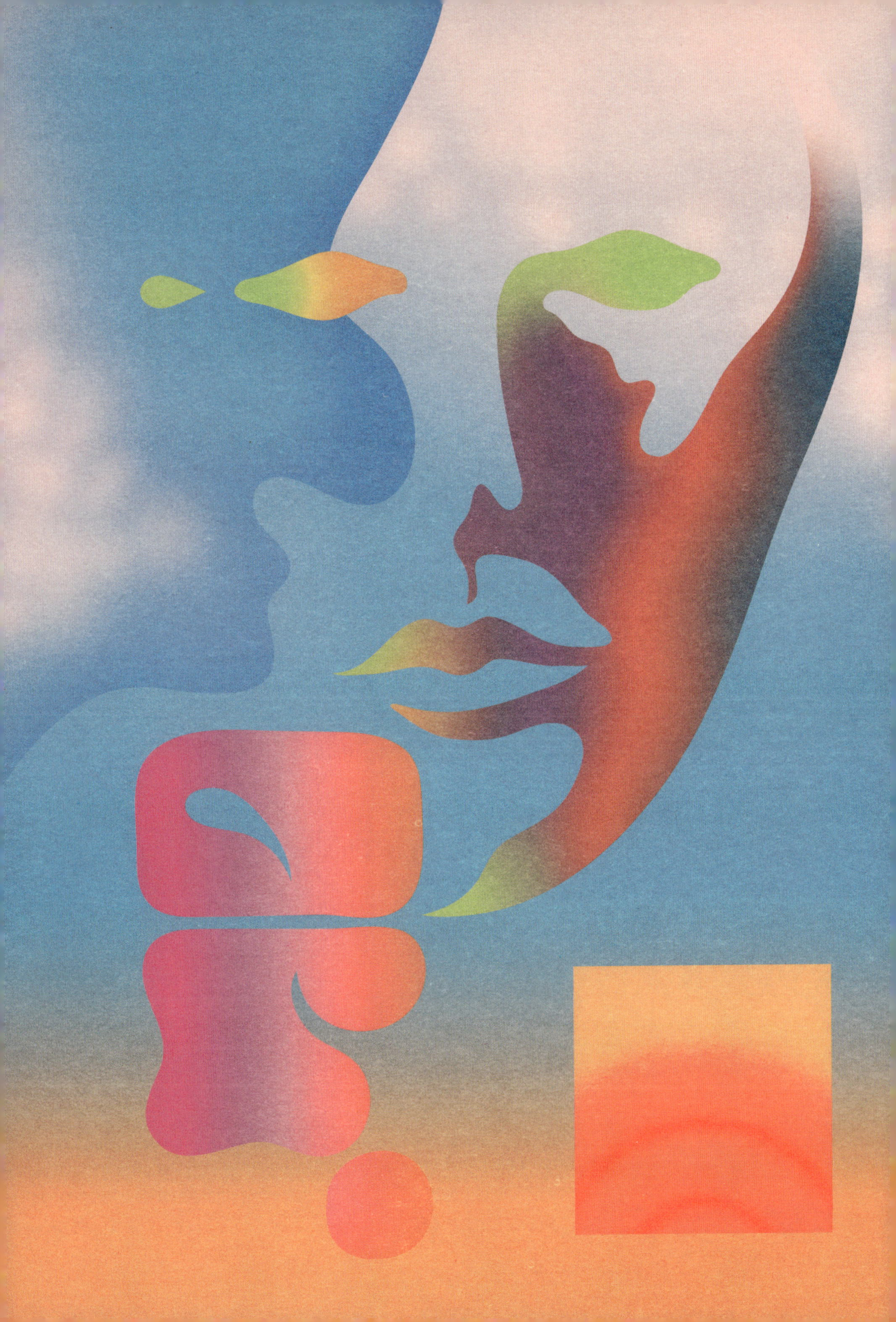

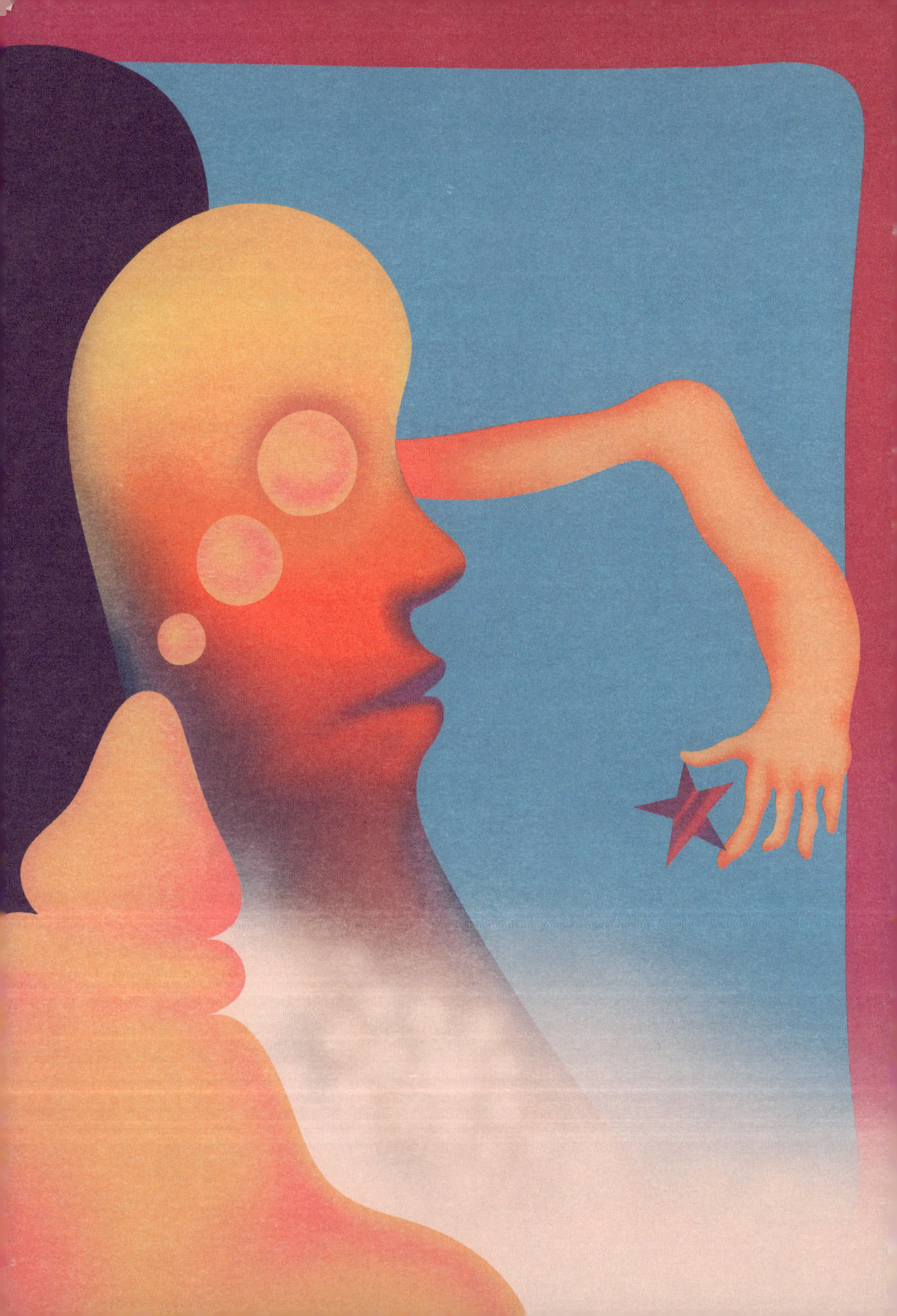

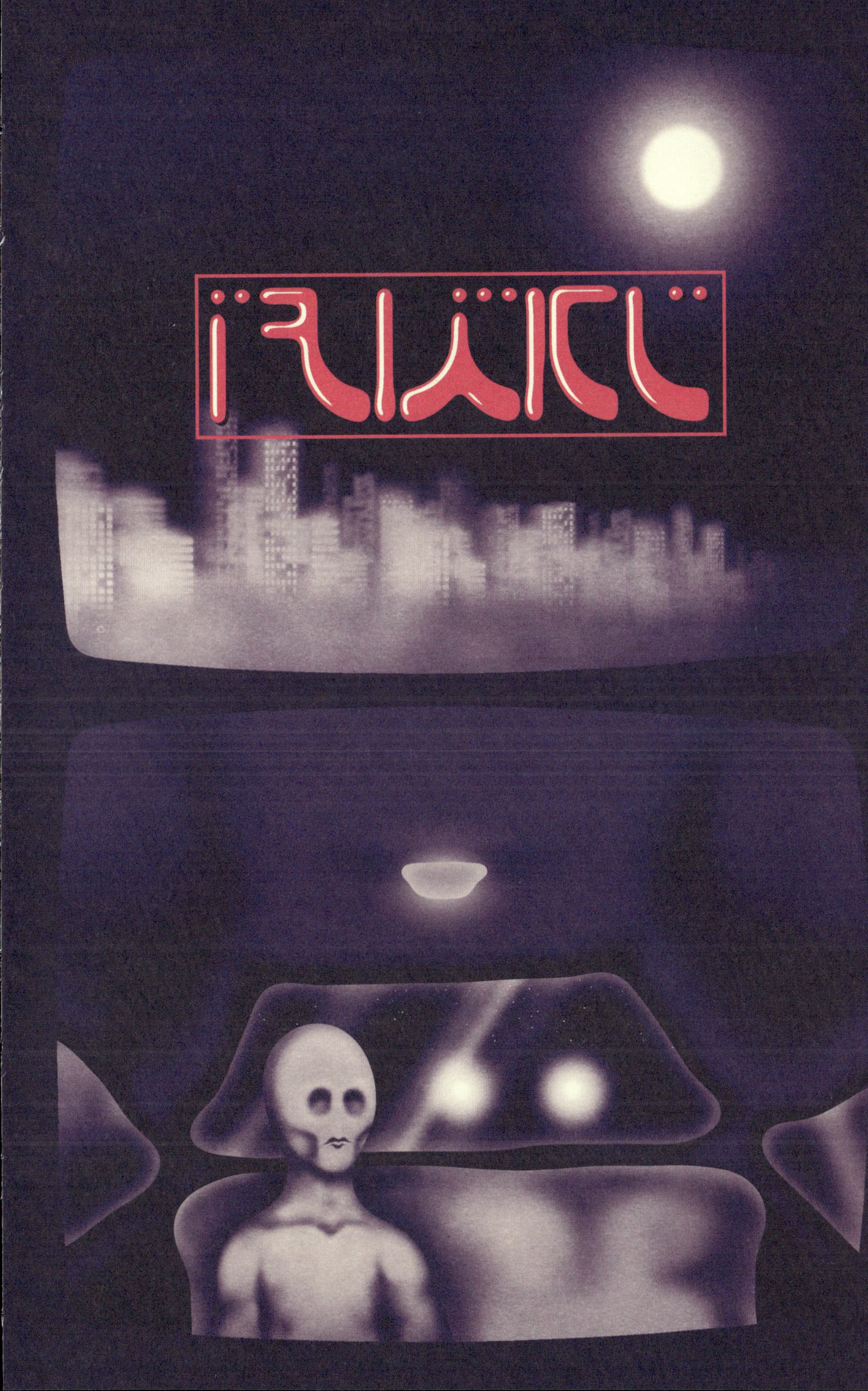

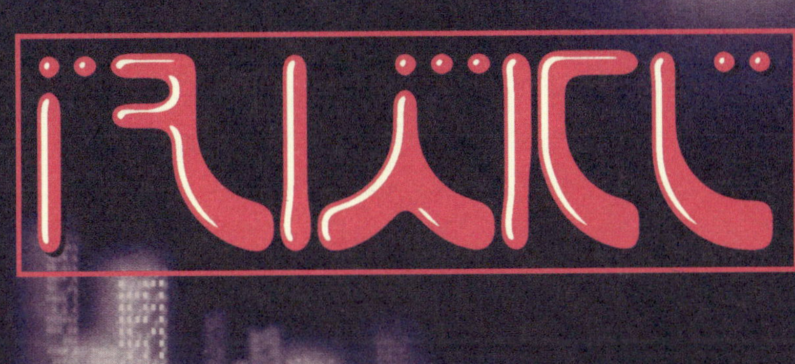

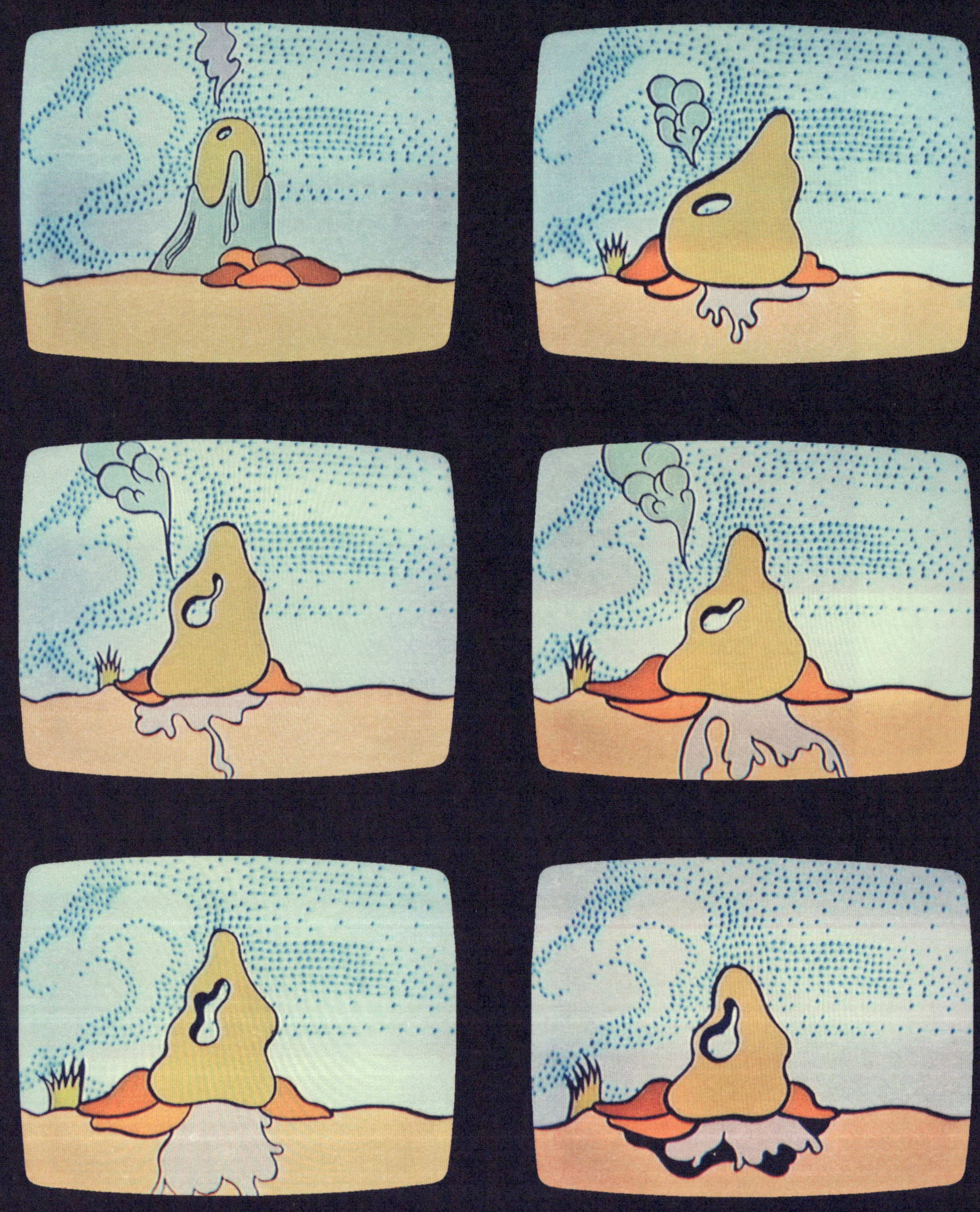

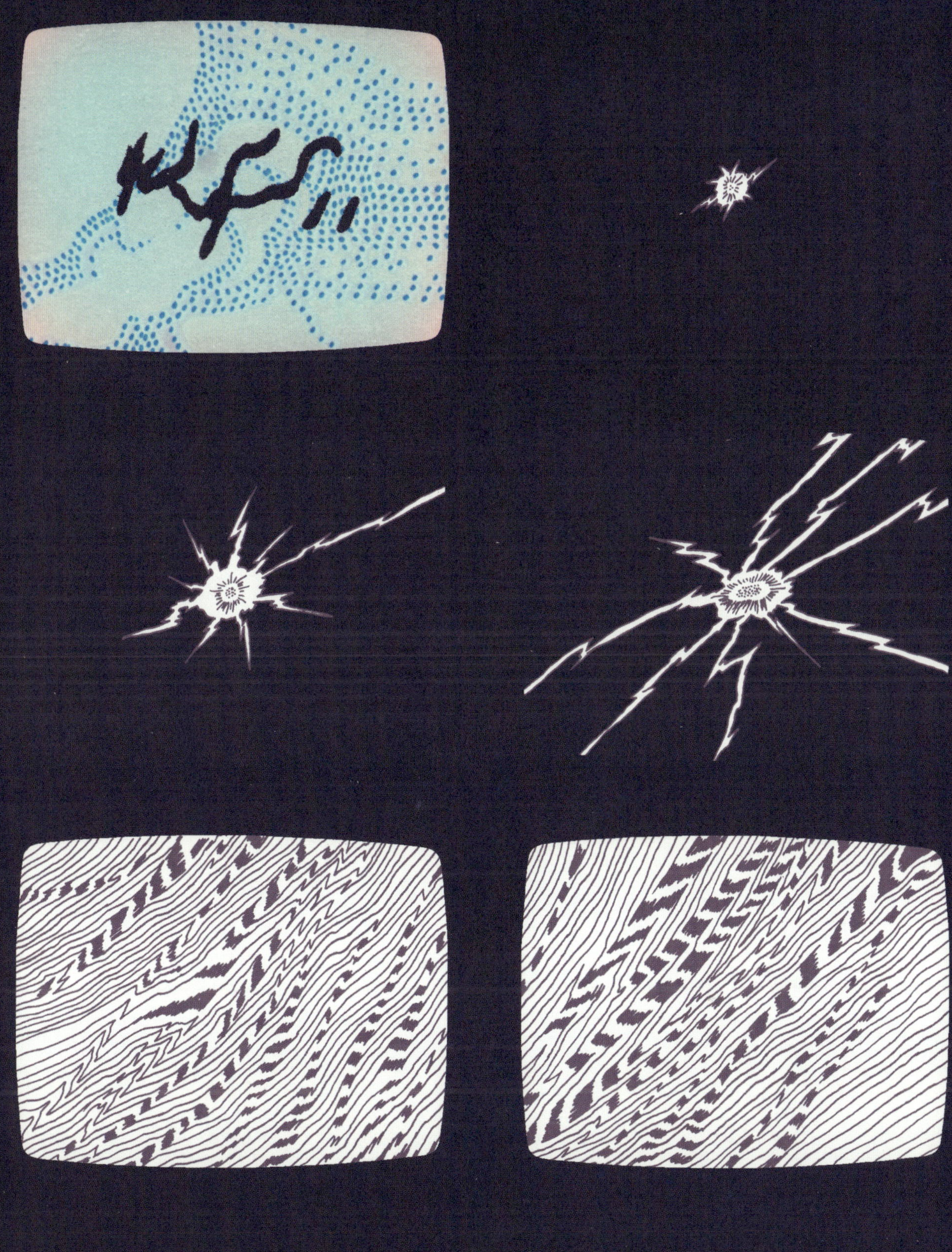

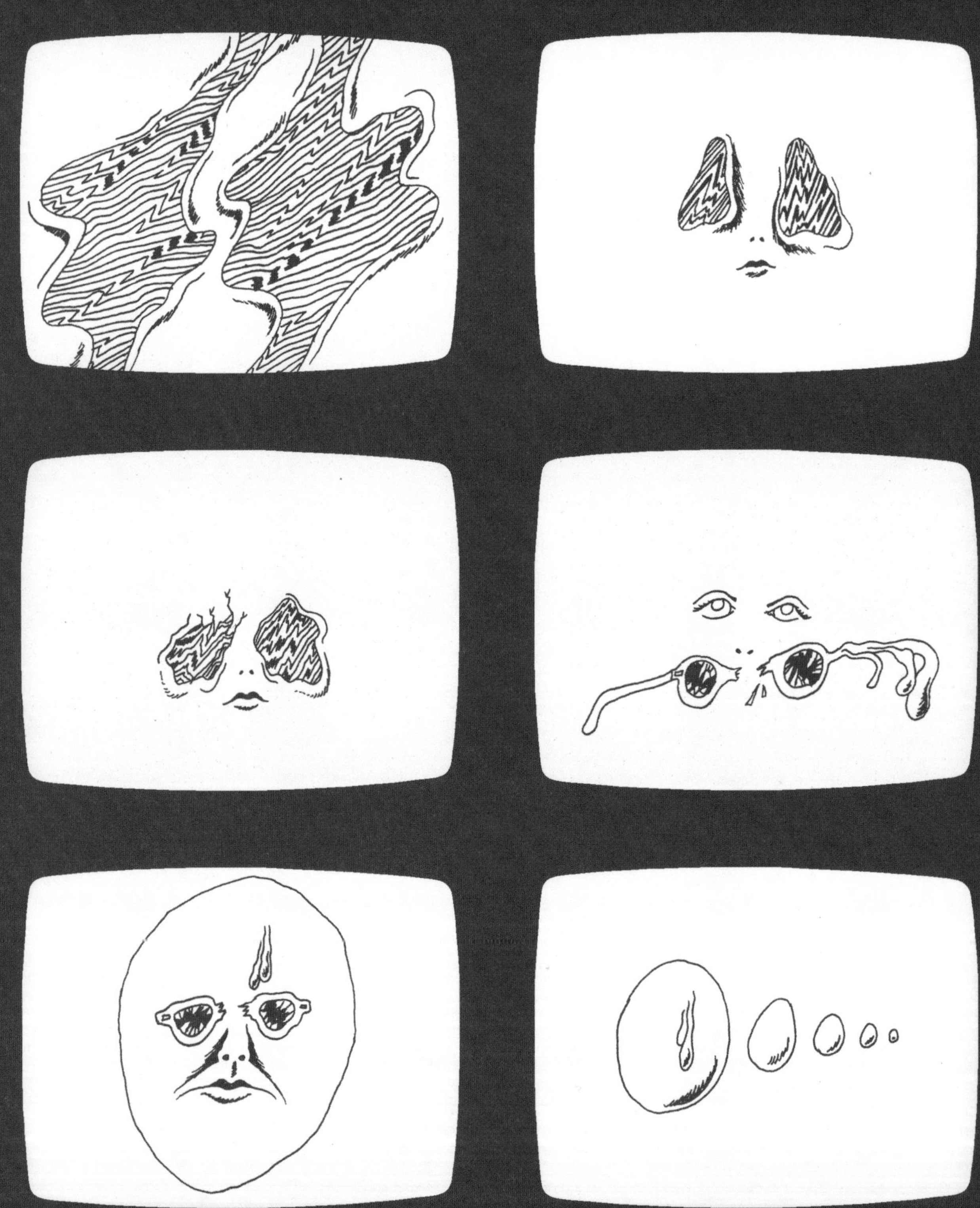

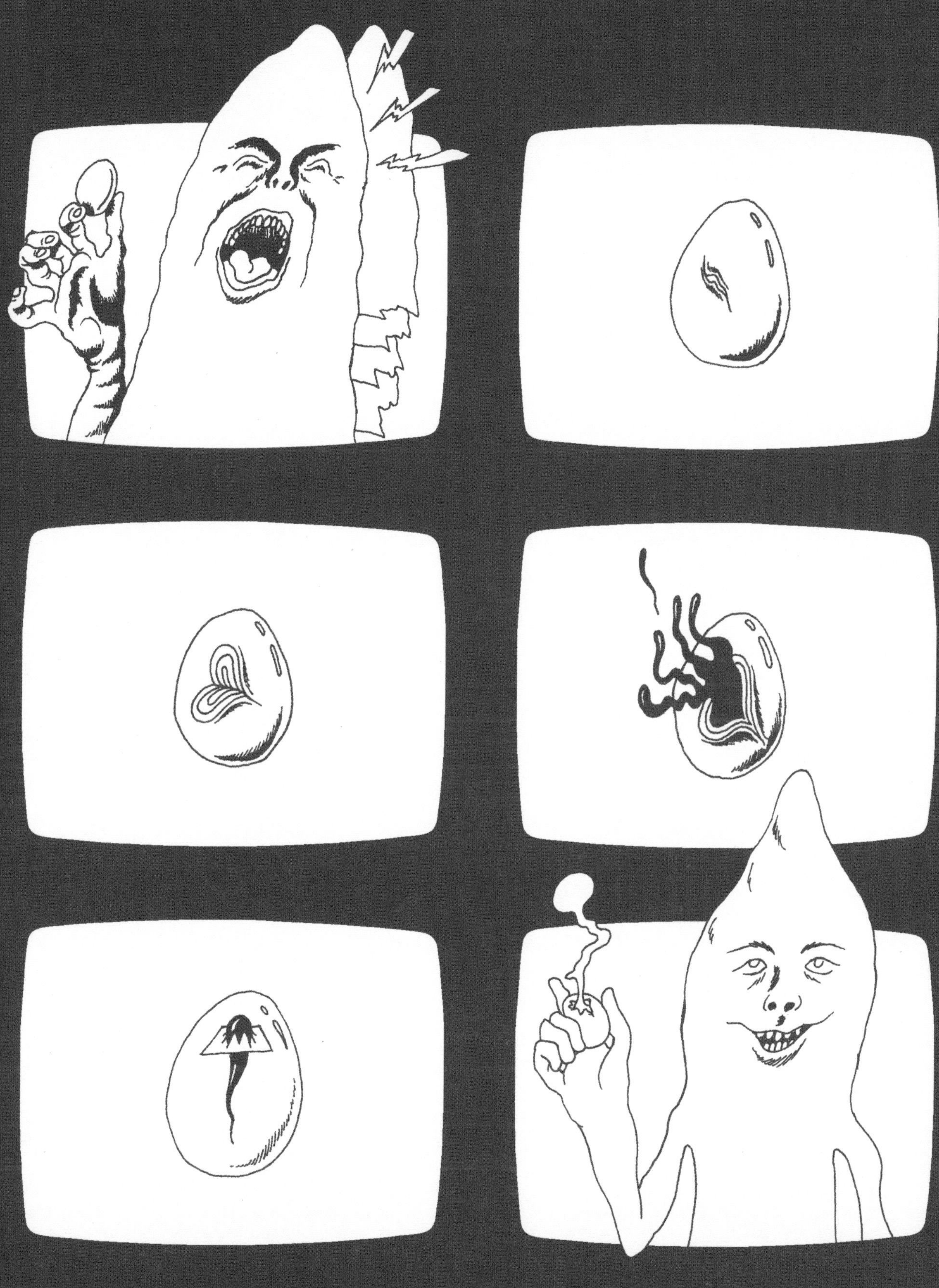

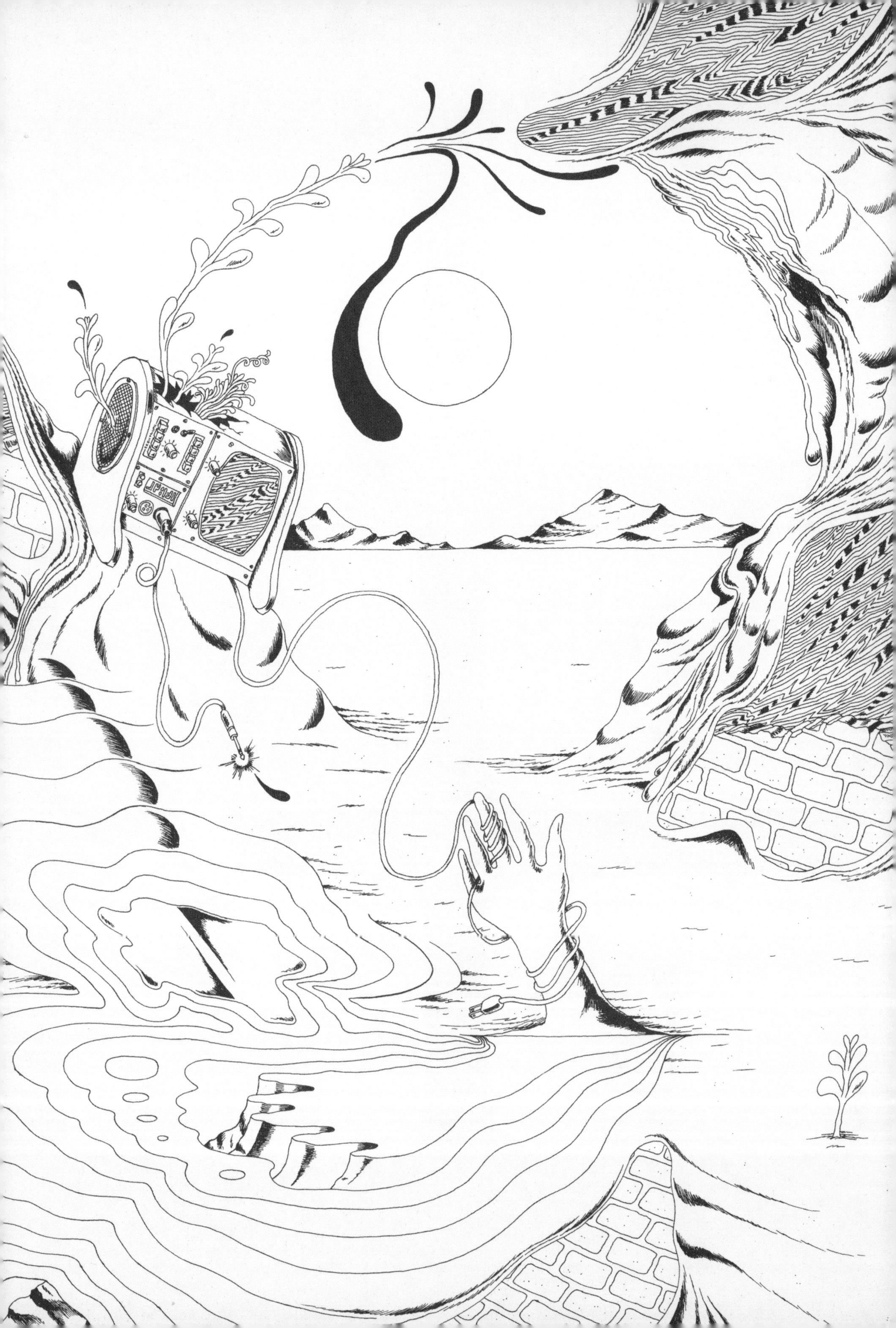

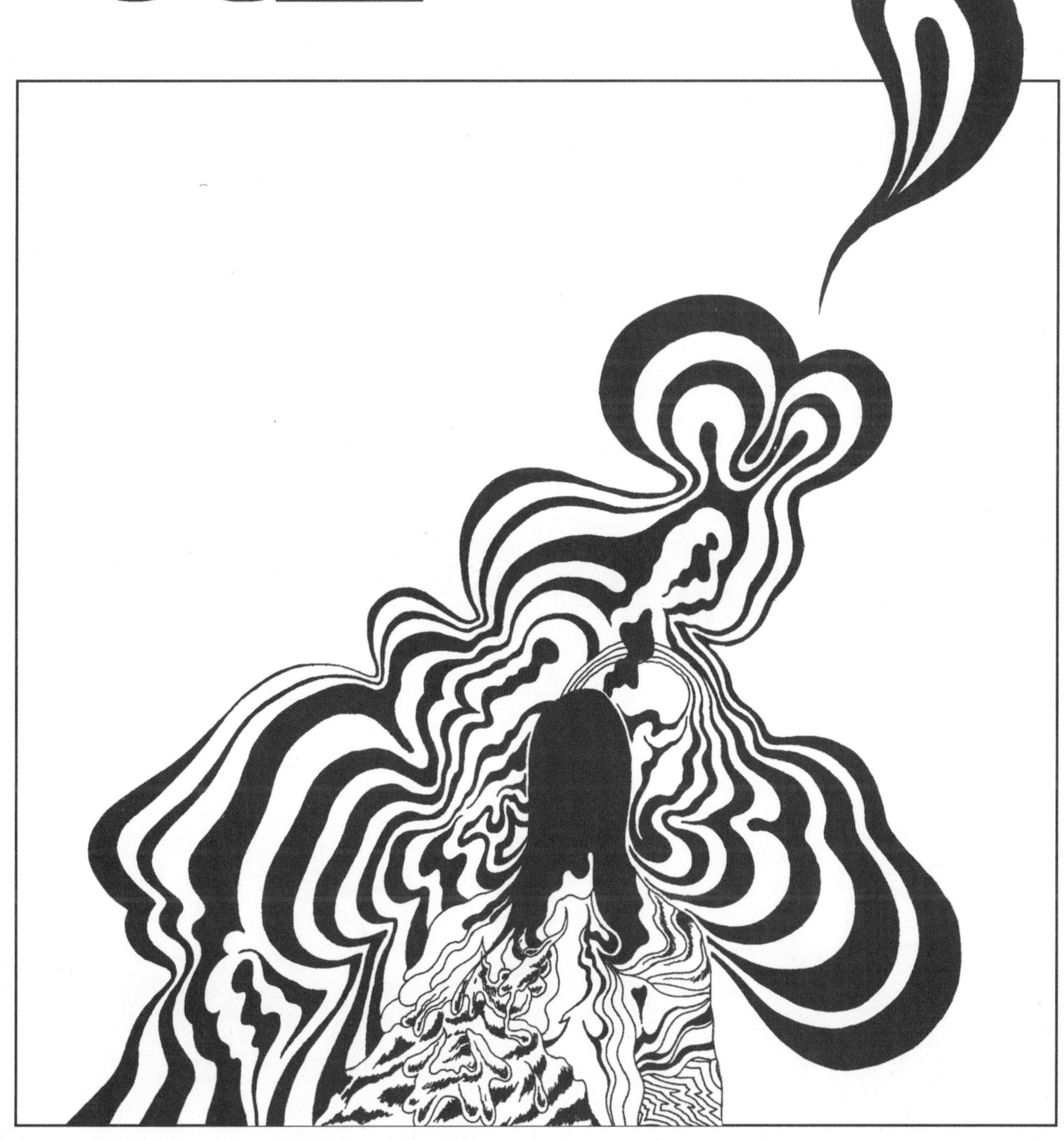

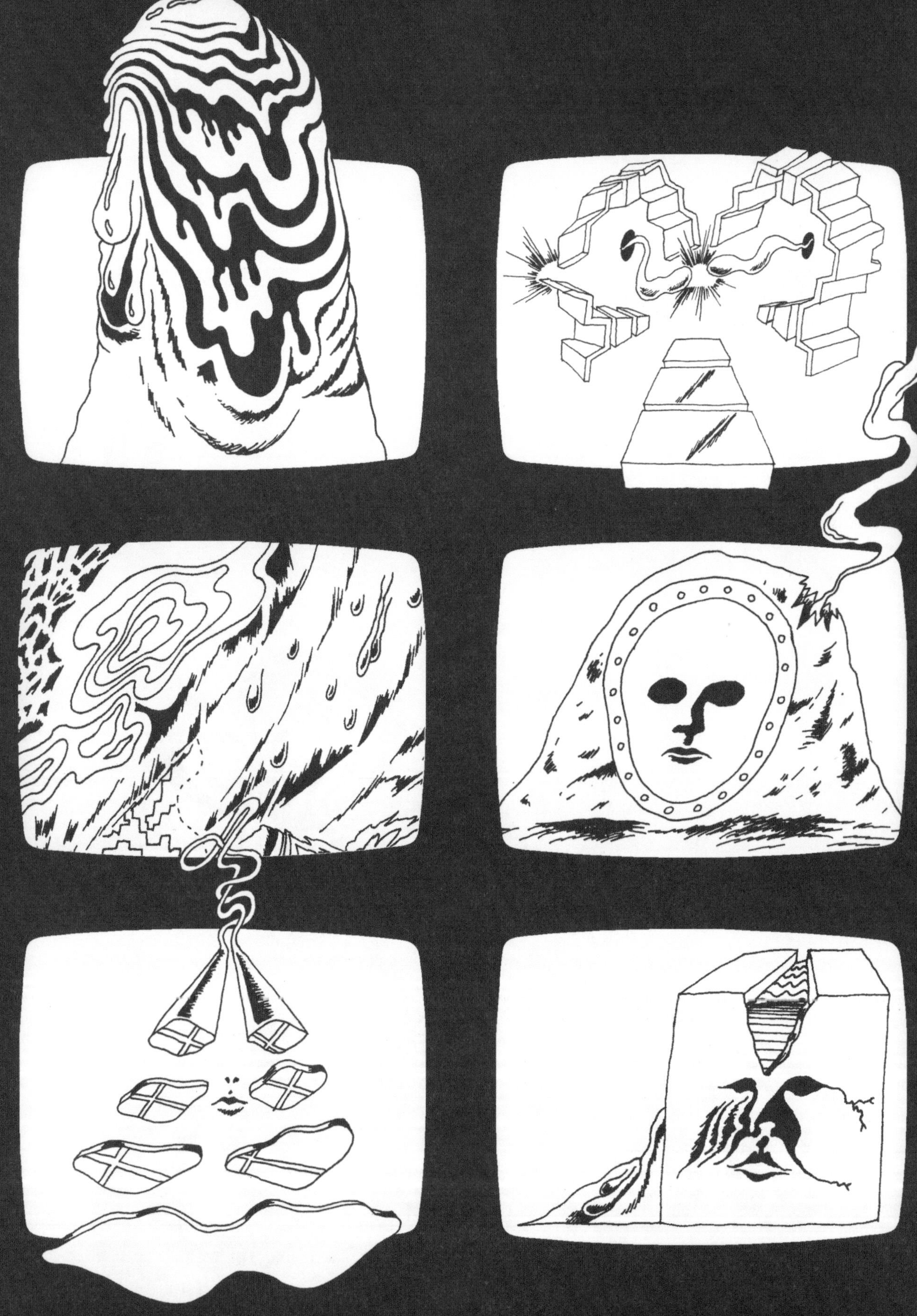

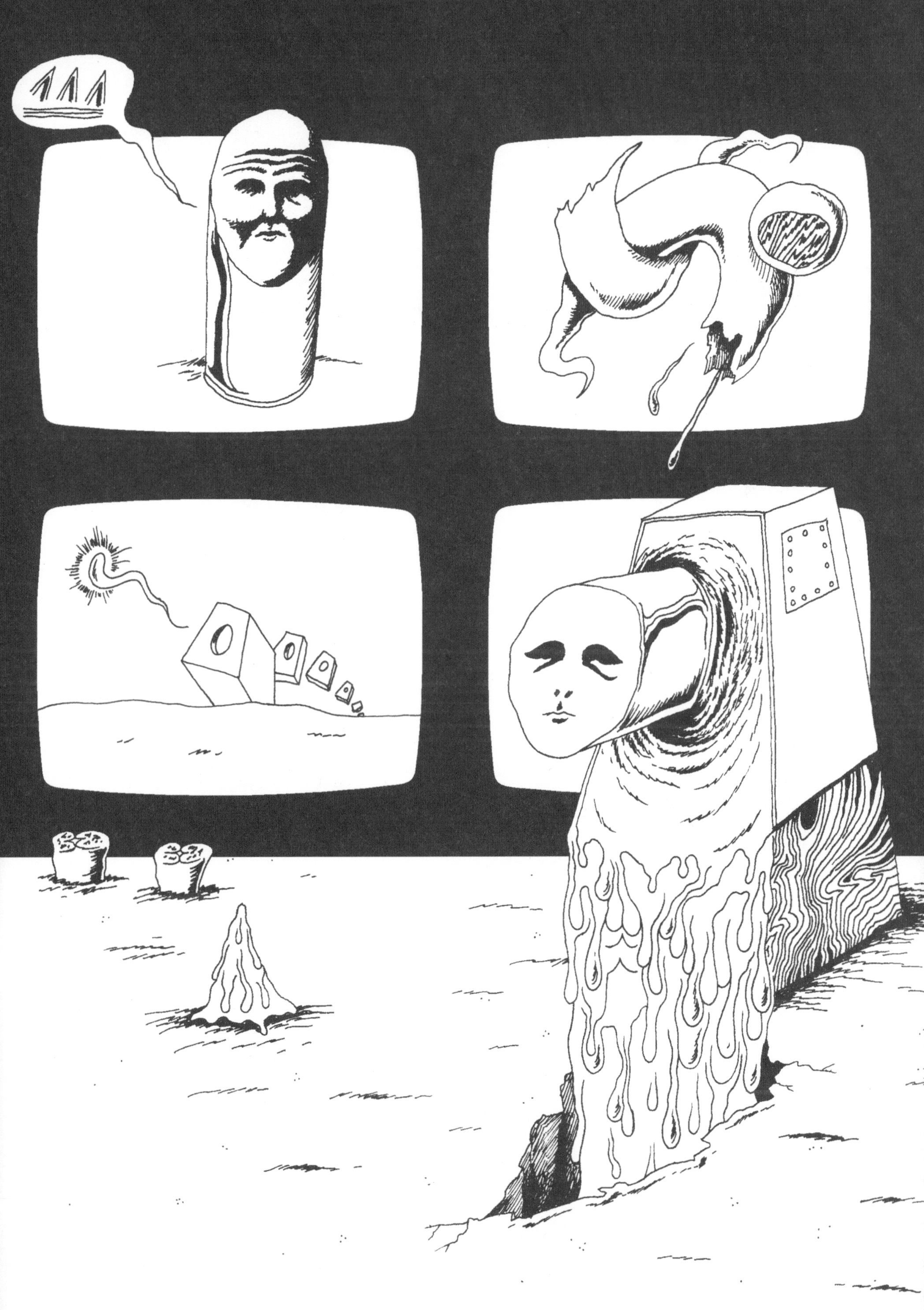

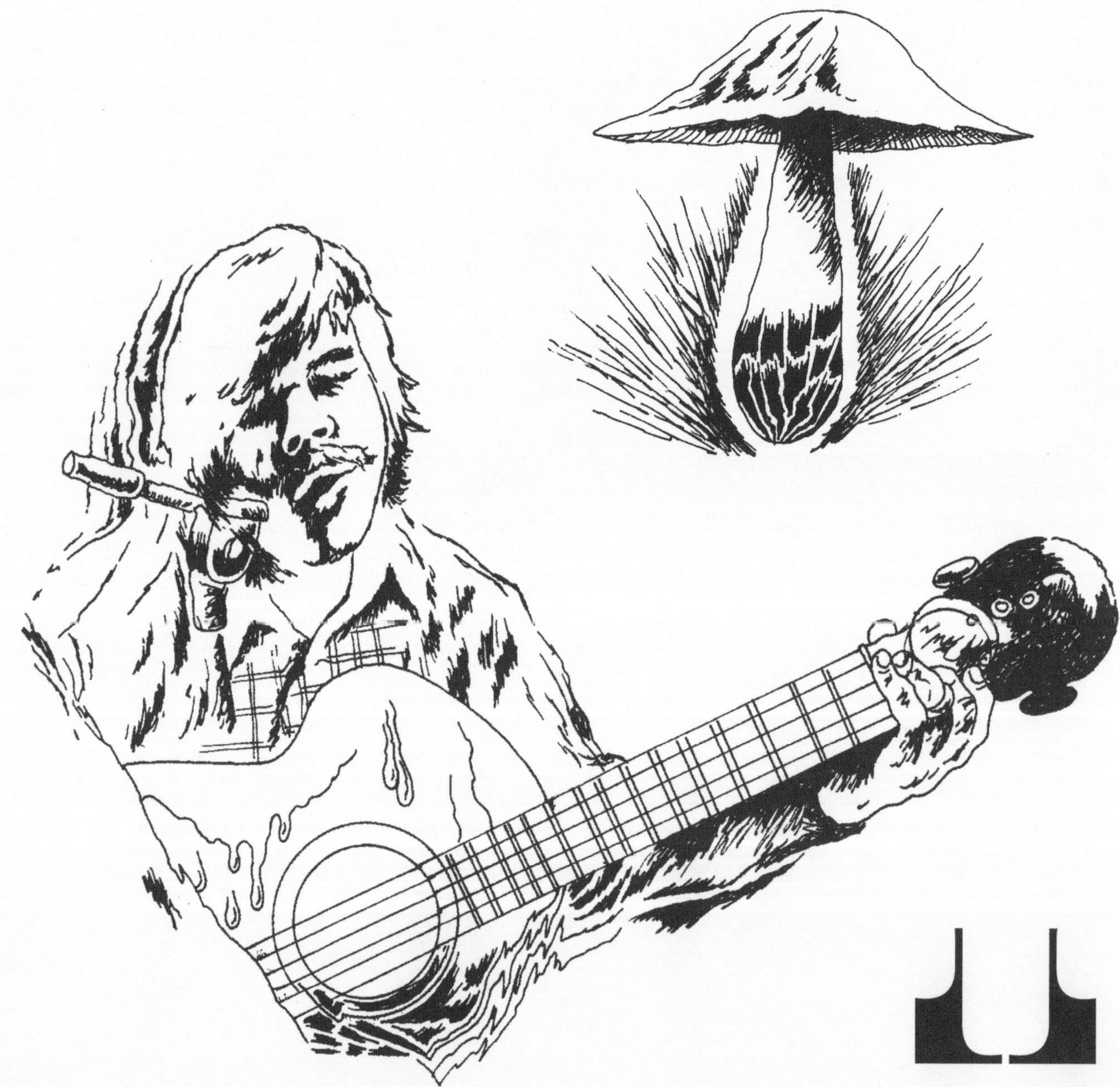

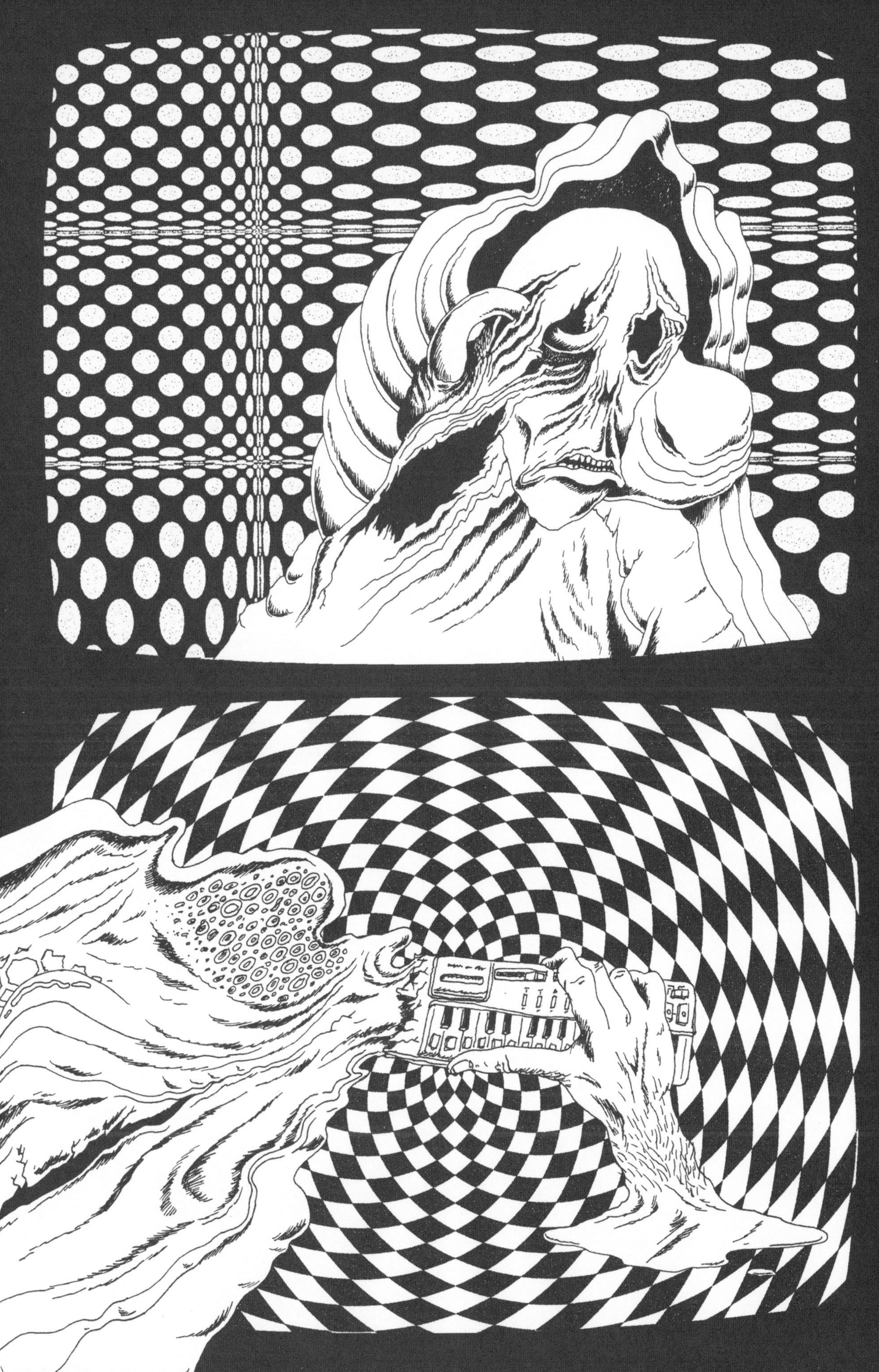

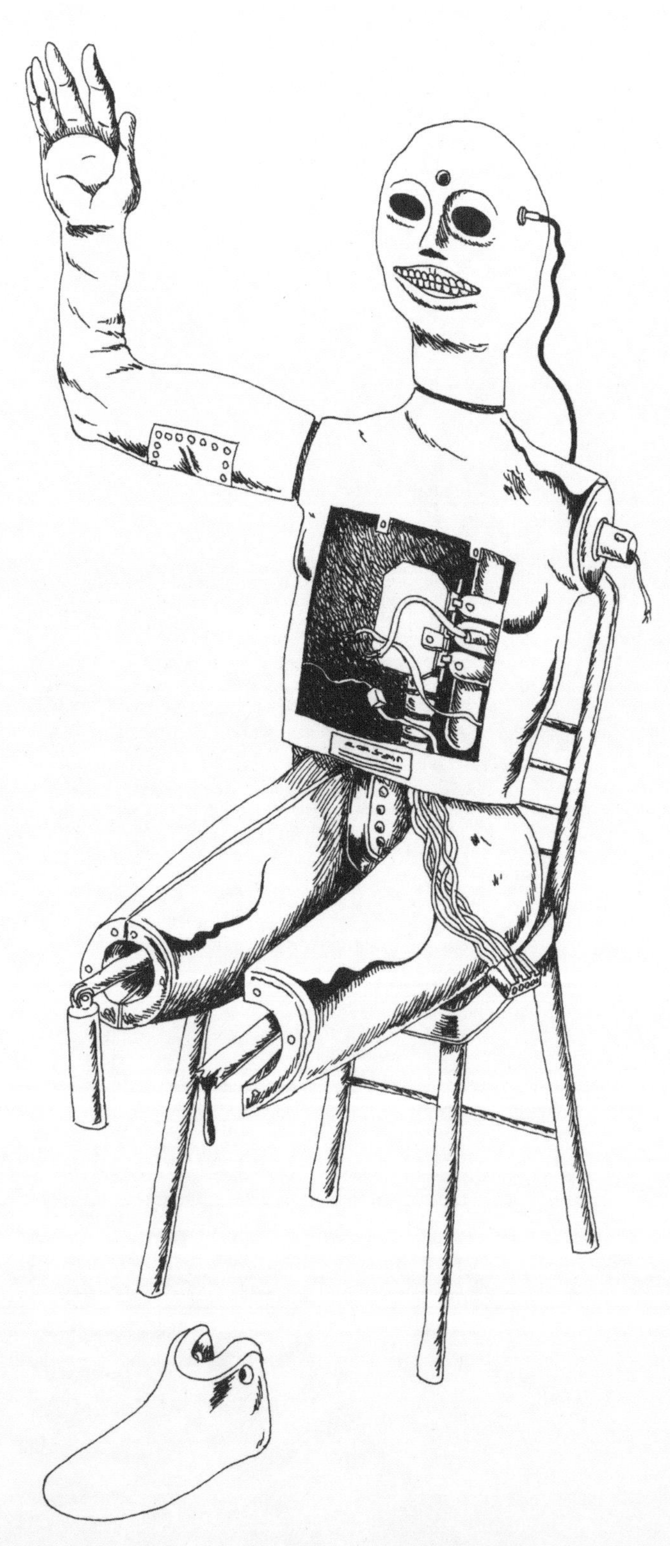

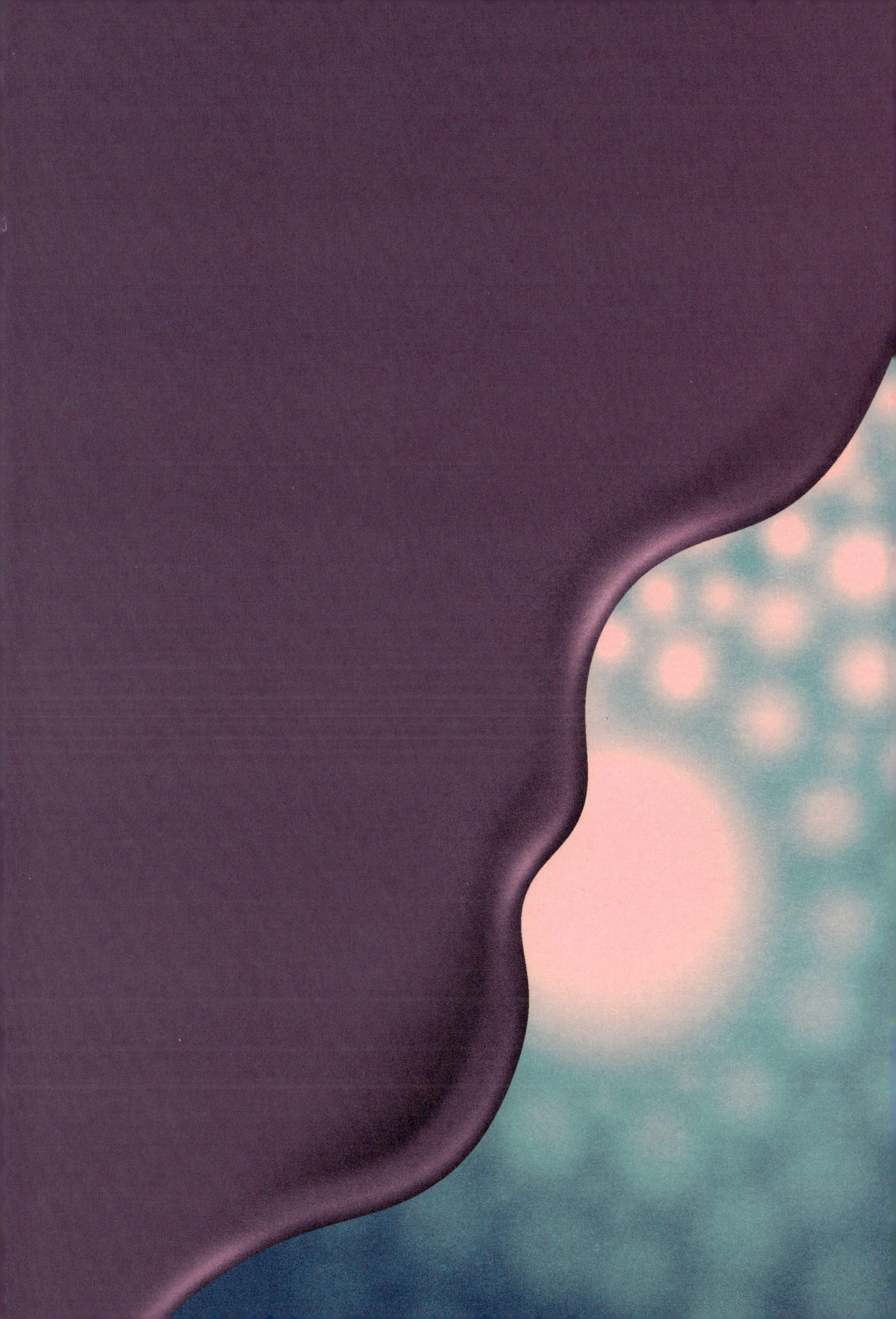

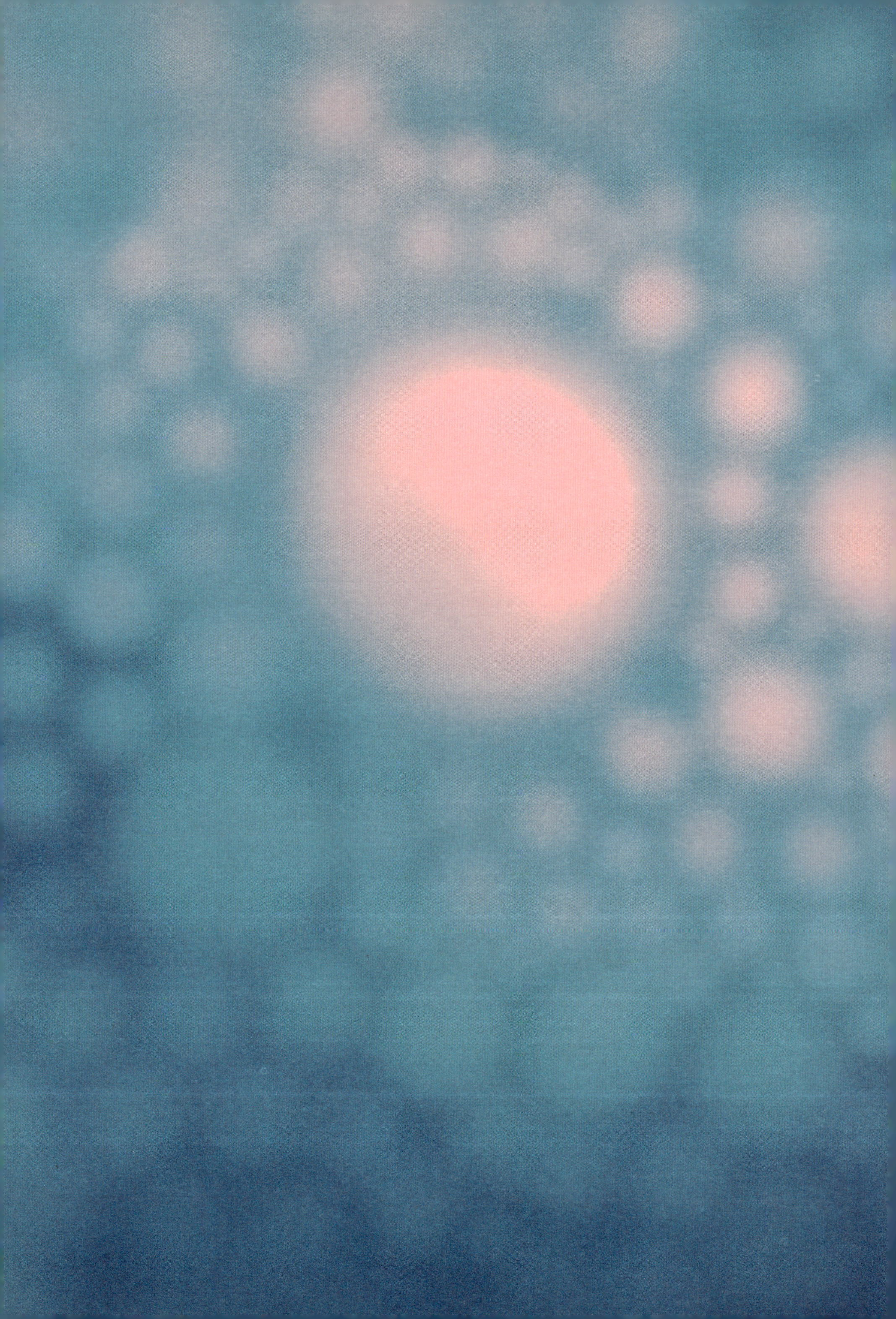

Floodgate Companion

All artwork and design by Robert Beatty, Lexington, Kentucky, USA, 2010-2016. Portions of this book have been reworked from Remains Street 3 (self published) & Remains Street 4 (published by Institute 193). Thanks to Kate for endless patience and support.

www.robertbeattyart.com

Floating World Comics
Portland, OR
floatingworldcomics.com

Third Edition: 2024
Printed in China.

ISBN 978-1-942801-98-6